AMERICA, OKINAWA, AND JAPAN

Case Studies for Foreign Policy Theory

Frederick L. Shiels

University Press
of America™

To My Mother and My Father

PREFACE

These pages are the result of two strong and independent, though related, interests: in the processes by which men at the very highest levels of government make decisions, and in the remarkable and eventful two and a half decades of American military rule in the Ryukyu Islands. The first and more general preoccupation developed over several years of reading about and discussing foreign affairs decisions-- mainly of the crises variety like Korea and Cuba-- and wondering if perhaps the theoretical literature of foreign policy was not too heavily geared to this type of episode, and not enough to more mundane but eminently study-worthy decision cases. The second interest was more circumstantial in origin, growing out of an unusual opportunity to work as the research assistant on the United States Army's historical study of the occupation and administration of Okinawa (as a civilian). My participation in the project during 1971-72 afforded me a unique chance to talk with figures in this unusual chapter in American history and access to confidential documents describing it from the inside. The research internship, which involved a useful minor role in an official history but considerable independence as a scholar as well, engendered a fascination with the subject matter enhanced by closeness of contact with it.

Chronologically, the period between the invasion of Okinawa and the promise of the island's return along with the rest of the Ryukyu Archipelago (1945-1969) is of primary interest here. The case studies which follow the introduction and historical background chapters focus on five major episodes within that span. They use these episodes to examine critically mainstream propositions from the political science sub-discipline of foreign policy.

The light that has been brought to bear on theory through case reconstruction, archival digging, extensive interviewing in the United States and Japan as part of my doctoral thesis for Cornell University was a joyful scholarly experience. I trust it will be a useful contribution to pedant and practitioner alike here in streamlined, revised, and updated form.

ACKNOWLEDGEMENTS

Thanks are gratefully given for assistance and support in this venture. First, a note of appreciation is
due Mr. Edward O'Flaherty, formerly of the Department
of the Army, for providing the initial Okinawa research
experience seven years ago and to Mr. Edward Freimuth,
also of the Department of the Army, for his counsel and
the use of his private collection of Ryukyus materials
(certainly one of the best, public or private, in the
country). I also owe a debt of thanks to Mr. William
Cunliffe of the Modern Military Records Branch of the
National Archives in Washington, D.C., to the staff of
the National Archives center in Suitland, Maryland,
and to Mr. Aijima Hiroshi and the staff of the National
Diet Library in Tokyo as well as the people at the Japan
Foundation Library in that city. The latter two groups
made work in foreign materials immeasurably simpler and
more pleasant. Also those in charge of the Okinawa materials at the University of Hawaii Library and the Ryukyus Research Center in Honolulu deserve credit.

The research could not have proceded very far with-
some generous financial support in 1975-76. A substantial
boost for Japanese field research came from Cornell University's Peace Studies Program underwritten by the Ford
Foundation. Important summer research funds were made
available by the Cornell Center for International Studies
and, especially, from the International Studies Association for whom I was a summer fellow in 1975. The China-
Japan Program provided much needed assistance during the
post-research write up stage that every scholar knows
can be the most crucial.

I should also like to thank Mrs. Yasuko MacDougall
for translating a number of useful sources from the Japanese. Special appreciation is also due Mr. Douglas Drei-
stadt who acted as my interpreter on Okinawa and to Ms.
Yvonne Yung and Ms. Shiraichi Aiko for their invaluable
assistance supplementing my rudimentary Japanese as interpreters in Tokyo.

Individuals who gave of their time and experience
in the interview process are too numerous to mention in-

dividually; all have been thanked personally. I owe a special debt, however, to historian George Kerr of Honolulu and Professor Edwin O. Reischauer of Harvard and to the staffs of the American Embassy in Tokyo and the Consulate in Naha, Okinawa in that regard.

Finally it is a pleasure to thank four professors: Robert E. Osgood of the School of Advanced International Studies of the Johns Hopkins University, and George Quester, Milton Esman, and T.J. Pempel of Cornell University for their encouragement and constructive, instructive criticism.

ABBREVIATIONS, PLACE NAMES, AND SPELLING OF JAPANESE

The use of abbreviations has been sparing in this study, and, except for the most common designations (e.g., "USSR"), all abbreviations are identified when the first appear in the text. The following list is also provided as a reference:

CIA	Central Intelligence Agency
CINCPAC	Commander-in Chief (of United States Armed Forces in the) Pacific (also informally and commonly used to designate the headquarters of that officer)
DOD	Department of Defense
FEC	Far Eastern Commission
IRG	Inter-Departmental Regional Groups (initiated under Johnson administration)
ISA	International Security Affairs (office in the Department of Defense)
JCS	Joint Chiefs of Staff
LDP	Liberal Democratic Party (of Japan)
NSAM	National Security (Council) Action Memorandum
NSC	National Security Council
NSDM	NS (C) Decision Memorandum
NSSM	NS (C) Study Memorandum
OLDP	Okinawa Liberal Democratic Party
OSD	Office of the Secretary of Defense
RYCOM	Ryukyus Command

SANACC	State-Army-Navy-Air Force Coordinating Committee
SCAP	Supreme Commander for Allied Powers in the Pacific (commonly used also to designate headquarters of that officer too)
SIG	Senior Interdepartmental Group
SWNCC	State-War-Navy Coordinating Committee (replaced by SANACC and ultimately by the National Security Council)
USCAR	United States Civil Administration in the Ryukyus

"Okinawa," the name of the main island of the Ryukyu Archipelago and the locus of the great bulk of the American military base structure is used interchangeably with "Ryukyus" in this study unless otherwise indicated.

All Japanese names and terms are rendered in the Hepburn romanization system spellings. Also, Japanese family names precede given names, in accordance with current scholarly practice, except when a quotation or citation places the given name first.

TABLE OF CONTENTS

CHAPTER ONE: INTRODUCTION

Part I

Okinawa and International Relations Theory

Why Okinawa? The American occupation there has been investigated before; square mile for square mile the Ryukyu Archipelago, long neglected by scholars, has fairly recently become one of the most intensively studied targets of Washington's foreign policy (although interest has waned since its return to Japan in 1972). Ironically, between the quieting of the guns in 1945 and the end of the Cold War decade in 1960 only two English language books dealt with the subject of the occupation there at all, and these only tangentially. The first was the official history of the American military campaign in the islands in 1945, Roy Appleman's Okinawa: The Last Battle (1948); the second was George Kerr's definitive Okinawa: The History of an Island People (1958), characterizing the first postwar decade in a short, powerful introductory chapter, but essentially stopping after the landing of American troops in its detailed treatment.1

During the 1960's a small stream of articles emerged, largely stimulated by the increased consciousness of an Okinawan problem in United States/Japanese relations. Yet only two book-length works appeared in English, Okinawan scholar Higa Mikio's Politics and Parties in Postwar Okinawa and the anecdotally readable Okinawa: A Tiger by the Tail by a former Army officer, M.D. Morris? Three works much more focused on American policy have been produced in the 1970's, all having the advantage of looking at the 24-year period between Okinawa's capture and the promise of its return (1969) comprehensively. The first of these, Japanese political scientist Watanabe Akio's The Okinawa Problem: A Chapter in Japan-U.S. Relations (1970) is well described by its title, discussing the occupation intelligently in rather traditional diplomatic-historical style with some attention to the literature of international relations qua social science.3 The second work, The Dynamics of Okinawan Reversion, 1945-1969 (1973) by Johannes Binnendijk, appeared in a book of case studies on "public diplomacy," and utilized a cybernetic/communications-flow model derived from Karl Deutsch.4 The most recent study, dealing with related economic and security problems in addition to Okinawa, was produced in 1976 by the Brookings Institution under the title Managing an Alliance: The Politics of U.S.-Japanese Re-

1

lations.[5] The authors-- I.M. Destler, Priscilla Clapp, Fukui Haruhiro, and Sato Hideo were concerned with the reversion (i.e., return) of Okinawa to Japan and the decision making leading up to that event, as well as other themes. They leaned toward the bureaucratic politics perspective, which I discuss in considerable detail further on. Their descriptions and analyses are meticulous and sophisticated; however, they do not much concern themselves with explicit links to the international relations literature. Instead they preferred to treat the politics of reversion, textiles, etc., as unique cases (which in many ways they are), made more comprehensible by certain selected insights from foreign policy theorists, but not likely to provide the basis for useful generalization.

The present investigation, which owes an unquestioned debt to several of its predecessors mentioned here, attempts to go considerably beyond them in connecting American policy-making for Okinawa to important works of political science, to test propositions from these works and generate new ones, with the following objectives in mind:

1. To use extensive research on a fairly narrow and focused period in American foreign relations to judge certain contentions of the "bureaucratic politics school" and the counter-attack on heavily rationalist strategies of decision which is labeled incrementalism or "muddling through."

2. In examining such propositions rigorously, if without broad attempts at quantification, to develop an analytic framework useful in understanding and applying knowledge about a wide variety of foreign affairs decision types.

3. In striving to accomplish objectives 1 and 2, to contribute badly needed empirical follow-up to theoretical work in international relations, a discipline in which theory and case study do not serve each other nearly well enough.

More specifically, hypotheses for which the Okinawa cases are mined for evidence and answers include:

1. Bureaucratic politics, advanced in the work of Graham Allison and Morton Halperin as a long-overdue focus for understanding decision processes, supplements rather than supplants "classical"

2

sources of policy explanation.

   2. Incremental models of official choice-
making, epitomized in the work of Charles
Lindblom, supplement rather than supplant
rational models of decision processes.

   3. Routine, often incremental, decision
patterns are occasionally broken by critical decision-sequences, which are frequently much closer to the rational end of the
rational-incremental spectrum.

   Rather than viewing the Ryukyuan chapter of American foreign policy as of interest primarily to the historian, I strive to put a thorough historical investigation of the episode in the service of the craft of decision analysis within political science. To accomplish
this, studies of the five most pivotal decisions related
to Okinawa are made with an eye to examining critically
two central trends in the literature of policy analysis
during the past two decades (reflected in the hypotheses
above). The first trend has been toward increasing skepticism about the practical wisdom of rationality, means-
ends analysis, and the comprehensive consideration of
alternatives in governmental decision-making. In place
of such scientific and rational models, the skeptics
have given us models which portray policy as unfolding
in small increments of change with rather limited action-
choices being seriously considered. A second trend has
been toward the rejection of the state-as-actor in international relations in favor of "governments as aggre-
gations of not-always-consistent bureaucratic actors."

   The rudiments of a new model of American foreign
policy decision-making will be advanced as part of a
framework for decision analysis which may be useful for
a variety of case-types, not exclusively American. Some
descriptive observations and propositions for foreign
affairs decision-making will be advanced, based on what
is found in the Okinawa cases and what is perceived as
the relationship between these findings and the wider
literature just alluded to. These perhaps extravagant
claims for enlightenment from what may appear to be a
largely unique series of events require some elaboration
and explanation; they are by no means self-evident. Again
we are confronted with the question, "Why Okinawa?"

   A second question which is fair to ask is "Why the
pre-occupation with decision-making theory?" Is this not

3

overly confining and arbitrary? The answer must come from
a consideration of what is to be accomplished. I have
said that I am concerned with the questions of choice
and rationality in foreign affairs and with the examination of a real-world case to see if there do seem to be
non-unique factors in what appears to have been a unique-
ly successful and therefore attractive policy-creating
sequence.

Decision-making concerns itself with the position
of individuals with power and influence in the determination of "national behavior" in the global amphitheatre.
Choice and reason are attributes of individuals and, with
qualifications, groups and organizations ultimately, and
not states, regions, systems, etc. Systemic theories of
international behavior are certainly relevant but not
central to the consideration of choice and rationality
in foreign policy. Aggregate data and field theory (the
latter the study of state behavior by determining the
state's position along a number of specified and interrelated dimensions) almost definitionally have not been
oriented to individual behavior, but rather aimed at
properties of large collectivities of people and resources. Of more relevance is the recent acceleration
of interest in game theory and economic models of international relations, but these presume a certain rationality and predictive probability that would be unwise to
adopt as a premise in studying a policy-case at this
point.6 This is especially true if one is leaving open
the question of competitive v. cooperative plural decision making centers within the foreign policy establishment as is the case here. Decision-making not only
allows the question to be left open, denying rationality
as an a priori assumption, it actively encourages us to
define and investigate rationality as a characteristic
of the complex process of choice.

Background to the Okinawa Case Study

Unlike the unfolding of many policies involving
American objectives in particular geographical areas,
the evolution of Ryukyus policy-- that is, the supervision of the islands as the most crucial United States
Pacific bases-- took place within a clearly identifiable
time-frame and represented a sharp departure from any
past policy. While no governmental activity can be isolated historiographically as if it were a speciman in
the laboratory experiment sense, the Okinawan occupation
comes as close as can be imagined to an isolated inter-

4

lude presenting an opportunity for innovation by major
organizational and individual participants. Many aspects
of the post-1945 period were novel for the world (and
for American leaders, of course): nuclear and other long-
distance strategic weaponry, super-power bi-polarity,
dissolution of colonial empires, etc. Yet few called for
as many departures from past experience as the conquest
and near absolute rule over a province of an advanced
rival power with a culture profoundly different from the
Anglo-American one and the stocking of a vast complex of
military bases with a dazzling array of high technology
weaponry within a geopolitical stone's throw of Asia.[7]

The Philippine experience offers certain attractive
parallels: rule over Asians, a strategic prize resulting from a big-power war, experiments with democracy,
etc. Suffice it to say here that two crucial differences
must be kept in mind: the fact that Japan regarded Okinawa as part of her home territory and not a colonial pawn
lost in a round of strategic chess (as was the case with
Spain and the Philippines), and equally important, that
Spain never became an intimate American ally, the role
which befell Japan with surprising swiftness following
the Pacific War.

In addition to the clean-slate aspects of this case,
which make it possible to begin the historical analysis
on a fixed date without fear of leaving too much out,
there are a number of dimensions of that experience which
make it a desirable study for comparativists and theory-
builders who seek to generalize and do so significantly.[8]
In relation to other contemporary foreign policy problems,
Okinawa offers its important geographic position and relevance for political-military formulas like the Forward
Base Strategy and the Nixon Doctrine, its importance to
the American Japanese partnership, and its significance
as an example of direct, massive penetration of a largely traditionalist agricultural society by American technology and culture useful for comparison with other cases
of United States interaction with Third World or Third
World-like societies.

From a different perspective, in light of problems
raised in the literature of international relations regarding the process of concocting policy, and indeed for
the practitioners of foreign policy themselves, the Okinawa case would appear promising. An immensely important
cluster of questions centers around the broad query: "How
do foreign policy decisions really get made?" This can
include probes into whether the processes vary comprehensively from decision to decision or whether there are

5

salient "constants," whether decision-making is ever rational and wide-ranging in its examination of alternatives, or whether it is always characterized by incremental movement and compromise; whether the unitary, "rational actor" model can be an adequate explanatory framework for particular policies, or whether organizational, bureaucratic interaction variables must necessarily be taken into account.[9]

Warner Schilling, acknowledging a debt to Gabriel Almond, has portrayed key components of the foreign policy making process as:

> ...an elite structure characterized by a
> large number of autonomous and competing
> groups; and a mass structure characterized
> by a small, informed stratum, attentive to
> elite discussion and conflict, and a much
> larger base normally ignorant of and indifferent to policy and policy making.[10]

This kind of evaluation is widely accepted by political scientists today as applicable to the great majority of foreign policy questions. If this is so, the Okinawa case is quite typical. As Binnendijk notes, Ryukyus policy was for 24 years largely a problem for a small group of elite decision-makers with even less public-- including "informed stratum"-- salience and input than usual.[11] For the analyst the advantage stemming from this fact is that he can focus his attention on inter-actions among relatively few individuals and groups concerned with Okinawa and study them more intensively. Okinawa can thus be seen as a conveniently pronounced but unquestionable example of an important class of decision-making types, those involving few people outside of a limited number of participants. The same factors which make this case a poor and atypical example of foreign policy-issue relevance for the mass public in American domestic politics (cf. Vietnam or the Middle East), make it particularly useful in answering the previously posed questions about the nature of foreign policy decision-making, at least as it applies to those decisions with few domestic players outside the foreign policy establishment.[12]

As for the prescriptive merits of the Okinawa case, that is insights from the way certain aspects of the situations were handled as events unfolded, I will refrain from commenting here except to say that several of the participants regarded the major decisions, at least after 1960, as instances of highly successful policy-making.[13]

One former high-ranking official even went so far as to term the reversion decision-making as his "dream case" of successful problem solving.14 In evaluating this assessment, of course, it would be necessary to separate factors which appear to be unique from those which seem to be replicable (i.e., one-of-a-kind circumstance v. standard procedures).

At this point a quick summarization of the foregoing would seem useful. American postwar policy in the Ryukyus involved a number of important substantive issues related to broad questions of strategy, alliance politics, and the impact of great powers upon tiny ones. Scenes related to the hammering out of this policy took place on a relatively small stage and involved a limited number of players, retrospectively allowing careful focus on the decision-making processes themselves in the search for answers to puzzles about foreign policy-making in general. The time period involved is similarly circumscribed; an understanding of the events themselves, I will attempt to show, is not to the usual degree dependent upon a consideration of previous policies or limited by the failure to consider such policies. For the Okinawa story, the importance of background values and historical precedent is less impressive than the novel problems and challenges presented. All of this is essential for putting the case study into perspective; we can now turn to a brief consideration of case studies per se and how they fit into the building of a social science.

All single case studies are to be contrasted with comparative studies, the latter covering more than one case with attention to the same variables in each case and assuming that measurements of these variables will differ (i.e., "vary") from case to case. Eckstein argues that the potential of single-case studies for the development of theory has been badly underestimated by social science in favor of comparative studies, because of a failure to recognize the full potential of the single case, a failure which he attempts to rectify.15 I do not want to go into the sophisticated arguments he presents for and against each approach; essentially I accept his claims for case-studies and will demonstrate by the handling of a body of data, its analysis, and its implications for theory that the claims are justified.

The Okinawa study can be thought of as a case in the general sense of the term, which examines a number of component cases. I am not primarily concerned with relating individual important decisions I will be examining with each other (i.e., the comparative approach). Rather, the decisions are single cases to be examined individually in the light of certain propositions and used to generate new propositions. In this sense the enterprise strongly resembles "heuristic" case-studies, consciously seeking to determine the "fit" of the case to theoretical propositions (for example, whether a decision more closely conforms to an incremental model of policy or a rational, "all-alternatives-considered" model). It might be asked "if one is going to analyze several decision-making cases within the Okinawa policy study, why not compare them with each other, as well as determining their individual fit to various propositions of international relations theorists? The answer here is that to employ the Okinawa decision cases that way would not make effective use of the comparative method, would not tap its strengths. To use the previous example, I might find that four out of five of my decision cases fit well with the incremental model and only one with the so-called rational model. What would that entitle us to say? Certainly not that "four fifths of foreign policy decisions appear to be incremental," nor even that factors contributing toward incremental decision-making appear to be stronger than those which favor rational decision-making. Why? Because too many elements affecting decision-making in the Okinawa case over time could plausibly be expected to be constant; in short a wider variety of cases should be examined (and ideally a much larger number of cases) to take advantage of the comparative method, and to begin to make use of probabilistic statements about theoretical propositions.

Why not then examine a broader range of cases with fewer pegged directly to Okinawa policy? The answer in part comes from the notion of configurative or "clinical" case studies as described by Eckstein, but actually applies to case studies in general and the economies of different research strategies. Case studies emphasize depth rather than breadth; one of their main strengths lies in their intensive focus on a limited area with payoffs in richness of detail offsetting not being able to make impressive generalizations, or even lesser probabalistic statements in any mathematical sense. A crucial point and one implicit in Eckstein's own presentation is that theoretically "aware" case studies, such as the heuristic type can, by themselves, lend weight to or cast doubt on the validity of propositions if they are well chosen. Two simple examples can illustrate what I mean by "well chosen." Suppose we have a proposition that says "states with large populations are very likely to belong to more than one alliance." If we examine the case of India and see that that country is not now the member of any alliance, nor has it been in the past several centuries, then a certain amount of doubt is cast on the proposition, because India has a very large population and the total number of very populous states in the world is not large. A state like Spain, with a population closer to the international median, would obviously be a less well chosen example to test this proposition. Of course one could examine all of the world's states and derive correlations between population size and alliance membership, but if such a comparative survey were time-consuming or the data in many cases inadequate, there would be a considerable advantage to using just the India case, which alone casts serious doubt on the proposition.[17] Or take a somewhat different kind of proposition and one that applies to the Okinawa case: "a low apparent level of public awareness of a salient policy problem implies a low level of Congressional input into its solution." Regardless of the specific outcome wrested from the data, the Okinawa case is clearly a better one to start with for this particular proposition than, say, Middle East policy. And while the Okinawa case would not necessarily be conclusive for the proposition if Congressional output were found to be low, it would certainly raise questions about the statement if that input were found to be high.[18]

Propositions and hypotheses for which a single case-study is very well chosen fall into the category of crucial case, which Eckstein defines as:

> ...a case that must closely fit a theory if one is to have confidence in that theory's validity, or, conversely, must not fit equally well any rule contrary to that proposed.[19]

To borrow from the earlier illustration, China might be a crucial case, having by far the largest population of any country, if it were not involved in any alliance. Graham Allison, in his Essence of Decision, appears to regard the Cuban missile crisis as a crucial case for the proposition (simplified somewhat here): "no foreign policy decision is immune from bureaucratically self-interested influences which impair the rational solution of the problem." The Cuban missile crisis is the acid test (crucial case) for the proposition, because if any foreign policy decision could be expected to be free from cumbersome, self-serving bureaucratic impediment, a

9

serious crisis engaging the full-time attention of the President and a small group of hand-picked men would be expected to be that kind of decision. Allison points to evidence which he feels shows that in fact there was harmful bureaucratic-political interference, giving heavy support to his proposition.[20]

Do any component cases of the bigger Okinawa case qualify as crucial cases of anything? Perhaps. In a sense three of the major decisions we shall analyze, leading sequentially to reversion, may constitute a critical test of bureaucratic politics by coming from the opposite direction from Allison's own case. The reversion decision sequence-- actually three separate decisions arrived at in 1961-62, 1966-67, and 1969-- involved an issue largely free from crisis pressures, essentially free from public awareness, only occasionally brought to the attention of the President, and traditionally managed by the military and, to some extent, the State Department bureaucracies. If it could be shown that non-bureaucratic influences played an important role in shaping the decisions and that bureaucratic politics as Allison has defined it did not figure prominently, then his thesis would be gravely undermined.

Consequently I see the advantage of the type of case study approach being used as two-fold. First, by seeking aspects of individual cases that can shed light on specific hypotheses from the literature of foreign policy decision-making, I hope to be able to make the cases theoretically useful, perhaps casting doubt on thers in varying degrees, but always in a constructive manner that encourages and facilitates further investigations. Secondly, by emphasizing individual cases within a single, focused substantive area we can probe much more deeply into and uncover more about the dynamics of the general Okinawa case without losing sight of our goal of contributing to theory in the process and without sacrificing more than we have gained by avoiding the comparative or multiple-case method.[21]

A Review of Select Literature on Decision-Making

Within the decision theory arena of international studies this research is most concerned with what I believe to be two of the most profoundly important and inadequately treated problem areas in that discipline in spite of some brilliant and promising advances: 1. the building of a framework for the analysis of foreign policy decisions that is useful for describing and explaining a wide range of cases in a way that non-trivial,

10

policy-relevant propositions and models may be developed, and 2. the question of rationality in foreign policy-making: how can it be defined,once defined is it desirable, if desirable is it achievable? Attention to the first problem is essential if we are going to move from the sometimes penetrating but configurative and thus limited case study and, conversely, from the complicated and cumbersome analytic schemes of Snyder or Rosenau,[22] to the development of a means of preserving some of the richness of the former and the collapsing and simplification of some of some of the variable factors of the latter. The ultimate and widely sought goal of inquiry in the first problem-area, framework construction, is quality of description, prediction, and explanation.[23] The comparable goal of the second area is the use of our strengthened capabilities in these areas to _improve_ the policy-making process.

The interest in decision-making is a natural one for students of global affairs; its focus can be traced well back into history-- at least to Thucydides and later Machiavelli. Indeed, the decision of the statesman representing large numbers of people is such an obviously paramount component of all but the most deterministic approaches to history that to isolate it and talk of it self consciously seems both artificial and trite. Yet it seems necessary to risk this artificiality because decisions themselves-- acts of choice-- make up only part of the picture of events. Consequences, including the implementation of, reaction to, and generation of further decisions are the other side of the picture, and the endeavor to specify what consequences come from what decisions-- if any-- is not any easy one.

Efforts to analyze decisions systematically have been the province of social science, and as such they are relatively new. This holds especially true for the analysis of foreign policy decisions, as a subset of decision-making in general. The first widely recognized attempt in this area was by Richard Snyder and his associates Burton Sapin and H.W. Bruck at Princeton in 1954 (hereafter cited as "the Snyder group") and entitled Decision-Making as an Approach to the Study of International Politics.[24] The monograph (expanded into a book in 1962) has a curious history: it attracted immediate if not universal acclaim, and has been widely cited and argued about for two and a half decades, but its analytic tools have rarely been used in anything like a comprehensive way. The notable exception to this has been Glenn Paige's The Korean Decision, which in view of the

11

author's repeatedly acknowledged debt to the Snyder group is, somewhat surprisingly, highly praised and one of the few serious political science case studies widely read by government officials and others outside the discipline.[25] I say "surprisingly" because it would seem that Paige's success should have injected new enthusiasm for the Snyder approach.

What the are the major attractions and problems of the Snyder-group framework for analysis? Concisely stated they offer us first categories general enough to apply to a wide range of cases and and specifically designed to relate government actors to those aspects of their surroundings which appear most relevant for the understanding of their decision. Clearly influenced by their mentors at Princeton, the Sprouts, they are careful to account for the phenomenological question. As Joseph Frankel describes:

> ..Following Professor and Mrs. Sprout a distinction is made /i.e., in Snyder/ between psychological and operational environments, the former as apperceived by the decision-makers, the latter as could be perceived by an "omniscient observer.' The psychological environment determines the limits of possible decisions while the operational environment determines the limits of possible effective actions. The two environments do not necessarily coincide.[26]

They also distinguish spatially between an internal (domestic political) and an external (foreign phenomena) setting, and characterize the relevant group operating at the interface of these settings as the decision unit, made up of a carefully organized aggregation of individuals, groups, and organizations (or parts thereof) connectable to a particular decision[27] They describe their technique of extracting decisions analytically from the complex welter of human interaction by defining decision-making for us as:

> ..a process which results in the selection of a socially defined, limited number of problematical, alternative projects of one project intended to bring about the particular state of affairs envisaged by the decision makers.[28]

The ingestion of information relevant to the decision

event by policy-makers over time they call "successive overlapping definitions of the situation." [29] They are careful to tell us that the study of statements and writings by participants-- made both contemporaneously and retrospectively-- are to be used to reproduce, admittedly imperfectly, these "definitions" of situations. It is up to the decision-analyst himself, however, to gather sufficient data to reconstruct an "objective situation" within which to place this "situation as perceived by the participants at the time," (those participants generally-- but not always-- having had more limited kinds of input).[30] Three major sets of variables of the decision units themselves are held to exist and they are derived from answers to certain questions: organizational variables- what organizations participate in the decision or at least attempt to and to what extent?, informational variables- what are the sources of fact and opinion available to the decision unit?,and motivational variables- what background values and situational incentives appear to influence the participants? [31]

Because of the large number of variables and substantial data demands of the Snyder group categories, it is not surprising that studies which have drawn on their framework have treated specific short-time-frame decisions, involving a very limited number of actors. Cases in point in addition to the Paige Korean intervention study are analyses of the outbreak of World War One by Charles and Margaret Hermann (and by North, Holsti et al.) with the obvious common denominator of crisis characteristics: seriousness of situation, short decision time, and elements of surprise.[32]

The crisis decision combines real world relevance and interest with normally manageable proportions for the analyst making retrospective examinations, which make it attractive for case studies and amenable to the use of the Snyder framework. Importantly, however, there is no predisposition on the part of Snyder and his associates to regard their analytic equipment as exclusively suitable for crisis investigations; to the contrary their pre-theoretical machinery would be less useful if it were so limited. This framework has not yet been applied to a series of related cases over time, even with modifications.

Detractors have referred to the Snyder framework as "a checklist" or a taxonomy, but even as such it is impressive. The surest proof of this is that easily the most widely discussed and provocative recent model of

decision-making, Allison's _bureaucratic_ _politics_,33 owes
an intellectual debt to the Snyder group (one than may
not be adequately acknowledged). Allison has made strong,
though not immodest claims, which he illustrates with
his in-depth treatment of the Cuban missile crisis, that
foreign policy processes cannot be understood as rational
processes controlled by a cohesive group of actors who
"choose." Rather, organizational structure and goals,
and subjective, partisan bureaucratic considerations--
competing sub-agency "shops," career enhancement, budget
politics-- must be factored into the formulae of explanation. The motivational and organizational variables
proposed by Snyder laid much of the groundwork for this
theoretical development; Allison's forte was an elegant
and tighly argued presentation of three competitive-
complementary models to explain in detail an actual case.
Since the appearance of Essence of Decision in 1971,
others have drawn on Allison and his predecessors' work,
adding their own refinements (_e.g._, Halperin's treatment
of the ABM controversy).34 This investigation runs through
the five major decisions selected, employing the (somewhat simplified) frameworks of the Snyder group, Lindblom
and Allison competitively to see what each would be likely to help us account for and what each might have missed
in describing explaining and "predicting" the decision
outcome (_i.e._, "predicting meaning using their categories
for analyzing the early stages of the decision and also
for anticipating the outcome). Following this experiment
I attempt to construct my own framework, in part synthe-
sizing the useful ingredients from the earlier approaches
and discarding less helpful components, and drawing from
other writers (but in a more limited way).

The short review of Allison's thesis provides a
good transition to an equally selective and abbreviated
excursus on rationalism in policy decision-making. The
concept of rationality in policy formulation comes under
direct and intense fire in Allison: even if policy inputs are "rational" in the parochial terms of individual
organizations and interests, the combining of these inputs could not possibly be considered rational.35 Counter
attackers have asserted that Allison's approach is wrong-
headed, that it dilutes the focus of responsibility for
action or exaggerates the impact of bureaucratic intrigue
which can be and has been neutralized in many cases by
effective Presidents. One of Allison's severest critics,
Steven Krasner, has even gone so far as to argue that
his former Harvard professor's thesis is dangerous in
a normative sense because it reduces foreign policy effectively to _process_ and robs the electorate of the

ability to turn to the traditional center of responsibility -- the White House-- for blame or credit.[36] Allison's critics appear affronted by the implications of his arguments (and I confess that I agree with these people by and large), but Allison is not the first to take on rationality as an ideal or as a workable process. He is not even the first theorist of consequence within postwar decision analysis to do so. Since the mid-to-late 1950's a prominent group of social analysts led by Charles Lindblom, focusing on American domestic policy making and Herbert Simon, writing about complex organizations and economic decision-making have strongly challenged not only the workability of rationality in decision making, but-- especially in the case of Lindblom-- have questioned it as a desirable goal.[37]

Simon and the Carnegie School (also including scholars James March and Richard Cyert) have produced a number of influential books and monographs arguing that the demands of rationality, i.e., wide-ranging means-ends analysis and consonance of values with action strategies, are burdensome in highly complex organizations dealing with equally multi-faceted problems. In their studies of firm and public administrative behavior they assemble a lot of evidence to show that what really takes place in these bodies is a sort of reductionism that limits the alternatives considered and the quality of results expected.[38] This satisficing concept has gained wide currency in the social sciences as a more realistic description of decisional behavior in an environment of limited informational resources and intricate problems (note: in spite of absolutely better information resources it often appears that the magnitudes of the problems pursued makes these improved resources less relatively adequate than the simpler resources used to attack much simpler problems formerly).

Charles Lindblom, in his own writings and in collaboration with David Braybrooke, has gone further than Simon and the Carnegie School to argue that in virtually any complex modern decision-making problem, rationality is a hopelessly uneconomical and difficult ideal, dispersing resources and requiring an unhealthy degree of centralization and concentration of power. In place of rational/comprehensive problem solving, Lindblom and Braybrooke have offered a decision "strategy" with pluralistic groups of decision-makers effecting marginal changes based on the limited consideration of practical alternatives.[39] Describing the strategy as "disjointed incrementalism," they hold that it not only better describes the hard world of policy making with limited resources and multi-faceted problems, but that the improvement of this process is a more palatable ideal than attempting to employ a rational-comprehensive approach.

The thinking of Lindblom, Simon, and the rest has had considerable impact and become so widely accepted as to seem in a skeptical era like orthodoxy rather than iconoclasm. Criticism has been directed at them, however, and at the center of it has been the belief that they overstate their case and deny rationality too much. For example, Robert Rothstein takes Lindblom to task for in effect making a virtue (the incrementalist strategy) out of necessity (the many limits on rationality):

> ..Marginal change is acceptable only to the extent that existing policies yield satisfactory results.. If there is sharp disagreement or dissent about prevailing policies, a system that can alter them only in minor ways is bound to be attacked... In short, incrementalism was and is an adequate approach to policy making only in periods of great stability, which is to say where there is wide consensus on non-ideological goals, continuity in problems, and plenty of money to paper over the cracks.[40]

The relevance of the Okinawa case to the widely accepted Lindblom principle, I believe, lies in the strong claims of rationality and "model" international affairs problem solving made by participants in the Okinawa decisions, at least in the last three policy sequences being studied-- under Kennedy, Johnson, and Nixon respectively. Given the limited boundaries of the Okinawa problem and the amount of highly trained "reasonable" manpower brought to bear in these decisions both on the Japanese and American sides, we might expect Okinawa to be something of a critical case for Lindblom's major hypotheses. If decision-making regarding the Ryukyus was disjointed, incremental, and made at the margins of existing policy, then Lindblom surely has a powerful case for pervasive disjointed incremental policy-making, as most comparably important policies seem to have been more difficult and less well handled than the decisions on the Okinawa problem. If, on the other hand, it could be shown that aspects of the decision strategies for Okinawa were strongly rational, that wide ranges of alternatives were considered, and that when decisions were handled in the way that Lind-

16

blom and Braybrooke describe decision-making, the results were decidedly less satisfactory, then we would
have to call this new orthodoxy into question and perhaps hold some hope out for rational strategy approaches
to the improvement of the entire foreign affairs decision making process.

Some Key Terms Defined

Up to this point I have defined a number of terms
(used repeatedly) in an informal, sometimes implicit
manner. It seems appropriate here to be more specific
about the most salient concepts being used. I do not
want to be confined at this point to only one starkly
operational use of "decision" or "actor," but I do
want to be more explicit about what I do and do not mean
by these words. Vague, trite, but hard to replace terms
like "policy" may or may not take on a certain life in
the context of a good essay or article, but definitional
guidelines can set useful limits on them. Expressions
I am concerned with defining now fall into the category of foreign affairs action-types.

The relationship between policy and decision, two
principal foreign affairs action types, is an important
one. Snyder has defined policy as:

> actions and rules of action, reaction, or
> interpretation. Accordingly policy can be
> anticipatory, cumulative, specific and gen-
> eral.'To have a policy means action and/or
> rules with respect to a problem, contingen-
> cy or event which has occurred, is occurring
> or is expected to occur. Action and rules may
> be among the givens preceding a definition
> of a situation by the decision-makers.41

Lindblom and Braybrooke distinguish between decision making and policy making by noting that:

> the latter encompasses both decision-making
> and the course that policies take as a re-
> sult of the interrelations among decisions
> and/or in which the latter term incorporates
> certain political processes in addition to
> analytical processes into the determination
> of action courses.42

I draw on both of these to formulate this distinction:

17

Decisions are specific actions normally based on the selection of one from a list of concrete alternatives for action. The action is nothing more than the act of deciding itself: it may be an articulation or modification of policy, or the announced intention that an action be carried out in the name of the deciding group and, in the case of foreign policy, often in the name of the government as a whole. The action carried out is decision implementation.

Policy is composed of decisions, guidelines for action, and the interrelationships among decisions and guidelines. A policy may also be thought of as the aggregate of a number of decisions regarding the proper actions of the government toward another international or transnational actor (i.e., another government, a corporation, classes of individuals, regional bodies, intergovernmental organizations, etc.) A policy may also relate to a functional area, i.e., "national security," "oceans," "immigration" and so on.

Decisions are more focused in time than policies, they can be dated more readily, and they are usually more issue-specific. I will refer to decision sequences as:

events-- including past decisions and their implementation-- leading up to a given decision, but because decision sequences cannot be defined with the operational precision of decisions or policies, because one can never know what all of the "past decisions" leading up to a given decision are, precisely, I regard my presentation of decision-sequence as informal definition or description.

To give a specific illustration: the choice made by President Kennedy in 1962 to initiate reforms in the administration of Okinawa was a decision. The events which can be identified as leading up to that decision-- including past decisions (e.g. appointing the Kaysen commission to investigate United States rule in the Ryukyus) and their implementation (e.g., the carrying out of the Kaysen study mission and the submitting of a report to the President)

18

are considered the decision sequences. The Kennedy guidelines, the decisions made about how to implement them,
and their implementation constitute a policy. It is essential to note that in this study policy and action cannot be separated or contradictory; policy is guidelines
(intentions) and how those guidelines are carried out
(implementation).

Having made a brief survey of the important theoretical literature relevant to the empirical work of this
study and having attempted to define the central terms
to conclude Part I of this introduction, Part II focuses
on the specific decisions and a more detailed treatment
of how the specific propositions of Snyder, Allison, and
Lindblom will be applied in analyzing them. As background
to the application of this analytic perspective to these
five decisions (in Chapters 3 through 8), Chapter 2 will
offer an extensive survey of American involvement in Okinawa for the entire period 1945-69.

The Decisions

The five decisions of this study were chosen with
only one criterion in mind: their historical importance.
Each represents a critical episode in the development of
American policy in the Ryukyus. If there are other critical episodes-- and it is arguable whether there are--
none is referred to in the secondary source literature
or the accounts of Japanese and American policy participants and experts as often as any of these five:

Decision 1- to upgrade and make more permanent
the American military presence on Okinawa in
1948 and early 1949, as described in National
Security Council (NSC) Report 13/3. The status of the Ryukyus, which were administratively
separated from Japan in January, 1946, had been
extremely uncertain. In spite of military arguments for retaining the islands (which were
populated by several hundred thousand Japanese)
since their capture in 1945, a hard commitment
had not been made. The Department of State had
opposed the retention of administrative control
over the islands as offensive to the Japanese,
who were increasingly seen as a potential ally
against the Soviet Union. The NSC document,
signed by the President, clarified the matter
and implied an open ended presence for the United States, at least pending a treaty of peace
with Japan.

Decision 2- to give legal weight to the de
facto separation of Okinawa from Japan in the
1951 peace treaty, while allowing Japan to retain "residual sovereignty." This was the compromise worked out by John Foster Dulles (officially "Advisor to the Secretary of State,"
but virtually peace treaty "Ambassador Pleni-
potentiary," which preserved United States
military rule and administrative rights but
appeased the State Department (by appeasing
Japan) to some extent through not annexing
Okinawa. Rather, Japan promised in Article
III to "concur in any proposal" to make the
Ryukyus an American trusteeship under the United Nations system, and, pending such a proposal, to agree to complete United States
jurisdiction there.

Decision 3 - to allow for the expansion of American and--more importantly -- Japanese economic aid to the Ryukyus and substantially more civilian control in the United States administration of the islands through an Executive Order signed by President John Kennedy in March, 1962. The Army, especially Ryukyus Command Lt. Gen. Paul Caraway (also High Commissioner), were very reluctant to have large increases in Japanese assistance to the Government of the Ryukyu Islands. They tended to equate aid with influence and the undermining of the American position. They were also not particularly happy about the prospect of a civilian Civil Administrator (the executive under the High Commissioner who in principle worked more closely with the local Okinawan government than his superior did). The State Department position and the investigatory commission under Carl Kaysen apparently won the president over, however, in their recommendations for policy liberalization.

Decision 4- to promise the return of the Ryukyus "within a few years" as part of the Johnson/Sato communique of November, 1967. A series of joint State-Defense policy reviews between 1965 and 1967 gradually wore down the opposition of the uniformed military (i.e., the Joint Chiefs of Staff; the Commander in Chief, Pacific; and the Ryukyus Command), to the extent that the Johnson commitment to reversion of the islands to Japan (in the not-distant-future but not immediately either), was at least minimally acceptable if not ideal.

Decision 5 - to commit the United States to the actual return of the the Ryukyus to Japan during 1972 made by President Richard Nixon to Prime Minister Sato in their 1969 joint communique. Domestic opposition to the Prime Minister's patient, tactful policy on Okinawa (he had pledged to seek the islands' return as early as 1965) was forcing the hand of the new American administration across the Pacific: either support Sato by a specific reversion pledge or undermine his position, perhaps paving the way for a less pro-American LDP faction takeover or even an opposition party coalition.

21

Each decision case-study opens with an effort to
reconstruct the environment in which the decision took
place. This includes a very brief reconnaissance of the
historical context of the decision and then a zeroing-in
on the decision sequence itself. For this reconstruction
I draw on the conceptual framework developed by Richard
Snyder et al., and applied explicitly to date in only
one published case study, that of Paige on the Korean
intervention.

In talking of "reconstructing" a decision environment, which is after all not much more than a methodical
and ordered historical exercise to begin with, one is
confronted by some of the same problems of vast amounts
of information sorting which plagued the policy-makers
who originally confronted the problem. Vital has described
the challenge of information magnitudes in practical foreign policy work:

> Confronted with a multiplicity of phenomena--
> political, economic, military, social, admini-
> strative-- which may be thought to bear some
> prima facie relation to the behavior of gov-
> ernments, societies, and individual personali-
> ties in each of the 140 sovereign states (and
> in a further group of dependent territories)
> the administrators of foreign relations must
> insist upon selectivity. If they do not, their
> colleagues in the ministry of finance will
> surely do so for them: the collection and as-
> similation of information is costly and time-
> consuming and unless bounds are set on the
> categories and quantities of data no useful
> bounds can be set on the costs in time and
> money. 43

In reconstructing a decision environment one does
have the mixed blessing of working with much processed
information, i.e., the reports of administrators, duty
officers, intelligence analysts, with their charting
and cataloguing and abstracting of information. This
allows the researcher to some extent to recapture what
was regarded as relevant information, but one always
runs the risk of missing information of the ephemeral
sort: private remarks and gestures, confidential conversations, etc. One can attempt to pierce this veil by
petitioning for classified documents and talking at
length with individuals involved in the decision from
many angles (as I have attempted to do in this study,

22

see the methodological appendix), but one can never be sure of having enough data and enough of the right kinds of data to say that one has "completely" explained something. And even when one is right, it may not be for the right reasons. Figure I-A represents the information problem greatly simplified. We are talking about four kinds of information, basically: 1. the totality of information relevant to a given decision, which is only a theoretical construct (i.e., it is vast and open-ended); 2. information known to key participants in the decision process, but forgotten, lost, held confidential, or otherwise not available to the analyst; 3. information available to the analyst now that was unavailable or as best we can tell unperceived by the key decision-makers; and 4. information available to both the contemporary participants and the analyst.

FIGURE I-A: Categories of Information in Decision Reconstruction*

1. Totality of information relevant to decision

2. That part of totality of information known to some participants but unavailable to analyst.

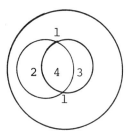

3. Information available to analyst but not to participants

4. Information available to participants and analysts.

Category 1 includes much information that is, properly speaking, never "known" or "perceived" by anybody or only by a few, such as "the opinions of the Japanese mass public on a specific issue" or "the intentions of the Communist Chinese leaders regarding Japan and Okinawa." Categories 3 and 4 comprise the stuff of which history is made, literally, and they are surprisingly fruitful in view of their being a limited percentage of the whole. Occasionally information will be divulged or otherwise unexpectedly become available, moving-- for the historian's purposes-- from category 2 to category 4,

---

*Technically speaking, "categories" 2,3, and 4 should be called sub-categories, as they are subsets of category 1.

23

FIGURE I-B- Snyder-Bruck-Sapin
Decision Analysis Schema as Originally Presented in Foreign Policy
Decision-Making. Copyright© 1962
by Richard Snyder, H.W. Bruck and
Burton Sapin. Reprinted by permission of MacMillan Publishing Co. p.72.

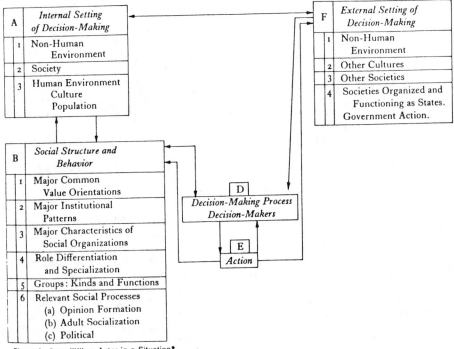

Figure 1. State "X" as Actor in a Situation*

Figure I-C- Adaptation of Snyder-Group Schema for Foreign Policy Decision Analysis

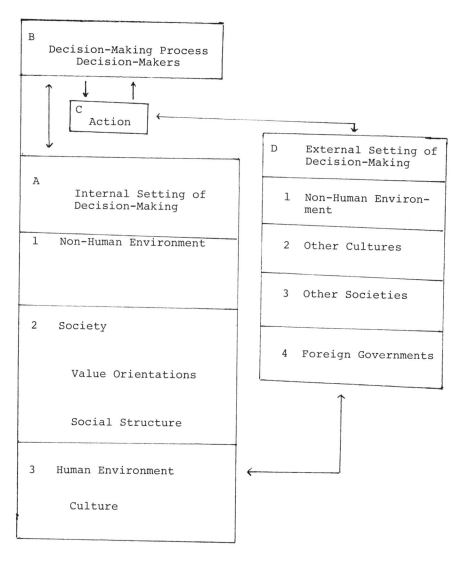

i.e., "newly discovered evidence," or "previously unavailable documents," which make for historical revision,
a process which goes on all the time. The Dead Sea Scrolls
are as relevant in that regard as the Pentagon Papers.

Snyder and his associates developed the useful distinction of internal and external settings for organizing phenomena and data pertinent to a given decision
(see Figure I-B). External setting is defined as:

> ..factors beyond the territorial boundaries
> of the state-- the actions and reactions of
> other states (their decision makers) and the
> societies for which they act and the physical
> world... Setting is an analytical device to
> suggest certain limited kinds of historical
> relevances and to limit the number of non-
> governmental factors with which the student
> of international politics must be concerned.
> The external setting is constantly changing
> and will be composed of what the decision-
> makers decide is important. 44

Internal setting is regarded as a somewhat more objective and knowable body of phenomena (although it is not
made clear why) and is:

> ..loosely labeled 'domestic politics", 'public
> opinion', or 'geographical setting'. A somewhat
> more adequate formulation might be: some clues
> to the way any state behaves toward the world
> must be sought in the way its society is organ-
> ized and functions, in the character and behav-
> ior of its people and in its physical habitat.45

These very large compartments bear close resemblence to
the domestic and international dichotomy that has almost
always run through treatments of national behavior, at
least since the rise of the nation-state in the 17th and
18th centuries. The categories within each compartment
are frankly regarded best as checklists for the analysis
of a given foreign policy decision. The Snyder group categories have been somewhat simplified and streamlined in
Figure I-C for use in analyzing the Okinawa decision episodes. Snyder and his associates justified their intricate breakdown of categories in the following way:

> There are two reasons for insisting that the
> analysis of the society for which state X acts

be pushed to this fundamental level. First, the
list invites attention to a much wider range
of potentially relevant factors than the more
familiar terms like morale, attitudes, national
power, party politics, and so on... Second, if
one is interested in the fundamental "why" of
state behavior, the search for reliable answers
must go beyond the derived conditions and factors (morale, pressure groups, production, attitudes, and so on) which are normally the focus
of attention.[46]

Because of the widespread consensus of those who
have studied the Okinawa problem that the major decisions
were taken by small elite groups within the defense and
diplomatic bureaucracy advising the President, it seemed
that a detailed linking of the decision processes to all
of these societal factors in each of the five cases was
unnecessary. Such streamlining may appear to be a departure from the originally stated intention to apply frameworks comprehensively, but as the Snyder group describes
its checklist as "crudely suggestive" there would have
been few tangible gains in "reliability" and trueness to
the original to have left the categories untouched.

Harold and Margaret Sprout have made a distinction
between psychological and operational aspects of settings
in international relations, which in turn influenced their
student, Richard Snyder, and his associates.[47] In describing the nuances of the two terms, Joseph Frankel points
out that:

The two environments do not necessarily coincide.
The decision-maker may believe that there are opportunities for effective action which do not fully exist, in which case his psychological environment is broader than his operational one. He may
likewise ignore existing possibilities, thus nar-
rowing his psychological environment in relation
to the operational one. He may also do both consecutively, as the result of disappointed expectations, or even simultaneously in different sec-
tors of the environment.[48]

Snyder defines his external setting in a way that
seems almost to preclude an operational version which one
can analyze. For the decision-makers, he says, the external
setting is:

what the decision-makers decide is important.

This 'deciding' can simply mean that certain lacks--such as minerals or guns-- not imposed on them, that is must be accepted. A serious native revolt in South Africa in 1900 was not a feature of the external setting of United States decision-makers; it would be in 1963.[49]

Snyder's usage is modified in my application of environments in the Okinawan cases, and occasionally I draw the distinction between the psychological environment of the policy-maker [50] and what appears in retrospect to be part of the operational setting at the time of the events, which policy people may have missed. The internal setting also has psychological and operational aspects. The domestic variables that appear to be constantly taken into consideration are part of the psychological internal setting, but there may also be influences which we can point to in the operational domestic setting which impacted on a decision, but were not consciously perceived as doing so. As an example, it appears that the attentive American public's consciousness of the rapidly heating Okinawa issue in the late 1960's may have been almost completely blocked out by the overwhelming Vietnam issue, thus freeing Okinawa policy-makers to operate in more of a vacuum than would otherwise have been the case. Few of the policy-makers whose interviews or writings I have encountered indicate that this was consciously considered by those in decision roles, but there are strong signals that it was the case.[51]

The internal and external settings are fundamental ordering devices in the Snyder group's investigation schema, but not the only ones. The authors also separate decision-making actors, who maneuver within these double environments, into organizational and individual categories. The individuals involved are the actual decision-makers, an important part of the decision-unit (Snyder's definition presented earlier in this chapter). Snyder, [52] collaborating with James A. Robinson in a refinement of some of the former's theoretical work, breaks down the attributes of individual-decision makers into personality characteristics, social backgrounds, and personal values. While detailed data for all actors in all of the decisions being analyzed is well beyond the scope of the present research, the three individual attributes are kept in mind when the analytic equipment is set up for each decision-case. To use our second decision, the residual sovereignty formula as an example, the role of John Foster Dulles in this was so large as to logically compel

28

us to examine his individual qualities in some depth, and for this the Snyder-Robinson categories are useful. For an individual with superficial involvement in a decision, such as Robert McNamara in the Kennedy decision, a detailed individual-attributes analysis would be too time consuming and not likely to yield productive results. If it appears that the individual traits did seriously affect an official's role, it is assumed that some hint of this will manifest itself in interviews, either with that official or some of the people with whom he came in contact in the course of the decision-sequence.

The other category of foreign policy actor is the organizational one, which Snyder separates analytically from the individual category in his article with Robinson (although elsewhere he combines the categories into "actors: individual and organizational aspects.") In reconstructing decisions we not only seek out the individual actors, but also are concerned with the network of organizations (presumed to change over time) which comes into play for each particular decision-sequence.

There are two important and related dimensions of the question of how individuals, working in an organizational context, perceive and react to internal and external settings. The first deals with the way in which individuals "incubating" a decision (which may not at the time even be perceived as a decision) process the information they get in very large quantities, although it need not be the specific information they want or should have. Information, phenomena, signals-- whatever this intake is called-- much of it must be discarded as noise (interference, either irrelevant or spurious), to use the application of the term developed by Roberta Wohlstetter.[53] Although Wohlstetter applied noise to a crisis analysis of Pearl Harbor, it seems applicable in a limited way to more "normal" policy-making procedures as those in the Okinawa decisions. Policy-makers in the State Department and Defense Department relied heavily on the information intake of the embassy in Tokyo, USCAR, and the Japanese (and to a very limited extent the American press) for their evaluations of how serious the pressure was becoming at the local level in Okinawa and Japan for American administrative concessions. Statements by Japanese politicians from the Prime Minister on down had to be weighed and evaluated as to intention, desired audience, etc. Noise also complicates the problem of accurate decision reconstruction by throwing an element of uncertainty into the way in which decision-makers deal

29

with their external setting. It is difficult to know
what incoming signals were never regarded, and which
were deliberately disregarded: reports and documentation of contemporary foreign relations information processing are almost always sketchy.[54]

Related to the problem of noise versus significant
signal discrimination (the latter a barrier of complexity to the understanding of how decision-relevant news
is digested), is that of reproducing the reactions of
policy-makers to incoming information: arguments of colleagues, intelligence reports, statistical data, etc.
Joseph DeRivera, in his lengthy consideration of the
psychological complexities of decision reconstruction,
tells us:

> I should like to be able to describe exactly
> what went on in the minds of the President and
> the Secretary of State: the thinking with its
> creative insights and its subtle distinctions;
> the arguments that occurred to each man-- and
> those that failed to occur; the emotions that
> were provoked by the various alternatives; the
> sub-conscious meanings that affected the course
> of the process but weren't revealed until later
> free association brought them to light; and
> the final process of commitment as it reflec-
> ted the impact of each man's personality. Un-
> fortunately, just a bit of this is available;
> there is no reasonably accurate record of any
> of these important decisions. The major reason
> for this fact is that the investigators are
> not fully aware of the decision-making process
> and do not know what questions to ask.[55]

It is not enough to know individuals and organizational habitats that appear to have been salient in a
given decision then. One must try to examine the information processes, at least those at the upper end of the
policy-making chain, to uncover patterns and significant
irregularities that may make a crucial difference in outcomes.[56] An excellent example of the significance of
this problem for the proper explanation of a decision
can be found in the case of the 1967 communique between
President Lyndon Johnson and Prime Minister Sato Eisaku
at their autumn summit. Somehow in the process of drafting the English and Japanese versions of the communique,
a discrepency occurred which remained in the final public texts of the document. The English version talked
about looking forward to the reversion of Okinawa "within a few years", while the Japanese counterpart used the

30

term <u>ryosan</u>-<u>nen</u>, which was translated back into English
as "two to three years" and read exactly that way, <u>i.e.</u>,
as a specific time commitment. The resulting difference
the two versions led to harsh criticism in Japan and an
unfortunate misunderstanding between the two allies. It
is difficult to believe that the discrepency could have
been accidental; yet if it were purposeful it is amazing
that the contradictory time references were allowed to
remain, given the concern with the timing of Okinawa's
return on the part of both parties. Who knew about the
discrepencies in advance? The President? The Secretary
of State? The Japanese negotiators? The language barrier
is a formidable one; could this have been accidental? The
answers are interesting, and necessary for an understanding of the decision outcome itself.

The one essential concept in Snyder's work which
remains to be incorporated into our decision-analysis
equipment is that of the <u>situational</u> <u>properties</u> of decisions (what might also be called "core context")5.7 These
are the often unique situational details which give shape
and color to the decision as a result of circumstance and
coincidence rather than more stable factors like the individuals involved, organizational structure, societal
differences, <u>etc</u>. It is not easy to separate these properties from <u>internal</u> <u>setting</u> and <u>external</u> <u>setting</u> as Snyder has described these; the distinctions are largely ar-
bitrary. How does one separate the more immediate elements of any particular situation from its environment?
Situation and setting are intellectual constructs-- artificial boundaries. Snyder has referred to contextual rel-
evancies of a situation, which, although very general,
may be a good way of combining the setting of a decision
and its situational properties. 58 The former are more permanent, ingrained factors, while the latter can be thought
of as more immediate and specific factors.

Specific situational variables have been catalogued
by Snyder and Robinson under the heading "occasion for
decision."59 The variables include: anticipated v. unanticipated situations, the amount of time allowed for response (is it "crisis" or "routine"?), and the demands
on the participants during the time which they have. The
magnitude of the values at stake are a related situational
property. The annual budgetary considerations regarding
the size of the Coast Guard are one kind of decision
(routine); the decision about whether the Coast Guard
should be dispatched to surround a group of trawlers in
American waters (mild crisis); the decision to send the
United States Navy to surround Soviet vessels believed

31

carrying offensive ballistic missiles to Cuba is a third and quite different breed. None is like the other in its mix of time and value magnitude variables.

The conceptual framework of Snyder and his associates has been designed as a method of reconstructing the ingredients of decisions. As an ordering device it has the advantage of careful description and attention to often neglected elements in the how of a decision and sometimes the why. Two simple and key questions about policy action and choice have been posed by Snyder and Paige, which summarize much of what these analysts are after: 1. why was a decision made at all? and 2. why this particular decision?[60] I believe that the intellectual equipment that they have provided us can help us to answer questions about how and why foreign relations decisions get made, useful for the investigation of the Okinawa cases, but that other approaches, including more specific and focused hypotheses about why actions unfold as they do, need to be employed.[61] (See Figure I-G, p43 summarizing the Okinawa decisions analytic scheme).

The second major foreign policy theorist whose contributions are assessed and incorporated into this analytic framework is Graham Allison. As mentioned, Allison's signal work has been the application of paradigms or conceptual models to explain particular foreign polcies, notably the October, 1962 crisis over the missiles in Cuba. With his competitive explanatory techniques he has created a heuristic device of considerable interest as a means of getting a better grip on decisions such as those made on Okinawa policy. One reason for this is that his work has been highly influential and his vocabulary of bureaucratic politics is achieving increasing currency in discussions of the domestic determinants of foreign policy-making.[62]

If Snyder's analytic framework provides us with a means of creating a map of the five major decisions on Okinawa, Allison's rational, organizational, and bureaucratic politics models allow us to move through the decisions, with corresponding different points of emphasis on each excursion. Before I outline the aspects of the three models that will shape my application of them to the Okinawa episodes, it is worth emphasizing that the bureaucratic politics approach is the one Allison is most attached to, and represents his most innovative thinking. The rational actor paradigm is his portrayal of the conventional wisdom about government behavior, the

32

FIGURE I-D— Summary Outline of Allison Models and Concepts. Adapted from Graham T. Allison, Essence of Decision: Explaining the Cuban Missile Crisis, p. 256. Copyright © 1971 by Graham T. Allison. Reprinted by permission of Little, Brown, and Company.

The Paradigm	Model I	Model II	Model III
	National Government	National Government	National Government
	Goals Options Consequences Choice	Organizations Goals SOPs and Programs	Players in positions Goals, interests, stakes Power Action Channels
Basic Unit of Analysis	Government Action as Choice	Government Action as Organizational Output	Government Action as Political Resultant
Organizing Concepts	National Actor The Problem Static Selection	Organizational Actors Factored Problems Fractionated Power Parochial Priorities Action as Organizational Output	Players in Positions Parochial Priorities Goals and Interests Stakes and Stands Rules of the Game Action Channels
Dominant Inference Pattern	Governmental Action = Choice	Governmental Action= Output Determined by SOPs and by Organizational Goals	Governmental Action= Resultant of Bargaining
General Propositions	Substitution Effect	Organizational Implementation Options Incremental Change	Action and Intention Chiefs and Indians Styles of Play Problems and Solutions

33

organizational model a curiously incomplete explanatory
device between the other two.

Allison presents the rational model (Model I) as
the implicit body of assumptions of the vast majority
of both real life policy-making incidents and accounts
of such incidents. The "basic unit of analysis" (Allison's term) is held to be "Governmental action as choice"
with the national actor as the major performer.[63] Thus,
when one talks of "Japan doing this" or "Washington considering that", one is talking in rational model terms.
Action is conceived as response to problems, with a conscious choice among alternatives being made. What Allison calls the dominant inference pattern (method of applying information) amounts to choices made to favor certain ends using the best means possible, i.e., "value-
maximizing" choices. Component propositions of the paradigm include: "the greater the costs of an alternative,
the less likelihood of its being chosen", and "the less
the costs, the greater the likelihood of choice."[64] The
various elements of the model are so familiar as to seem
like truisms, implying that we have internalized "the
model" completely in our thinking about decision-making.
We will examine the Okinawa decisions as deliberate conscious choices of the part of "Washington" or "the United States government" through the lens of this model.

Allison's second paradigm or Model II breaks the
governmental actor down into organizational components,
a process which he describes as qualitatively changing
explanations and ways of thinking about decision-making.
Here the basic unit of analysis is "Governmental action
as organizational output," with organizational configurations determining both the way in which information is
processed and the choices which are made on the basis of
that information.[65] Organizational actors are the central
performers, and major organizing concepts include "factored problems and fractionated power" and "parochial
priorities and perceptions." This means that organizational operating procedures, the stress between central
control and the decentralized division of labor, and various other organizational imperatives (budget, performance evaluation) may determine the way in which decisions
are made as much as the choices among objective policy
alternatives of the rational model. The dominant inference pattern is that any action of a government is largely explanable in terms of set procedures, established
routines, and choices circumscribed by these fixed processes. Among the general propositions growing out of
this depiction of the decision-making apparatus are:

1."Routines guide choices among options and thus effectively limit the options," 2. the health of the organization is always a consideration in selecting among options (e.g., feasibility, organizational costs, etc.),"
and 3. change directed from above (i.e. the political
leadership) is possible, but difficult because it must
almost always be channeled through the established or-
ganizatinal network. In the case of Ryukyus decision-
making one would have to look to the working arrangements of the Army (notably the United States Civil Administration in the Ryukyus) within the Department of
Defense, the State Department, the White House, and
Congress for managing the Ryukyus within the double
contexts of Japanese alliance policy and American national security requirements.

   Model III, based on the bureaucratic politics paradigm, has provoked the most attention (of Allison's models) within academic international relations. Here neither actors nor organizational machines are sufficient
for an understanding of individual and sub-organizational
interests and motives. The basic unit of analysis becomes
"Governmental action as political resultant." By "resultant" Allison means the outcome of "compromise, conflict
and confusion" rather than choice per se (although multiple choices may be involved).[66] The organizing concepts revolve around a central metaphor, bargaining games,
with the relevant questions "who plays?" "what determines
a player's stand and his impact on the outcome?" and
"what is the nature of the game being played?" The dominant inference pattern is that of actions as resultants
of bargaining and intra-bureaucratic pulling and hauling
rather than organizational game-plans or national choices.
The general propositions applicable to bureaucratic politics are difficult to formulate because of the tremendous complexity of the process. Allison offers these notions, among others: there are a large number of factors
in the governmental games that intervene between issues
and results; governmental action is not the result of
intention, but the outcome of a composite of intentions;
and intentions and actions are influenced by whom the
players represent, how well they communicate, their style
of play, and the importance of various sub-issues to different players. As applied to the Okinawa decisions and
analytic framework I am using, the bureaucratic politics
model will be a valuable and interesting set of guidelines for linking individual and organizational actors
(cf.Snyder). It is necessary to know not only the issues
and costs and organizational configurations in these
cases, but also the bureaucratic political variables im-

35

pinging on the major actors.

The work of Charles Lindblom, David Braybrooke and Herbert Simon has been treated earlier in this introduction. I focus on the work of Lindblom rather than Simon here fully recognizing that the latter is the true pioneer in the study of organizations, the first important critic of "classical" rationalist assumptions about problem-solving, and an influence on Lindblom. Lindblom's work, however, has the advantage of having focused heavily on governmental decision-making and having drawn a sharp contrast between rationalist organizational problem solving and disjointed incrementalism in a way that makes his assertions easier to "test" and more capable of being tested in convincing ways with the Okinawa decisions than would Simon's. An important dimension in Lindblom's thinking-- and an important departure from Simon's-- is his normative argument for the desirability of decentralized decision-making "at the margins" rather than centrally directed, comprehensive-review methods. He and Braybrooke support their claims for the benefits of incrementalism with an elaborate utilitarian argument in A Strategy of Decision and then he continues that argument, coupled with a detailed analysis of decentralized policy processes ("partisan mutual adjustment"), in his The Intelligence of Democracy (1965).

In spite of its interesting aspects, Lindblom's normative case for the decentralized, uncoordinated decision-making process would be beyond the scope of this study, either in relation to the Okinawa decisions or in a separate critique. We must limit ourselves to a consideration of his two central models of decision-making, the rational-comprehensive (or synoptic) and disjointed-incremental strategies. In discussing the two strategies as alternatives at one point Lindblom posits two variables, 1. level of understanding, and 2. degree of change, with four possible outcomes (as indicated in Figure I-E, a four-quadrant graph). Decisions can involve either high or low understanding (i.e., information processing resources) and either incremental or large change in this deliberately reductionist schema of decision-making realities. In this diagram quadrants 1 and 4 indicate large changes with high and low understanding, respectively. For Lindblom quadrant 1 situations are exceedingly rare, and quadrant-4 (low understanding, great change) situations are exceptional, e.g., wars, crises, and revolutions. The synoptic method is empirically applicable only to small changes with high understanding. The disjointed incremental decision,

36

FIGURE I-E- Lindblom Models:
Key Variables and decision Ty-
pology from A Strategy of Deci-
sion. Copyright © 1963 by Donald
Braybrooke and Charles Lindblom.
Reprinted by permission of MacMillan
Publishing Co.

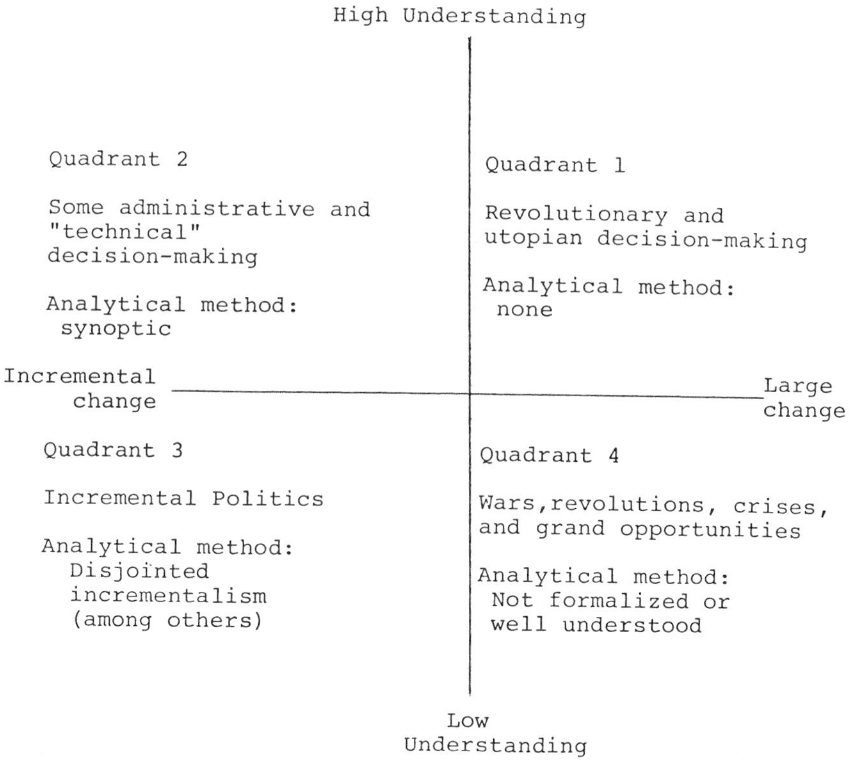

High Understanding

Quadrant 2

Some administrative and
"technical"
decision-making

Analytical method:
  synoptic

Quadrant 1

Revolutionary and
utopian decision-making

Analytical method:
  none

Incremental
  change

Large
change

Quadrant 3

Incremental Politics

Analytical method:
  Disjointed
  incrementalism
  (among others)

Quadrant 4

Wars,revolutions, crises,
and grand opportunities

Analytical method:
  Not formalized or
  well understood

Low
Understanding

37

applying to the majority of decision-making situations, calls for small changes with moderate amounts of information.[67] For even modestly complex policy-making problems, truly rational-comprehensive methods would be staggeringly expensive and time-consuming.

The process of testing Lindblom's models (to see whether the rational-comprehensive or his preferred disjointed incremental model corresponds better to the facts of the five Okinawa decisions) will not be a terribly sophisticated one. The analysis will rest on the descriptions of the decision-making process by the approximately forty key American decision participants interviewed who were involved in the 1961-62, 1966-67 and 1969 episodes.[68]Secondary source descriptions, newspaper accounts, etc., also contribute to the assessments.

One of the problems of Lindblom's characterization of the rational-comprehensive problem-solving method is that he demands more of it than is ever demanded in real life situations. His checklists of the requirements of synoptic problem-solving include the following: nearly limitless quantiies of information and exhaustive investigations of the widest range of alternative actions, consequences and implications of consequences. In the real world, of course, such comprehensiveness is rarely achieved, although it may be approached. The Lindblom alternative of changes stemming from standard procedures and involving marginal and continually adjusted movements, however, is by no means the only one to his idealized view of rational strategy. (He admits this, without offering a specific instance or description of decision-making which is close-to-rational yet neither rational-comprehensive nor disjointed incremental). His own proposed alternative strategy has been elaborated more recently to incorporate many surprisingly rational sounding elements, but it also reminds one of Allison's bureaucratic operators:

> In using such terms as 'muddling through' and 'disjointed incrementalism' especially the term 'disjointed', I have perhaps made a mistake. I have used the terms to acknowledge some obvious surface characteristics of certain decision-making strategies so that they could be quickly identified. Perhaps it would have been better to stress the subtle and systematic character of these strategies. A skillful practitioner of muddling through is by no means muddled; he is

38

instead an extremely shrewd, sensitive and
skillful decision-maker. Nor is the mind of
a practitioner of disjointed incrementalism
disjointed.[69]

The application of the Lindblom analysis to the Okinawa decisions offers two attractions: 1. Few foreign
policy studies have explicitly drawn on his model of
disjointed incrementalism, yet it seems eminently suitable a representation of the extremely complex puzzle-
solving in foreign relations (if it turns out not to be
a very reliable representation then it can be criticized
as a policy analytic device), 2. if the Okinawa policy-
making cases are well accommodated by the incremental
model, then a persuasive case for the limitations of
rational comprehensive policy-making will have been made,
and there may well occur the question of whether a process so fragmented and uncertainly coordinated can be
improved by any known method of organizational innovation. We would expect that to the extent that the decisions reflect disjointed incrementalism, they are also
characterized by Allison's bureaucratic politics, as
the models overlap considerably.

An alternative formulation to the Lindblom hypothe-
sis, and one favored by the analyst less skeptical about
synoptic techniques, might state that: "while the complexity of organizations and intricacy of problems in the
Ryukyus decisions might well favor the incremental evolution of policy, for certain major innovative policy
needs the synoptic method as an alternative and as an
explanation of actual outcomes and processes is superior."
It was noted in passing that the interviews and document
investigations in this study provide the source by which
to judge the appropriateness of Lindblom's polar models,
but what specific indicators within the interviews and
archival materials should be examined? For the synoptic
model Lindblom provides some criteria (here paraphrased):
an agreed-upon set of values held by most of the policy-
making parties, the aims of policy formulated clearly in
advance, comprehensive reviews of options and problems
related to each discreet decision, and coordinated execution of the option alternative chosen.[70]

Attention has been called to the fact that Lindblom
exacts rather stringent requirements from the rational
model which he sets up, almost to the point of creating
a straw man. For the purpose of dissecting the Okinawa
decisions most of these requirements are adhered to,
being relaxed only when it appears that by doing so we

39

can still confirm that the procedures used by the decision makers resembled the synoptic model far more closely than the disjointed-incremental one. In this regard one should look for evidence of synoptic approaches such as broad, detailed statements of policy goals related to a certain decision (e.g., a position paper calling for the decision in the first place); statements of options and arguments for those options; the number and scope of those agencies which appear to have been brought into the decision in a coordinated way; the appearance of fundamental or truly non-marginal changes among the options; and the explicit relating of alternatives and techniques for implementing them. On the other hand, when a decision is examined for incremental features, one can expect to find an absence of authoritative policy-goal statements; limited or contradictory lists of options or option papers clearly confined to marginal changes; a reluctance to widen the scope of participation in solution-finding, and haphazard entry into and exit from participation by various agencies and components (stimulated by factors of organizational need, bargaining success, career considerations of major individuals rather than issue - orientation): and uncertain or imprecise relating of means to those ends which are specified.

In tying together the theoretical concerns of the case studies, it will be well to recall two of the major concerns of this research, laid out earlier in this chapter: 1. the construction of a useful and widely applicable framework for foreign policy decision analysis, and 2. an appraisal of rationality in decisions, including constraints on officials and ways to maximize the intelligent consideration of alternatives within these constraints. To achieve the first goal, the Snyder framework is used, with certain modifications, to pull together the salient variables of the five decision-sequences, including individual and organizational participants, those aspects of the participants' environments bearing most directly on the decision being analyzed, and properties peculiar to the decision-sequence being considered. Allison's work alerts us to the strong possibility that no single national or governmental decision strategy will exist for attacking the problem, but rather a cluster of strategies based on organizational imperatives and bureaucratic political interests at least as much as purely substantive considerations. By providing us with fairly discreet and detailed rational actor, organizational and bureaucratic political paradigms, he contributes to our framework by permitting us to draw on these to generate alternative explanations for the events we are describing. Lindblom, in turn, gives us criteria for

40

evaluating the way in which alternative solutions are actually considered by those responsible for producing results. A description which may help simplify the framework building technique would go as follows: Snyder and his colleagues direct our focus to decision origins and structure, Allison to decision mechanisms and explanations, and Lindblom to decision strategies and their limitations. (See figures F and G on the following pages).

The second area of inquiry critically assesses the arguments of those who seek to challenge the very notions of coordinated and centrally controlled decision-making conducted with a frank consideration of real alternatives. Here again the Snyder group offers methods for outlining the configuration of participants and their milieux in a given decision-sequence. Allison and Lindblom provide the more central contentions about rationality and the rational limits of these participants and the processes in which they are engaged. For the Okinawa decisions the latter two theorists in effect encourage us to question both the extent to which individuals can use resources to evaluate alternatives and the extent to which groups of individuals (i.e., as organizations or other, sub-organizational, units) can coordinate and reconcile diverse views of these alternatives.

Figure I-F – Schematic Diagram of Decision
Theorists' Contributions to Oki-
nawa Decision Analysis Framework,
Including Interconnections Among
Their Basic Concepts.

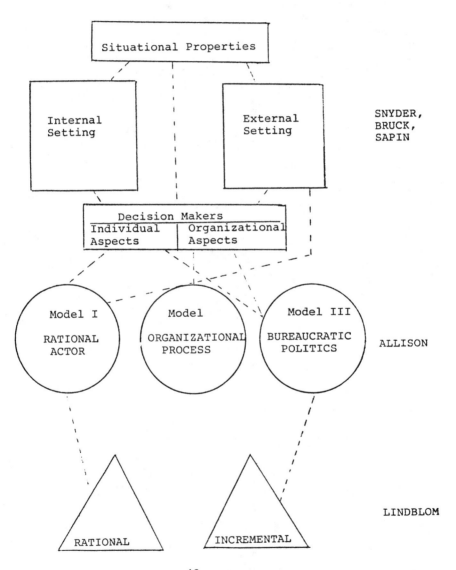

The Snyder-Group Framework

Internal Setting	External Setting	Individual Actors	Organization Network	Situational Properties
Non-Human Environment	Non-Human Environment	Personality		Anticipated v. Unanticipated
Society Values	Other Societies	Social Background / Experience		Routine v. Crisis
Structure	Other Cultures	Values		Value Magnitudes
	Foreign Governments			

The Allison Models

Rational Actor Paradigm	Organizational Paradigm	Bureaucratic Politics Paradigm
Action-as-Choice Rational Actors Value Maximizing Inference- Pattern Means-Ends Analysis and Consistency	Action-as-Organization Output Organizational Actors Factored Problems and Parochial Priorities Organizational Needs and Procedures Inference Pattern Routines and Organizational Health v. Change from Above	Action-as-Political Resultant Sub-Organizational Actors Bargaining Games Bargaining and Complex-Motives Inference Pattern Game Strategies, Style of Play, Values Determine Outcome

The Lindblom Models

Rational/Comprehensive	Disjointed/Incremental
Means-Ends Consistency Much Information / Understanding Many Options Considered Central Coordination	Ends Determined by Available Means Limited Information / Understanding Only Marginal Changes Considered No Central Coordination

NOTES

1

See Roy Appleman et al., Okinawa: The Last Battle, (Washington: Historical Division, United States Department of the Army, 1948); George Kerr, Okinawa: The History of an Island People, (Rutland, Vermont: Charles E. Tuttle Company, 1958).

2

Higa Mikio, Politics and Parties in Postwar Okinawa, (Vancouver: British Columbia University Publications Centre, 1963); M.D. Morris, Okinawa: A Tiger by the Tail, (New York: Hawthorn Books, 1968).

3

Watanabe Akio, The Okinawa Problem, (Melbourne: The Melbourne University Press, 1970).

4

Johannes Binnendijk, "The Dynamics of Okinawan Reversion, 1945-1969," in Gregory Henderson, ed., Public Diplomacy and Political Change, (New York: Praeger Publishers, 1973), pp. 1-187.

5

I.M. Destler, Priscilla Clapp, Fukui Haruhiro, and Sato Hideo, Managing an Alliance, (Washington: Brookings, 1976).

6

See for example Thomas Schelling, The Strategy of Conflict, (New York: Oxford University Press, 1963) and Anatol Rapaport and A.M. Ghammah, Prisoner's Dilemma, (Ann Arbor, Michigan: University of Michigan Press, 1965) for applications of game theory to decision-making.Also Norman Frolich and Joe Oppenheimer,"Entrepreneurial Politics and Foreign Policy," World Politics, (Supplement, Spring, 1972) pp. 151-178, and Warren Ilchman and Norman Uphoff, The Political Economy of Change, (Berkeley, California: The University of California Press, 1971) for quite different but skillful applications of economic paradigms to political decision-making.

7

To say "near-absolute rule" does not mean that the American administration was in any sense brutal or totalitarian. I refer here rather to the final veto

power of the High Commissioner over virtually any measure that might have had an impact of the United States'
position in the Ryukyu Islands and the generally tight
supervision by the Military Government (after 1950 the
United States Civil Administration in the Ryukyus) over
the activities of the Okinawan-run Government of the
Ryukyu Islands and its predecessors, at least until
the mid-1960's.

8
By "significantly" I mean generalizations which go beyond the obvious, the truisms; see for example Marion
Levy's discussion of "trivially true" statements as
contrasted with "useful" statements which may not be
wholly true, in Klaus Knorr and James Rosenau, ed.,
Contending Approaches to International Politics,
(Princeton, New Jersey: Princeton University Press,
1969) pp. 93-94.

9
While we are not ready for a formal definition of "rational" and "incremental" at this point, generally the
former can be thought of as "the conscientious effort
to consider alternative means to specified ends objec-
tively," and the latter as "marginal changes in which
the alternatives considered cannot differ markedly from
the status quo."

10
  Schilling in Strategy, Politics, and Defense Budgets
(with Paul Y. Hammond and Glenn H. Snyder). (New York:
Columbia University Press, 1962), p. 19.

11
  Binnendijk in Henderson, op. cit., pp. 141-142.

12
  I believe that previous studies have somewhat underemphasized the importance of outside influences (non-
foreign-policy-elite) om the Okinawa issue. I shall
attempt to correct that imbalance in this study with
information based on interviews and other field research, without contending that policy on the Ryukyus overall involved more than limited inputs from
outside the specialized elite.

13
  Based on numerous interviews with American officials.

14
   Interview with William Bundy, Princeton, New Jersey,
January 21, 1976.

15
   Harry Eckstein, "Case Study and Theory in Political
Science," in Fred Greenstein and Nelson Polsby (eds.),
Handbook of Political Science, Vol. 7, (Reading Mass.:
Addison-Wesley, 1975) pp. 79-137.

16
   Ibid., pp. 81-85 and 96-99.

17
   Of course, one could give a more facile example:"states
with large populations always join alliances."

18
   It should be pointed out that Eckstein's claims for
the utility of case studies apply to macro-political
situations in which the total sample size, e.g., numbers of countries or numbers of salient foreign policy problems is relatively small and inappropriate
for probabilistic statements.

19
   Eckstein, op. cit., p. 118.

20
   The merits of that claim have been widely debated; I
won't discuss them here.

21
   The research value of Verstehen, or empathy for the
group one is studying and a feel for its subjective
viewpoints (as opposed to sheer, cold observation)
is an important one for the social sciences and one
which distinguishes them markedly from the natural
sciences. It is an important element of my preference
for an in-depth study of the Ryukyus case. For a related discussion see Eckstein, op. cit., pp. 122-123.
Glenn Paige notes, in his discussion of objectives in
his use of the Korean intervention case, that the
boundaries of a case must be made as clear as possible, some assessment of the representativeness of the
case must be attempted, and a serious effort must be
made to treat the case in a way that maximizes its
potential for replication and comparison. I adopt
these as worthy and indeed necessary goals for the
best use of the single-case research strategy.

22

Richard C. Snyder, H.W. Bruck and Burton Sapin, Foreign Policy Decision-Making, (New York: The Free Press
of Glencoe, 1962); James Rosenau, Linkage Politics,
(New York: The Free Press, 1969).

23

On the interrelationship and stresses between explana-
tion and prediction in scientific knowledge see Stephen
Toulmin, Foresight and Understanding, (Bloomington,
Ind.: Indiana University Press,1961).

24

Snyder, op. cit., is an expanded treatment with criticism of the original Princeton monograph published in
1954.

25

Glenn Paige, The Korean Decision, (New York: The Free
Press, 1968).

26

Joseph Frankel, The Making of Foreign Policy, (London;
Oxford University Press, 1963), pp. 4-5.

27

Snyder, op. cit., pp. 95-96.

28

Ibid., p. 90

29

Ibid., pp. 77-80.

30

As per the distinction made by the Sprouts and cited
in Note 26.

31

Snyder, op. cit., p. 105. I do not explicitly incorporate these variables in my own application of the
Snyder framework, but they are very much taken into
account in my use of Snyder's and Allison's analytic
techniques.

32

Charles F. and Margaret G. Hermann, "An Attempt to
Simulate the Outbreak of World War I," in the American Political Science Review, LXI (1967) pp. 400-
416; Robert C. North, Ole R. Holsti, et al., Content
Analysis, (Chicago: Northwestern University Press,1963),

33
Allison's terminology changed from "bureaucratic politics" in his "Conceptual Models and the Cuban Missile Crisis," American Political Science Review (September 1970) to "governmental politics," in Essence
of Decision, (Boston: Little, Brown, 1971). I, like
most of Allison's friendly critics, prefer bureaucratic politics as more descriptive, however.

34
Morton Halperin, Bureaucratic Politics and Foreign
Policy, with Priscilla Clapp and Arnold Kantor, (Wash-
ington: Brookings, 1974).

35
This is not to say that such decisions are inept,
ineffective, or destructive, but-- precisely-- "not
rational."

36
Stephen Krasner, "Are Bureaucracies Important?" in
Foreign Policy,(Summer 1972), pp. 159-179.

37
Herbert Simon, Models of Man: Social and Rational,
(New York: John Wiley and Sons, 1957) and Administrative Behavior (New York: Macmillan Company, 1959);
Charles E. Lindblom and David Braybrooke, A Strategy
of Decision, (New York: The Free Press of Glencoe,
1963).

38
Simon, op. cit.; Richard Cyert and James March, A
Behavioral Theory of the Firm, (Englewood Cliffs,
New Jersey: Prentice-Hall, 1963).

39
Lindblom and Braybrooke, op. cit., pp. 85-86.

40
Robert Rothstein, Planning, Prediction, and Policy-
Making in Foreign Affairs, (Boston: Little, Brown,
1972), p. 25.

41
Snyder, op. cit., p. 85.

42
Cited in William Bacchus, Foreign Policy and the Bu-
reaucratic Process, (Princeton, New Jersey: Princeton
University Press, 1974, pp. 21 -22.

43
 David Vital, The Making of British Foreign Policy,
 (London: George Allen and Unwin Ltd., 1968), p.15.

44
 Snyder, op. cit., p. 67.

45
 Ibid., p. 68.

46
 Ibid.

47
 Snyder himself states a preference for the term setting over environment because he feels the latter has
 either too technical or too broad a connotation many
 times. Ibid., p. 67.

48
 Frankel, op. cit., p. ix.

49
 Snyder, op. cit., p. 67.

50
 Psychological environment is not a precise thing,
 after all, because different individuals and groups
 may have rather different perceived settings.

51
 Binnendijk, op. cit., has made a strong point about
 the lack of salience of the Okinawa issue for Americans, as has Clapp. Vietnam, on the other hand, was
 an issue in which a remarkably high number of Americans became directly involved, were at least minimally knowledgable about and it dominated the foreign
 policy sections of the newspapers. It is very probable that Okinawa would have received more public attention had their been no Southeast Asian or comparable conflict situation as a centerpiece issue.

52
 Richard Snyder and James A. Robinson, "Decision-
 Making in International Politics," in Herbert Kel-
 man, ed., International Behavior: A Social-Psycholog-
 ical Analysis, (New York: Holt, Rinehart and Winston,
 1965), pp. 435-459.

53

Roberta Wohlstetter, Pearl Harbor: Warning and Decision, (Stanford, California: Stanford University Press, 1962), pp. 55-56.

54

Government decision-making and information-processing may be better documented than that of any other organizational type (business, etc.) as any form-filling, beleaguered bureaucrat will attest.

55

Joseph DeRivera, The Psychological Dimension of Foreign Policy, (Columbus: Charles E. Merrill, 1968), p. 106.

56

DeRivera makes a useful distinction between attentive and perceptual processes:
"The construction of reality depends on two intertwining processes: An attentive process which determines what is selected as the stimulus and a perceptual process that determines which of several alternative views of the stimulus is actually perceived. The attentive process depends on the response categories which a person has learned in the past and on the person's goals and beliefs. The perceptual process depends on the nature of the stimulus which the person confronts and on the person's beliefs." Ibid., p. 45.

57

Richard Snyder and Glenn Paige, "The United States Decision to Resist Aggression in Korea," in Snyder, op. cit., p. 212.

58

From a conversation with Richard Snyder, Columbus, Ohio, August 28, 1975.

59

Snyder and Robinson, op. cit., p. 440.

60

Snyder and Paige, op. cit., p. 209.

61

One of the criticisms leveled at Snyder and his associates regarded their conceptual framework is that it is rich in categories but poor in theory, presenting few why questions in the search for how decisions are made. See Herbert McCloskey, "Concerning Strategies for a Science of International Politics," in World Politics, (January 1956), pp. 281-295.

62

Examples of works which draw on Allison's insights include Destler et al. op. cit., and Halperin, op. cit.

63

Allison, Essence of Decision, p. 32.

64

Ibid., p. 30. Propositions set up in quotation marks to indicate that they are propositions have sometimes been paraphrased rather than precisely quoted; in no case has the substance been altered.

65

Ibid., p. 78.

66

Ibid., p. 132.

67

A tempting criticism of Lindblom, but an ultimately ineffective one, would be to say that serial, incremental changes can never bring one to a qualitatively different goal because elements of the last decision are definitionally embodied in the next one (therefore "change is impossible"). This is an interesting variant of Zeno's "Stadium Parable" in which the runner is always faced with a halfway point between himself and his goal but can never reach the goal because of an infinite number of halfway points. The circle diagram below helps show that qualitative change can take place through tiny increments over time once all elements of the first circle are outside the set of elements of the fourth circle.

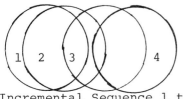

Incremental Sequence 1 to 4
Via 2 and 3

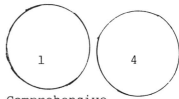

Comprehensive
Change: 1 to 4 Direct

51

68
For the earlier decisions-- in 1948-49 and 1951-- I
depend on documentary evidence of the type that was
used in the historical background chapter. Secondary
source descriptions, newspaper accounts, etc., will
help fill in some of the gaps to allow for an adequate assessment.

69
Charles Lindblom, Strategies for Decision-Making,
(Urbana, Illinois: University of Illinois, 1971),
p. 3.

70
Lindblom and Braybrooke, op. cit., p. 38.

CHAPTER TWO: HISTORICAL BACKGROUND

Okinawa is the largest of an 800-mile cascade of islands extending offshore from southern Japan (Kagoshima)
almost to Taiwan.[1]More populous than the state of Rhode
Island and only a third of its size, Okinawa has long
been important to the interests of vastly greater Pacific powers. American strategists working with the Supreme Commander of Allied Powers in the Pacific (SCAP)
in the immediate postwar years recognized the extraordinary potential of the island, which lies within 1000
miles of Tokyo, Seoul, and Manila, and less than 500
miles from Shanghai and Taipei. This centrality, so pre-
cious to Air Age navigators, traditionally gave Okinawans a great deal of the privacy, protection, and iso-
lation they have always seemed to relish. For most of
the sea-travel era the island was a stopping point along
several important routes but was actually close to no
single power. Fishermen and growers of sugar, sweet po-
tatoes and rice, Okinawans have in the past been treated
as more valuable for where they were than who they were
or what they had accomplished.

Historical records place Chinese mariners in the
Okinawa vicinity as early as the seventh century A.D.
During the European middle ages, the island emerged as
an important if tiny client state of the Chinese empire,
whose geographers called it Liu Ch'iu, from which the
Japanese derived the current Ryukyu, and nineteenth century British and American navigators Loo Choo or Lew Chew[2]
During this period Okinawans were ruled by indigenous dy-
nastic kings, who were vassals of China's emperor, but
maintained autonomy over a peaceable and rigidly structured folk society. These people, related to, yet quite
distinguishable ethnically and linguistically from the
Japanese, were not "discovered" by their powerful island
kinsmen to the northeast until the fourteenth century,
for all practical purposes. Contacts with the southern-
most province of Japan (Satsuma) increased until 1609,
when Okinawa was invaded and the king captured and made
subservient to the shogunate (although he was allowed to
remain on the throne at Shuri, the ancient capital.)
From that time until the late 1800's the Ryukyus were in
a situation which has been referred to as dual subordina-

tion. An eighteenth century scholar, Hayashi Shihei, described the Okinawans' deft balancing act between Japan
and China:

> She subjects herself to both countries and
> pays tribute to both. She uses the Japanese
> calendar when she deals with Japan, and the
> Chinese calendar when she contacts China.[3]

The skill that Okinawans gained at maneuvering among
considerably larger powers would serve them well in the
twentieth century vis a vis America and Japan.

In the 1870's Japan used the internal weaknesses
of China and an exaggerated confrontation over the mur-
der of some Okinawan fisherman by Taiwanese as a pretext
for taking the Ryukyus and placing them under direct,
"protective" control. The men in Tokyo had been nervous
about the possibility that the expanding Western powers,
including the United States, might establish a protec-
torate or other foothold there. These Meiji rulers were
anxious to prevent further incursions like those of the
American Commodore, Matthew Perry, in the early 1850's.[4]

The Treaty of Shimonoseki (1895), ending a bitter
Sino-Japanese war to the distinct disadvantage of the
Chinese, terminated most effective Chinese claims to
the islands, and began a fifty-year period of ever increasing Japanese control over the Ryukyuan way of life.
Although they have been described as treating the Okinawans as second-rate second cousins, the Japanese did
raise the standard of living there until the onset of
the Second World War.[5]

The vast Pacific conflict turned the island into
a Japanese fortress. Citizens were pressed into a massive war effort and exposed to constant anti-American
propaganda. The final act of the tragedy came in 1945
with the Battle of Okinawa, a three-month bloodbath
that pales even Hiroshima and Nagasaki by comparison of
casualty statistics. In those cities combined, an esti-
mated 150,000 people died very quickly; on Okinawa during the long spring of the same year nearly 300,000 had
perished, including 12,000 Americans, 110,000 Japanese
soldiers, and perhaps one fifth of the entire civilian
population of the island in eleven weeks of horror.[6]

Hostilities ended on June 21, having begun on April
Fool's Day. The commander of the Japanese forces on the
island and his deputy committed hara-kiri, leaving Okinawa to the Tenth United States Army under the command

of General Joseph Stilwell. The scene these victors surveyed was described later by one of their number, intelligence officer Daniel Karasik:

> From personal observation of a greater por-
> tion of the island I would say that 90 percent
> of the private dwellings on the island were de-
> stroyed, and many of the remainder made at least
> temporarily uninhabitable. In addition, practi-
> cally all commercial buildings, warehouses, pub-
> lic buildings, schools and hospitals were de-
> stroyed. The public utilities and water systems
> in the cities were completely disrupted. The
> railroad and its rolling stock were completely
> wrecked; for a distance on the western shore
> not only were all the tracks torn up, but all
> traces of the roadbed were obliterated. The na-
> tives had retreated to countless thousands of
> caves with all of the possessions that they
> could move...
> The whole population was torn from its roots,
> mixed up, and disorganized. Children were sep-
> arated from their families and members of fam-
> ilies were lost... The whole society as it had
> existed was for all practical purposes destroyed.[7]

Along with all of this chaos, Stilwell inherited a
much beleaguered but remarkable surviving population.
Although some wariness of sweeping descriptions of national or racial characteristics is justified, one can
extract a fairly consistent "Okinawan personality description," which occurs with only slight variations
in numerous scholarly and journalistic accounts.[8] The
average Okinawan encountered by the American soldier
was shorter and somewhat swarthier than his Japanese
cousin, likely to display modesty to an extent that
might be misinterpreted as subservience, and a stubborn passiveness, yet was usually adaptible and fond
of "joining things" despite a basically tradition-
oriented life view. As an ethnic group Ryukyuans might
be described as a curious cross between a number of
desirable Buddhist, Shinto, and Christian types (although subscribers to the last mentioned faith are
rare). That is to say that they are extraordinarily
and consistently non-aggressive and peace-loving, wor-
shipful of ancestors and reverent about nature and the
land, and tend to place considerably less emphasis on
pride and cultural superiority than do many peoples,
including their Eastern neighbors. If other traditional
cultures clearly exhibit some of these traits, few dis-

55

play all of them to the extent that the Okinawans do.

Besides a relatively placid, if somewhat disoriented population, the United States found itself in possession of an interesting bit of terrain, a series of four
island clusters or guntos, called Amami, Okinawa, Miya-
ko, and Yaeyama in the order of their extension southward from Japan. The islands are coral with some vol-
canic upthrusts in Yaeyama, the soil is not particularly
fertile. Fishing is a crucial supplement to agriculture
in sustaining the population. Most of the American forces occupying the islands found them somewhat unfamiliar,
but not unlike southern Florida or the Bahamas, which
are about the same distance from the equator, halfway
around the globe. Rainfall is heavy (120 inches annually); the temperature and humidity are high, although
mitigated by sea breezes. The most distinctive and problematic aspect of the Ryukyuan climate is the typhoon
season, bringing fierce storms, sometimes several in a
year. The damage potential of the storms to buildings
and equipment is formidable, a fact which those guiding
American policy perceived only vaguely in 1945, but much
more clearly a few years and many millions of dollars
worth of damage later. In the summer of that year the
damage most concerning the Americans assigned to the islands was the massive physical destruction caused by
bombing and artillery fire over many months.[9] As Karasik suggested, it was feared that not only were the major cities and much valuable farmland lost, but that society itself and any sense of stability the Okinawans
knew might have been demolished in the process.

The Early Post-War Years: 1945-1952

Discussions of the possible fate of the Ryukyus
actually began among the Allied Powers nearly two years
before the Japanese surrender. At Cairo in November of
1943, according to Secretary of State Cordell Hull,
President Roosevelt and Chiang Kai-shek talked about
possible joint administration of the islands after the
war.[10] The Chinese generalissimo had for some time placed
considerable value on the Ryukyus, as is evidenced in
his controversial political manifesto, China's Destiny.[11]
He considered them not only rightfully China's histori-
cally, but also "essential" to the proper defense of the
country. It must be noted that in the actual text of the
Cairo Declaration of December 1, 1943, however, Roosevelt, Churchill, and Chiang stated that it was their

56

purpose that "Japan shall be stripped of all islands in
the Pacific which she has seized or occupied since the
beginning of the First World War in 1914 and all the territories Japan has stolen from the Chinese, such as Manchuria, Formosa, and the Pescadores shall be returned to
the Republic of China. Japan shall also be expelled from
all the territories she has taken by violence and greed."[12]
Whether this stern language was meant to apply to the Ryukyus was never made clear, perhaps purposely. Interestingly, even before Chiang's book was published, his chief
rival, Mao-Tse Tung, decried the imperialist (Japanese)
takeover of the islands, implying a belief that China
still had some claim to them.[13] Both Chinese leaders,
from their respective capitals, were involved in international disputes related to claims in the Okinawa area
after World War Two, although neither ever interfered
with the United States presence there.[14]

At least as important as the coordination of an Allied position on the Ryukyus at the international level
was the simultaneous and inevitably--if not openly--
connected secret planning for the postwar period by United States military strategists. A convincing indication
of the earliness of plans to establish a world-wide network of bases, approved at the highest levels, can be
found in State-War-Navy Coordinating Committee (SWNCC)
document 38/20, dated October 9, 1945.[15] It contains a
letter from the Secretary of the Navy, James Forrestal,
to Secretary of State James Byrnes describing the development of proposals for postwar base configurations which
had taken place in 1944. The letter is instructive enough
to merit quoting at length:

On 7 January 1944 the President forwarded
to the Secretary of State /then Cordell Hull/
a study of postwar island air bases which the
Joint Chiefs of Staff considered necessary for
the postwar period. The accompanying letter
from the President requested that the State
Department "as a matter of high priority, initiate negotiate with the governments concerned
to acquire permanent or long-term benefit of
the bases, facilities and rights required, at
the earliest possible moment."
On 1 February 1944, the President again
wrote the Secretary of State referring to the
letter above and supplementing the letter by
broadening the scope of the postwar bases to
include all military bases instead of air
bases alone and making certain other modifications in the original letter...

57

The Navy's concern in postwar bases other
than those in United States territory, falls
into three general categories, as follows:

(A)   Those   formerly under the sovereignty
       or control of Japan, including both
       Japanese owned areas and such islands
       as were mandated to Japan after World
       War I. In this category, and in which
       exclusive rights are desired, are the
       following:

              Marshall Islands
              Caroline Islands
              Ryukyus
              Bonin Volcano Group
              Marcus Island...

/note: the other categories of lesser bases
 are described and lists of base-sites pro-
 vided/[16]

It is quite clear from this and a number of related documents made available relatively recently that the Ryukyus were a coveted prize for the planned global defense
system even before their use against Japan in World War
Two was fully planned.

The next Allied pronouncement which was to have an
important bearing on Okinawa's fate was the Potsdam Proclamation (July, 1945), an ultimatum one of whose articles states that after Japan's surrender, "its sovereignty shall be limited to Honshu, Hokkaido, Kyushu, Shikoku,
and such minor islands as we determine."[17] (the we refers
to the United States, Soviet Russia, China, and Great
Britain). As with the Cairo Declaration this statement
left the Okinawa question open, and allowed the Allies,
especially the United States (who by the time of Potsdam had occupied Okinawa), time and latitude in working
out the question of who had what rights in the islands.
Between Potsdam and the Peace Treaty in 1951 (i.e., six
years after the fighting stopped), almost all policy developments concerning the fate of the Ryukyus were determined in the context of the islands' potential value
to the United States and based upon various American
experiences with postwar problems and opportunities.

Among the paramount problems, of course, was the
growing perceived threat from the U.S.S.R. and the requirement of American vigilence to head it off. In Octo-

ber, 1945 a major document entitled "Strategic Concept and Plan for the Employment of United States Armed Forces" was signed by Secretary of War Robert Patterson. Its assessment of the world situation was conservative and familiar enough:

> In the course of the defeat of the Axis powers, the United States and Russia have emerged as the preeminent world powers, with the British Commonwealth of Nations occupying a position definitely in a lower category...
> Neither the possession of the atomic bomb by the United States, Britain, and Canada nor the development of similar weapons by Russia can be expected to change materially the existing distribution of power among nations.

It pointed to possible areas of contention, including:

> the desire of Russia to insure friendly governments in neighboring countries..
> Opposition to the U.S. maintaining a strong position in the west Pacific..
> Social upheavals arising out of popular demands for a redistribution of wealth and political power..[18]

It alerted top officials to the need to "provide for securing vital U.S. installations against effective attacks by any potential enemy, including attacks with new weapons" and to "provide for the contingency of a breakdown of relations among the major powers and the possible resulting emergence of World War III."[19] Among the specific recommendations was the assembling of "an outer perimeter of bases from which to reconnoiter and survey possible enemy actions, to intercept his attacking forces and missiles, to deny him use of such bases, and to launch counteractions.."[20]

There are indications, moreover, that the U.S.S.R. was perceived by the military as a real threat in 1945, and in the fall contingency plans were being undertaken to deal with a possible conventional attack. In November the Joint Intelligence Committee had already produced the first detailed assessment of the "Strategic Vulnerability of the U.S.S.R. to a Limited Air Attack" (including atomic targeting of Soviet industrial cities),beginning a tradition of war plans which proceeded through the Cold War to the present.[21]

More germane to Okinawa itself is the JCS 570 series,

59

the Joint Staff Planners' "Over-all Examination of U.S. requirements for Military Bases and Rights," delineating four kinds of postwar bases, including:

a. PRIMARY BASE AREAS, strategically located, comprising the foundation of a base system essential to the security of the United States, its possessions in the Western Hemisphere, and the Philippines and for the projection of military operations /note: included Panama Canal Zone, Hawaii, Ryukyus, and Azores, among others/,

b. SECONDARY BASE AREAS, essential for the projection of and/or for access to primary bases, and for the projection of military operations. /included Midway, Bermuda, and Bonins, among others/,

c. SUBSIDARY BASE AREAS required for increasing the flexibility of the system of primary and secondary bases /included Formosa and the Canaries, among others/

d. MINOR BASE AREAS, and base sites at which transit privileges and varying military rights are required, if not already obtained, in order further to increase the flexibility of the base system /included New Caledonia, Dakar, and Curacao, among others/.[22]

The proposed base system included an employment of Okinawa pegged to the assumption that:

All Japanese Mandated Islands and Central Pacific Islands detached from Japan, including the Bonins and Ryukyus, will be brought under exclusive United States strategic control.[23]

It can be deduced from the foregoing that A. plans for a possible global base network were proceeding at least a year before Tokyo's surrender, B. the Ryukyus were viewed early on as a vital link in this strategic chain, and C. the U.S.S.R. was identified as the number one threat to a stable postwar order and a potential enemy worthy of planning a major counter-strategy against.

The concept of the strategic outpost or overseas base is, of course, a venerable one. The United States had used Hawaii and the Philippines in the late nineteenth and early twentieth centuries as lightly fortified semi-colonies and naval depots. The Southwest of America had been increasingly dotted with forts from 1850 to 1890 to protect against "incursions" on American expansion by the Indians and Mexicans. Plans for Okinawa and the West Pacific bases being contemplated by the cabinet and the Joint Chiefs in 1944-45 would be comparable in many respects to the British use of Cyprus in the eastern Mediterranean and Hong Kong at the edge of China or the French garrison of Djibouti (Somaliland) on the Horn of Africa. The goal in these cases was to secure a point with the following characteristics for the defense or domination of a nearby region: A. a location close to but not deep inside the region, B. a discreet and somewhat isolable bit of territory, ideally an island or peninsula, and C. a relatively stable and placid local population-- or, better still, no population.[24]

From the time of America's landing in April, 1945 until late 1950, a body called the Military Government (with minor variations of that name occurring) existed on Okinawa--at first make-shift and gradually much more sophisticated. After some inter-service shuffling in mid-1945 over who was to administer the islands, the Navy took over from the fall of that year until nine months later, when it was decided that the Army should take responsibility as of July 1, 1946. Obviously the most immediate problem of the Military Government was to deal with the devastation and social disintegration of the island's several hundred thousand survivors. A letter from the Commander in Chief of the Pacific (CINCPAC) of December 1945 had outlined the five prime goals of the United States in aiding Okinawa's recovery:

a. The physical restoration of damaged property and facilities.
b. The continued improvement of health and sanitation.
c. The early establishment of self-governing communities.
d. The institution of a sound program of economic development...which will assist in achieving the highest possible level of economic independence.
e. The establishment of an educational program.[25]

In attempting to achieve these goals the Military Government operated under a number of different handicaps, including the following: 1. the critical shortage of materials, machinery, and trained personnel, 2. the uncertain status of the sovereignty of the Ryukyus, 3. the early shifting of civil control of the islands back and forth between the Army and Navy, and 4. the formidable language barrier and shortage of Japanese speakers in the American ranks (this last-named was at least as important as the other factors).[26]

The military were by no means completely unprepared to deal with the challenges of reassembling the shattered Okinawan society; however, there were clearly inadequacies in what preparation had taken place. As early as a year before the invasion of the island, military social science specialists had been assembling data about the geography, social structure, and economic needs of the Ryukyus. A month before the invasion itself (code named: ICEBERG), many of these professionals met in Hawaii to share information about the area which could be important to the invaders and subsequent administrators in the American Pacific forces. When the landing finally did take place, much of this information proved valuable. Some misinformation (based partly on faulty military intelligence), however, was to prove counter-productive and actually contributed to logistical problems after the beacheads were established. The military were led to expect, for example, that a large, totally disoriented and anti-American local population would be encountered in the southern part of Okinawa. What was not known was that the preponderance of the heavy southern population had been transported to the North by the Japanese, while the Japanese army entrenched itself in the South. Consequently the United States forces in the northern two thirds of the island were ill prepared to handle the large numbers of civilians encountered, and invaders to the south met unexpectedly severe resistance from enemy forces unencumbered by a civilian population.[27]

After the three-month battle the surviving Okinawans were neither as helplessly disoriented nor nearly as hostile as had been expected.[28] By August of 1945 the Military Government was actually able to begin selecting and organizing an "Advisory Council" of prominent Okinawans who could be located, and even organize local elections-- all of this in the midst of debilitating shortages, dislocated refugees, etc. By the time the Navy had taken over the Military Government for its nine-month rule late in September, the main island had already been districted and councilmen elected in each district.

There began, through late 1945 and into 1946, two separate and somewhat contradictory trends in Okinawa which were to characterize much of the American policy there for a number of years. First there was the recognition, especially on the part of the Navy, of the desirability of Okinawa as a controlled base complex in the Far East and the taking of steps to make this complex a reality through a program of military construction of enormous size.[29] In what seemed to be a policy counterpoise, however, President Truman and Army Chief of Staff Eisenhower were issuing statements which reflected considerable high level doubt about setting strategic roots into the island.[30] The State Department had early gone on record in 1946 as favoring the return of the archipelago to Japan:

> For the United States to take over any part of the Ryukyu Islands would be contrary to its policy of opposing territorial expansion whether for itself or for other countries. Furthermore, from a practical point of view, control of the Ryukyus by the United States would in all probability require a considerable financial outlay by the United States for the support and development of the islands and would involve the United States in the thankless task of governing three quarters of a million people of totally alien culture and outlook.
>
> The establishment by the United States of a permanent base in Okinawa or elsewhere in the Ryukyu Islands would be likely to provoke serious international repercussions and would be politically objectionable. The existence of such a base, in addition to the other Pacific bases to be held by the United States might also come to be resented by China and would probably be regarded by the Soviet Union as a provocative threat rather than as a proper defensive move by the United States. If the United States should acquire such a base, it would be considered by other states as stepping outside the zone of its legitimate political and regional interests... Political and diplomatic considerations indicate that the Ryukyu Islands therefore should be considered minor islands which should be returned to Japan and demilitarized.[31]

These doubts stemmed not only from normal postwar isolationist sentiments (or at least tendencies) and legal
complications (the absence of a treaty), but also from
the questionable wisdom of trying to manage a substantial
indigenous population, who were already beginning to talk
about returning to Japan. These doubts seem intelligently founded in retrospect, especially if one considers the
relative ease of administering a less populated "base island" like Guam with Okinawa.

Even as construction proceeded into 1947, with run-
ways and barracks being expanded, the Japanese were ex-
pressing increasing interest in getting Okinawa back.
Political activism and tensions were on the rise on the
island itself. By fall, three political parties had been
formed, at least one of which was clearly in favor of being out from under the United States' authority (i.e.,
the Okinawan People's Party or OPP);the second a rather
moderate, reform oriented party (the Democratic Alliance);
and the third a vaguely pro-American party, in spite of
its name (the Socialist Party).[32]

To stay abreast of the new tide of political activism in the islands, the Military Government issued two
special proclamations in the fall of 1947: one for reg-
istering political parties, and the second for conducting
mayoral and assembly elections. The previous year the Advisory Council had been replaced by the Okinawa Civilian
Administration (briefly the Central Okinawa Administration). The new body was headed by a Chief Executive, an
Okinawan with an important representative and intermedi-
ary role, even though he was appointed by the American
military. At the same time courts were being established,
schools opened, and a massive influx of economic aid provided in the form of power stations, roads, hospitals and
the like.

Also in 1947 Secretary of the Interior Julius Krug,
who was making a tour of the Pacific islands under American control, and General Douglas MacArthur (still Supreme Commander of Allied Forces in the Pacific) issued
joint statements recommending accelerating democracy in
the American-occupied islands and the desirability of a
quick treaty with the Japanese.[33] Okinawa was singled
out for special attention by the two men, however, as its
unusually large population of over a half million and its
close cultural ties to Japan made it a unique case.[34] The
general and the secretary were not clear about the implications of this for the style of rule which was appropriate, but by describing the Okinawan situation as "unique"
it appears that they had in mind, at a minimum, more cau-

tion and vigilence there than in the former Japanese trust territories, which had much smaller numbers of people.

By 1948, although most local candidates were running as independents based on the sort of personalistic, elitist appeal found in the pre-war Okinawan political culture, the parties were gaining support and the United States experiment in controlled, developed democracy was beginning to succeed, perhaps too rapidly in the eyes of some. Even with the increasing initiative given to and accepted by the island population, however, ultimate decision-making power remained solidly in the hands of the Military Governor at the hastily reconstructed capital of Naha and, after 1950, for seven years with the Governor in Tokyo through his Deputy Governor in Naha.

Internal manifestations of what were perceived as external developments, namely rising Communist influence in Asia following the collapse of the Chiang regime in 1949, were also to vex the Military Government. The risks of unchecked Ryukyuan democracy in such an environment were clearly perceived by the spring of that year, as the following excerpts of a dispatch from Brigadier General John Weckerling of the Ryukyus Military Government Section of the Far East Commission (FECOM) to Colonel Jesse Green of the Military Government office in Naha indicate:

> The few Communists that you have in Okinawa are going to give you increasing trouble. I haven't the slightest doubt but that they are directed from Tokyo by couriers who illegally enter the Ryukyus from Japan. We had one such case which was reported to G-2.
> I recently wrote General Eagles /Military Governor on Okinawa/ and recommended that he consider the recasting of the personnel of the assemblies since they are appointed by him. Since you have the resignations of most members of the Okinawa assembly this might present to you a very good opportunity to include a few more useful and patriotic members. I think some action too might be taken to restate their missions, including the clarification of the legal status of their appointments, place and agenda of meetings, etc. You will have to be very careful in announcing these changes if you make any lest the Communists take advantage of your announcements and claim credit for bringing about improvements which you might make.[35]

65

Many tensions from within the Ryukyus and Japan itself seemed to derive more from the uncertainty of Okinawa's legal status than from any other factor. MacArthur had been arguing since 1947 that Okinawa, for strategic reasons, should be separated from Japan indefinitely as part of a peace treaty, preferrably to be negotiated as soon as possible.[36]His call for increased, though circumspect, local autonomy development in the Ryukyus in 1949 appeared at least in part to be an attempt to sweeten what would be a bitter pill for the Japanese, i.e. this separation. The general's chief justification for acquiring the island as a base complex was that not only would this presence allow the United States to fill the giant power vacuum created by the collapse of the Japanese empire, but also that it would protect an unarmed and neutral Japan from predatory powers in the area (e.g. Russia). That the actual treaty negotiations did not take place is now a matter of history; the reasons for the delay are numerous, but can be condensed or simplified by the observation that virtually any "clarification" of the Far Eastern situation at that time or attempt to make that situation permanent when it was more convenient to regard it as temporary would probably not have satisfied some major power or group of powers, whether it be the United States, the Soviet Union, China, or the Commonwealth. These nations thus followed what seemed to be the most expedient course and did nothing, at least as far as moving toward a quick conference which would bring together the contentious powers. They did stage behind the scenes maneuvers designed to help assure that once formal peace negotiations were begun, each would be in its most advantageous possible bargaining position.

In Washington by 1948 it had become apparent to top American foreign affairs officials that this formal Allied settlement with Japan was not possible; the various treaty proposals of 1947 had been dropped when it was decided that they would not be much of an improvement on the de facto Japanese-American relationship which had grown up, but rather more likely would damage that relationship. The Johnston Committee recommendations in the the spring in combination with the generally deteriorating state of relations with the USSR convinced them that Japan must be made more self sufficient. Interdepartmental exchanges on the problem produced a series of draft position papers. The Army's study of Spring, 1948 included the following assumptions, among others:

    a. The United States will attempt to strengthen its current world-wide strategic position in

order to contain Soviet expansion.
b. The United States will not allow itself
to be manuevered into a peace treaty with
Japan on terms unfavorable to United States
security interests.
c. Soviet influence will become progres-
sively stronger in southern Korea until all
Korea is Soviet dominated.[37]

In the Army's eyes, Japanese policy had to be turned
around to conform to these harsh new realities:

...Were Japan to succumb to Soviet domination,
our only effective foot in the door in the Far
East would be lost and the remainder of the Far
East would have little hope of resisting eventual Soviet domination...
    To insure against Japan succumbing to Sov-
iet domination Japan's economy must be rehabili-
tated and her territorial integrity and political
independence must be guaranteed by the United
States, with assistance by such Japanese forces
as may be permitted.[38]

Importantly, the Army also recommended modestly re-arming
the Japanese, i.e., beyond the then very limited, pistol-
equipped national police force.

    By late October planning for the new partnership
had advanced to such a degree that secrecy was difficult;
Newsweek was able to publish the story of the policy
about-face, including hints about an "Asian Marshall
Plan"and Japanese re-armament-- all based on leaked information. This caused an uproar in Japan and no little
consternation in the United States. The idea of moving
from humanitarian rehabilitation and reform to even a
cautious restoration of Japan's former economic and defense capacity seemed far more ambitious and risky at
the time than it has in retrospect, even taking into account public and Congressional dissatisfaction with occupation costs. The putatively "super-secret" document
embodying these changes (many of which were accurately
reported in the Newsweek article) was NSC 13/2, which
like the final draft NSC 13/3 specified that the Ryukyus
would be developed as a heavily fortified facility. It
also stated that the U.S. would implement a long-term
development plan there no longer financed from Japanese
occupation funds (the document text appears in the Appendix). The build-up of Japan as a potential ally in
the Far East, rather than an emasculated Switzerland of

the Pacific, was thus linked directly with the decision
to remain in the Ryukyus as the price of the lowered military profile in the main islands. Item eight of NSC 13/3
read it part:

> ...Responsibility should be placed to a steadily
> increasing degree in the hands of the Japanese
> Government. To this end the view of the United
> States Government should be communicated to SCAP
> that the scope of its operations should be re-
> duced as rapidly as possible, with a correspond-
> ing reduction in personnel, to a point where its
> mission will consist largely of general supervi-
> sory observation of the activities of the Japan-
> ese Government and of contact with the latter at
> high levels on questions of broad governmental
> policy.[39]

1948 was also the year in which China became the
number one concern of strategic intelligence experts in
Washington. The deterioration of the Chiang Kai-shek
forces' position caused the CIA to issue a secret paper
warning against any consideration of Chiang's perennial
claims to the Ryukyus:

> Recognition of China's claims would in-
> volve a tremendous risk. Chinese control
> might easily deny use of the bases to the
> US /sic/ and, in the event of final subju-
> gation of the National forces by the Commun-
> ists, might give the Soviets easy access to
> the islands.[40]

Echoing General Marshall's 1945 statement the study put
special emphasis on the effect of the loss of the Ryukyus to an unfriendly power:

> Withdrawal of US forces from the Ryukyus fol-
> lowing the eventual withdrawal from Japan and
> Korea would move the US line of defense in the
> Pacific back to the Marianas. Should an Asiatic
> conflict develop under these circumstances, the
> Ryukyus might become subject to the control of
> powers whose interests are antagonistic to those
> of the US. Any power occupying the Ryukyus and
> possessing an adequate air potential could con-
> trol an unarmed Japan. Furthermore, control of
> the Ryukyus by powers unfriendly to the US would
> obviously consitute a threat to US Pacific bases
> as well as tend to circumscribe any future action

of US forces operating in the Western Pacific.[41]

On the other hand:

> US control of the Ryukyu Islands would: (a) give the US a position from which to operate in defense of an unarmed post-treaty Japan and US bases in the Philippines and other Pacific Islands; (b) obviate the possibility of the Ryukyus falling under the control of a potential enemy; (c) neutralize, to some extent, the Soviet position in the Kurils, Korea, and Manchuria; and (d) give the US a position from which to discourage any revival of military aggression on the part of the Japanese.[42]

In 1949 the question of what to do with the strategic Ryukyus was further complicated by a natural disaster, a typhoon which took many lives and totally wrecked about fifty percent of the American military buildings, including much of the housing for military families, at a cost of over eighty million dollars to the United States. Army Under Secretary Tracy Vorhees surveyed the damage in the islands and concluded that if the United States were going to stay (the wisdom of which he doubted), then totally new and far more substantial construction would be necessary-- facilities considerably better than the jerry-built structures which had sprung up the length of Okinawa since 1945.[43] During the following two years, government allotments for the Ryukyus were substantially increased; nearly 90 million dollars was made available for the construction of facilities which could be used jointly by the Ryukyus Command and the local community as well as for the rebuilding of housing and barracks for the military and their dependents.[44] The decision to upgrade facilities on Okinawa on a large scale came, significantly, two years before the treaty negotiations were concluded in San Francisco and the future of the Ryukyus under United States administration made at least relatively more clear. Privately--that is within the classified information network of Washington-- the policy groundwork for the build-up had been laid with NSC 13/3, approved by the President in May 1949 and intended to provide high-level general guidelines on American policy toward Japan.[45]

Several events occurred at the end of the decade which seemed to force up the premium placed on Okinawa by American policy-makers. The two most notable were the final defeat of Chiang Kai-shek's forces by the Communists in 1949 and the outbreak of war in Korea the following year.[46] Secretary of State Acheson disclosed in early 1950 the United States' intention to propose strategic trusteeship status for Okinawa to the United Nations.[47] The use of the island as a staging ground for American support of the South Koreans that summer and for the duration of the conflict seemed to vindicate the Joint Chiefs of Staff (JCS) in their repeated recommendations to hold Okinawa as a strategic outpost even if the short-term costs seemed high.

In 1950 the fourth postwar Ryukyus governing body was established, the gunto (island cluster) governments, of which Okinawa was the most important. Soon afterward the Headquarters of the Far East Command (FECOM) redesignated the Military Government as the United States Civil Administration in the Ryukyus (USCAR),[48] trying to lessen the "occupied territory" implications of the term military government. The title Deputy Military Governor of the Ryukyu Islands was changed to simply Deputy Governor, Ryukyu Islands. This was held by the same officer who occupied the military position of Commanding General, Ryukyus Command (RYCOM). The Deputy Governor was responsible to the Governor of the Ryukyus, who was headquartered in Tokyo as the Commander in Chief, FECOM. In reality the latter assigned virtually all administrative functions to his deputy at Naha and to the Civil Administrator, who was a Brigadier General (the Deputy Governor was a Major General always until 1957, when the post was made a Lieutenant General's).

In the spring of the following year, 1951, a Provisional Central Government was established to coordinate Ryukyu wide activities, that is, issues involving more than just the island of Okinawa proper. The idea of a federated system for the Ryukyu Archipelago, embodied in the decentralized gunto governments) had proved impractical because Okinawa was so disproportionately dominant in population and influence. In the spring of 1952 a sixth and final (until reversion in 1972) body was established, the Government of the Ryukyu Islands (GRI) . This was headed by a Chief Executive who was appointed by the Governor in Tokyo on the recommendation of the Deputy Governor and the 31 member legislature at Naha, providing both Ryukyuan and USCAR influence in the selection process, although in fact the recommendations were always the same.

The permanence of the GRI, whose structure was to

70

remain essentially the same for twenty years,is linked
to the Japanese Peace Treaty having been signed in the
fall of the previous year. Although the Russians refused
to initial the treaty and the Chinese (Peking and Taipei)
had not participated in the proceedings, a number of important issues were acted upon. Among them was the fate,
or at least the provisional fate, of the Ryukyus. This
was achieved with some compromise from both the United
States and Japan. Negotiator John Foster Dulles, who had
discussed Okinawa's future with Japan's Prime Minister
Yoshida well before the start of the final negotiations
at San Francisco, managed to at least partly satisfy the
Japanese desire not to give up Okinawa by incorporating
the concept of residual sovereignty in interpreting the
Ryukyus related Article III of the treaty. [49] Under this
article Japan would recognize United States rights to
obtain a strategic trusteeship for Okinawa, with the understanding that Okinawa was still to be considered Japanese (but this is an interpretive statement not actually in the text of the treaty article; see the Appendix).

Through the innovative but legally controversial
concept of residual sovereignty, the United States was
in effect getting a carte blanche in the Ryukyus in return for the vague, tacit assurance to the Japanese that
the islands would be regarded as ultimately belonging to
them. A corollary that made residual sovereignty somewhat
more palatable was the argument that military facilities
in the Ryukyus would be an effective guarantee of Japanese security without the necessity for as large an American military presence in Japan proper. Needless to say,
this corollary argument did not impress the Okinawans,
who tended to resent the use of their island as a security annex, having had very unpleasant experiences with
another variant of this relationship during World War
Two. The significance of considering the islands as la-
tently Japanese even while in American hands administratively was to develop only gradually. The perspective
did seem to give the Okinawans more latitude than they
might otherwise have achieved, e.g. the setting up of the
GRI, which was able to establish both formal and informal
links with Japan over a period of several years. [50] However, it should be noted that these links were permitted largely at the discretion of the United States authorities, at least the formal ones such as permission
to fly the Japanese flag on holidays, travel regulations
liberalization and the like.

A related issue which surfaced from time to time

was the relevance of the Russian possession of the Kuril and other Northern Islands for the United States/Japan/ Okinawa triangle. Reference was made at the 1951 San Francisco treaty proceedings that the Soviets had received territorial fruits of conquest from a war in which they scarcely participated; why then, Americans asked, did the United States administration of the Ryukyus cause such indignation?[51] The Soviets regarded their prizes as sanctified by the Yalta agreement, whereas the American occupation of the Ryukyus was much less explicitly their prerogative-- in effect it was the transformation of temporary occupation into de facto conquest. When Americans bothered to reply they stressed that the Russians had possession and sovereignty in the Northern Territories; the United States administered but did not own the Ryukyus. More relevant, however, was the feeling of Japan about all of this. Japanese legal scholars and high officials, including Prime Minister Kishi at one point, reminded Americans (who couldn't understand the zeal with which the Japanese worked at regaining the Ryukyus and the comparable lack of interest in the Kuriles-- over which they had no sovereignty) of three points: 1.The American negotiators themselves had given the Soviets their territorial booty at Yalta; the Japanese would thus be in a much more difficult position trying to secure those islands, practically speaking, than from the Americans,who had not "conquered" Okinawa or received it as war spoils, but had "borrowed" it, 2. The Americans were allies and the Soviets adversaries; thus, more was expected from the former, including sympathy with irredentist sentiments, and 3. Of no moral but considerable practical significance was the fact that Okinawa was heavily populated with socially modern--if rural-- Japanese, while the northern islands were very lightly peopled and with mostly pre-modern, semi-nomadic Ainu and related ethnic groups.[52]

The Cold War: 1953-1965

The major development of the 1950's which was to give the Japanese and Okinawan pro-reversionists some cheer occurred somewhat unexpectedly in 1953. That summer Secretary of State Dulles announced that the northernmost cluster of the Ryukyus, the Amami group, would be returned to Japan.[53] The Amamians, who with the Okinawans and southern islanders had been separated from Japan for American jurisdictional purposes by SCAP Directive 677, were always closest to the Japanese spiritually as well as geographically. They had agitated for a "return to the Fatherland" for some time, even using hunger strikes on a mass scale as part of their tactics. By August of 1953 Dulles decided that the political gains from this concession to Japan would outweigh any strategic losses.[54] Lest the move be too freely interpreted-- as a prelude to Okinawa's relinquishment for example-- several rather firm reiterations of United States intentions to retain Okinawa itself for an indefinite period followed the Amami reversion. Vice President Richard Nixon in a November visit to Naha stressed that "the United States will continue to control Okinawa so long as a Communist threat exists."[55] Early the next year President Eisenhower reaffirmed the United States' intention to remain in the Ryukyus in his State of the Union message (the only time the Ryukyus have been specifically mentioned in this type of address):

> We shall maintain indefinitely our bases in Okinawa... American freedom is threatened so long as the world Communist conspiracy exists in its present scope, power, and hostility.[56]

The period 1954-1958 can best be viewed through this perspective of the United States having made clear its intentions to stay in Okinawa indefinitely, both politically and militarily. Thus, those Okinawans who chose to work with rather than around or against the Americans did not really think in terms of imminent return to Japan, but rather concentrated on maximizing both increased political autonomy and economic support from the Americans. The focus of most issues was domestic.

Perhaps the stickiest and most persistent problem of the 1950's was the land-acquisition dispute, of which we can give only a simplified account here. In a sense it epitomized the entire spectrum of clashes stemming from two fundamentally different premises: the Okinawan view of the needs and rights of the domestic population, and the American view that military imperatives came first even at the inconvenience of the locals. By 1955 the armed forces had expropriated about seventeen percent of the arable land on Okinawa for base construction-- a serious loss for an agricultural economy which was at best marginal in terms of feeding its people. Although a system of compensation evolved, Okinawans were unhappy about two of its features: 1. the inadequacy of the rent allotments themselves, and 2. the "lump sum" system of payment endorsed by the special subcommittee of the U.S. House of Representatives Armed Services Committee in

73

1956, that allowed the Civil Administration to compen-
sate farmers in one large payment rather than in annual
rent.[57]General Lyman Lemnitzer, Military Governor in Tokyo, formally approved this system in 1957. But even the
moderate and pro-American factions of the GRI were opposed to the plan because it was believed that rental
rates might appreciate more realistically if they were
spread out over a number of years (i.e., the duration
of the use of the land, which might become more valuable to the renters). Moreover, although farmers would
retain titles to their land under the lump-sum system,
there would be a more substantial sense of retained
ownership if rent were paid annually. Not until 1958
did the largely united Okinawans convince the American
authorities that the issue was of critical import, essential to good relations between the islanders and the
Civil Administration. It took two Okinawan delegations
to Washington to persuade American policy-makers of the
symbolic (and pecuniary) necessity of annual payments
to Okinawan farmers. The fact that the issue was resolved
largely to their satisfaction, through a newly formed
land tribunal in Naha, is indicative of the frequently
flexible and pragmatic nature of American administration
and the clever persistence of their administratees.

Others have disagreed that the land problem in Okinawa was ultimately successfully resolved, or an example
of big power,little power give-and-take. For them, the
American land confiscation program made Okinawa a micro-
cosm of a pattern of military capital penetration of
great intensity, as Mark Selden describes it:

> More than 20 percent of the arable land
> (the percentage was much higher in popu-
> lous central Okinawa) was turned into a
> sea of cement air strips, training grounds
> and missile installations. In one swift
> blow the livelihood and way of life of ru-
> ral Okinawa was destroyed and agriculture
> crippled...Yet Okinawa is of course no ab-
> eration. It is rather the very quintessence
> of a brutalizing American presence which in
> varying forms is found wherever American
> forces are stationed throughout Asia-- from
> Taiwan and South Korea to the Philippines,
> Laos, Thailand, Vietnam, and Micronesia--
> and the world. On Okinawa the silken glove
> of a "superior" colonial culture carried by
> administrators, businessmen, missionaries
> and teachers scarcely conceals the mailed
> fist of the military.[58]

74

In response to such charges, the American military and those sympathetic to its position responded that the usurping of prime acreage for base purposes was a necessary evil (the strategic argument) and that the farmers were well paid for the use of their land. They added that the American instinct for compromise and the dignity of the little man led to the working out of a solution by 1958 which essentially gave the Okinawans what they wanted. They also pointed to the 16 percent land rental rate increase between 1958 and 1962 (compared with a consumer price index rise of about 10 percent for the period) and the fact that after 1958 there were no major mass demonstrations against the USCAR land policies (and this not due to any sort of political intimidation). This was cited as at least superficial evidence of satisfaction with the accommodation. There are also the counter-arguments of developmentalists like former Secretary of the Army Stephen Ailes, who has asserted that the hardships wrought upon Ryukyuan agriculture by the base build-up were far outweighed by constructive tangibles like roads, water and communications systems, which raised the standard of living of every Okinawan.[59]

Compounding the economic problems felt by the Okinawans in the 1950's was the legal status of the islands. The preferred status of the Ryukyus was the subject of debate especially during the early years of the decade even though there was very little doubt about the strategic value of the bases there. The former head of the Office of Far Eastern Affairs (1944-45) in the State Department, Joseph Ballantine, noted that the United Nations trusteeship formula was never very seriously advanced once the peace treaty had been signed because American decision-makers knew that the Soviets would veto such a status for Okinawa. Ballantine advocated the return of the Ryukyus but with their military bases kept in a special status distinct from Japanese bases[60]

Ralph Braibanti, writing in the American Political Science Review, called attention to the painful inequities of the legal limbo in which the Okinawans found themselves:

> The present statelessness of the Ryukyuans is bewildering and degrading. Citizens of neither Japan nor the U.S., nor even of a Ryukyuan nation, Ryukyuans are subject to stringent travel restrictions. Japanese contractors and laborers on Okinawa have been regarded as friendly nationals since the ratification of the Japanese

75

Peace Treaty and have enjoyed various benefits, including American Army PX privileges /which have been denied to the Okinawans.[61]

Although many of the specific grievances of the Okinawans, caught between the needs of one giant power and the relative helplessness of the other power to do anything as long as these needs remained were eventually attended to, the basic problem of statelessness and being in an unprecedented, makeshift arrangement endured.

The second most volatile and stubborn issue of the decade (after the land controversy) was that of self-government, with the Okinawans pressing for more autonomy-- the popular election of the Chief Executive, for example-- and the United States reluctant to give much leeway because of the rise of leftist political groups, who in turn pressed even harder for popular support of increased autonomy and United States pledges of withdrawal. Also contributing to USCAR's seeming intransigence was an international atmosphere of suspicion of anything associated with communism; not surprisingly there was a tendency to link the more vocal leftwing,anti American groups to "international Communism"-- often by way of Tokyo marxists. Stresses between the normally limited-success leftist parties and USCAR boiled over in 1956 with the election of the island's most vocal and prestigious radical, Senaga Kamejiro, to the important position of Mayor of Naha (pop. 230,000). After several months of fierce political turbulence which ground municipal government there to a virtual standstill, city assembly conservatives finally persuaded Deputy Governor (General) James Moore to quietly intervene and change a procedural rule, allowing the assembly to oust the mayor. A great deal of bad publicity and ill will attended this incident, with much of the Japanese press castigating Moore's intervention as a "colonialist" move and as making a mockery of the American desire to exhibit Okinawa as a "showcase" of Western democracy.[62] Perhaps equally embarrassing was the fact that although the governor had gambled on public disenchantment with Senaga as softening the effect of American interference, in the new elections for mayor of the capital voters chose another strong leftist, Kaneshi Saichi, who had sharply criticized USCAR for 'meddling."

In the late spring of 1957 important high-level policy developments occurred which were to have mixed implications for Okinawans anxious to revitalize the reversion to Japan issue. At that time President Eisenhower

76

issued his Executive Order 10713, formalizing many of
the features of the USCAR-GRI relationship and changing
the title of Deputy Governor, Ryukyu Islands to High
Commissioner. The change also brought the removal of that
official's responsibility to report through Tokyo and
gave him much more direct contact with Washington (although formally through CINCPAC headquarters in Honolulu).
The indirect impact of this executive order was more important than its content. The formalizing imprimatur of
the President implied American intentions to continue
the status quo in Okinawa rather than move toward returning the islands.63 In a joint communique with Prime Minister Kishi, moreover, Eisenhower clarified the United
States' intent to continue to hold the island-base, but
tempered this with a reiteration of the residual sovereignty principle.

One other policy landmark with political multiplier
effects for Okinawa occurred during the Eisenhower administration. At the request of the Senate Foreign Relations Committee, the Conlon (Research Associates) Study
of the Asian situation recommended in 1959 that military
and political needs be better integrated in Okinawa with
a view toward returning the political adminstration of
the island to Japan in the "not-distant" future.64 Okinawan political scientist (and now Deputy Prefectural
Governor) Higa Mikio has characterized the study as the
"Bible" for Ryukyuan leaders (i.e., in the early 1960's).65
Its causal impact on policy formation is difficult to
establish, but it is widely felt to have paved the way
for trends in the next three administrations toward the
gradual return of the islands.

The administration of John Fitzgerald Kennedy saw
several important directional changes in Okinawan affairs. Although nothing quite as dramatic as the Amami
gunto reversion under Eisenhower occurred, considerably
more activity took place-- all things considered-- to
give Japanese irredentists and Okinawan reversionists
cheer.

During the first summer of the new Democratic administration, the Prime Minister of Japan, Hayato Ikeda,
met with the President in Washington. Although Kennedy
commented on the continued military importance of the
islands, there was a visible shift in presidential emphasis on recognizing the fundamentally Japanese nature
of the islands. Moreover, in their communique it was announced that channels would be opened for increased Japanese involvement in the area and a subtle move toward
an American-Japanese partner-stewardship was to bloom.

Although Japanese technical and token economic assistance had been permitted since 1952, the Kennedy policy was to open the gates-- within two fiscal years at least-- for a flood of new assistance from an increasingly prosperous and eager Japan.

Late in 1961 a Kennedy appointed investigatory body headed by Dr. Carl Kaysen of the White House Staff completed a study in the Ryukyus with two particularly important recommendations which were to be translated into actual policy, albeit in modified form: 1. substantially increased American assistance for the islands (through raising the ceiling on annual appropriations for their development) and, 2. increasing Ryukyuan control over their own governing mechanisms. The latter recommendation came to fruition in 1962 when the President issued his first important amendments to Executive Order 10713 (Eisenhower). These included the lengthening of the GRI legislative terms and nomination of the Chief Executive by the legislature.

The United States military presence on Okinawa during the Kennedy years was marked by controversy surrounding the personality of High Commissioner Lt. Gen. Paul Caraway. Energetic and forthright, Caraway was anxious to help Ryukyuans move in constructive directions, but his methods and mannerisms were sometimes offensive to Okinawans and the Japanese. What some have regarded as his tendency to talk down to GRI officials and his doubts about the Ryukyuan capacity for self-government because of inefficiency and "corruption" caused a storm of protest and the displeasure of the influential American Ambassador to Japan, Edwin O. Reischauer. Although General Caraway was recognized as having made some laudable personal contributions, his successor in 1964, Lt. Gen. Albert Watson, carried instructions to administer the islands in a more diplomatic, low-key manner and to mend as many rifts as possible, including some with United States personnel.[66]

The Cold War Thaw and the Nixon Doctrine: 1966-1972

Although a certain amount of resentment was indeed engendered during the Caraway tenure, a number of basic trends of the early 1960's were perceived as favorable by Japanese observers, at least relative to comparable periods in the earlier postwar years. The movement toward increased Japanese economic involvement as well as step by step--if slow-- realization of self determination

78

for Okinawans were to be accelerated under the Johnson administration following Kennedy's assassination.

By January of 1965 President Johnson had met with the new Japanese Prime Minister, Sato Eisaku, and reaffirmed the Kennedy policy of more closeness with Japan regarding the development of the Ryukyus (including the expansion of the official functions of the United States-Japan Consultative Committee).[67] Viewing the five year Johnson period as a whole, the question seems to be not whether the United States was allowing events in the archipelago to move Okinawa toward Japan, but in what ways and with what rationale in mind.

During the mid-1960's Johnson's High Commissioners oversaw an enormous 44 percent increase in land rental rates and a twenty one million dollar settlement of long-standing pre-peace treaty damage claims (the latter important because Japan had renounced the right to all such claims as part of the peace treaty agreements). Another development which pleased Okinawans, although not necessarily keeping pace with their aspirations, was the 1965 USCAR proclamation allowing the Chief Executive to select many of his own departmental directors and other personnel without consulting the High Commissioner.

The nexus between Japan and the Ryukyus was strengthened considerably in 1966 and 1967 with increased official contacts between Japanese officialdom and Ryukyuans, both governmental and the people themselves (e.g., Okinawan passport issuance duties were turned over to the Japanese).[68] This functional reversion process, the allowing of certain governmental and economic functions to be taken back over by Japan (many symbolically important), although not officially endorsed by the Americans, was being experimented with. The profile of USCAR was being lowered and that of Japan raised.

The easing of the United States grip would not have been possible, however, without some fairly profound changes in thinking in Washington-- especially when one considers the unquestioned strategic utility, if not essentiality of Okinawa during the peak of the Vietnam war. Overlapping reassessments of the importance of continuing to hold the Ryukyus administratively as well as militarily were percolating at high levels of the national security policy apparatus, and pivotal Japanese alliance-minded officials in the State and Defense departments were wearing down military resistance to concessions to Japan.[69]

The culmination of this trend of events during the Johnson regime came in November of 1967 when the President and Prime Minister Sato issued a joint communique from their summit conference. The document proclaimed the planned return of the Bonin (Ogasawara) Islands, a small group located approximately 500 miles east of the Ryukyus. This was regarded as a relatively small concession to Sato in view of the increasingly insistent demands at home to press for Okinawa reversion, but there were other critical points in the communique as well.[70]

Formal recognition was given, for the first time at this level, to the aim of returning administrative rights over the Ryukyus to Japan and a tripartite Advisory Committee to the High Commissioner was established to promote Japan-Okinawa unification in orderly, constructive ways. Although activist groups in both Japan and the Ryukyus criticized the Prime Minister for practically returning "empty-handed, full of promises", the steps taken at the summit were unquestionably decisive ones from a historical viewpoint.

By the time the Republican administration of Richard Nixon took office in 1969, pressures for returning political control of Okinawa to Japan were intense and being channeled more effectively than ever. This is not to imply that amid considerations of Vietnam solutions, NATO rethinking, international monetary problems, etc., that the Ryukyus were a particularly salient foreign policy problem area; but it was certainly one of those "major minor issues" to be reckoned with. This was especially true as Okinawa tended more and more to color all Japanese-American relations, which were themselves entering a period of unprecedented postwar delicateness.

At about the same time that Americans were going to the polls to elect Mr. Nixon, in November, 1968, Okinawans, by courtesy of one of the later gestures of the Johnson Far East policy, were voting in their first popular election for their Chief Executive. Elected by an impressive margin was Yara Chobyo, the head of the influential Okinawa Teachers' Association and an ad hoc reversionist coalition, the Reformist Joint Struggle council. Belying a grandfatherly appearance, Yara had a keen sense of political timing and an instinct for the jugular, as well as scholarly eloquence. Unlike his predecessor Matsuoka Seiho of the moderate, relatively pro-American Liberal Democratic Party, Yara minced no words in criticizing the United States, particularly on the politically fertile and sensitive issues of the latter 1960's, e.g., the American use of Okinawa in the Vietnam

80

War effort, the presence of B-52 bomber aircraft used in raids against North Vietnam, toxic gas storage, etc.[71]

The Chief Executive rode in on a tide of sentiment against almost any form of United States military presence from which an issue could be kindled. Popular demonstrations grew in frequency during the late 1960's and early 1970's, even as High Commissioner Ferdinand Unger and his successor Lt. Gen. James Lampert were rapidly rescinding earlier USCAR enactments which were considered restrictive and outdated. Attempts to grant political rewards as a trade-off for the easing of Okinawan pressures which might embarrass or impair the military were only partially successful. Okinawa's demands for reform, autonomy, increased economic aid and jobs, decreased military presence, and rapid American political withdrawal--simultaneously!-- were outpacing American attempts to placate or, as Japanese observers phrased it, "buy time."

In November of 1969 Sato arrived in Washington for a conference with Nixon with an enormous amount of press and public fanfare in Japan pressuring him to obtain a definite American commitment on Okinawa. These pressures derived in part from twenty years of Japanese irredentism met by American stalling tactics and in part from the cluster of symbolic incidents, such as the nerve gas storage affair[72] which served to weaken United States attempts to minimize the less favorable aspects of the military presence there. Moreover, in spite of the slowness of tension-reduction in Southeast Asia, the general pitch of global Cold War ideological clashes was perceptibly diminishing as was the "ramparts against Communism" mentality. Finally, the United States' disillusionment with its often frustrating role as preponderant spender of resources and lives among Western powers to keep various forms of Communism from making inroads into Third World areas affected considerations surrounding the Ryukyus. This more conservative, "realist" foreign policy approach was expressed in the Nixon statement at Guam in the summer of 1969 (henceforth labeled the Nixon Doctrine by an apparently doctrine-hungry press):

..as far as problems of international security are concerned, as far as the problems of military defense, except for the threat of a major power involving nuclear weapons, that the United States.. had a right to expect that this problem would be handled increasingly by.. Asians themselves.[73]

These were some of the key trends of thought and event
influencing this meeting of the two most important non-
Communist Pacific power leaders. Their joint communique,
announcing the immediate commencement of consultations
aimed at reversion in 1972 was the result. In turn the
Japanese pledged that the American military facilities
on the islands would not be jeopardized, although they
might be somewhat reduced (for communique text see Appendix) . The announcement was dramatic but not unexpected: Secretary of State William Rogers and Japanese Foreign Minister Aichi Kiichi had been negotiating since
the summer and sources both within the government and
the press indicated in advance that an agreement would
be reached. The main question was what the terms of the
agreement would be.

Within the fairly broad guidelines of the Nixon-
Sato agreement came three crucial"concretes": first,
the setting of a definite time framework in which to
operate; second, the establishment of a Preparatory Commission headed by the High Commissioner and a Japanese
ambassador to coordinate plans for the transfer of authority at the Okinawa level; and finally, the actual
commencement of negotiations on the specific terms of
the treaty through a Consultative Committee. The complexity of these negotiations is hard to over-emphasize.
They were to require the better part of two years of intensive bargaining concerning the multitude of issues
implicit in an arrangement which would transform Okinawa from an American quasi-trusteeship into a prefecture of Japan once again. This involved the transfer of
numerous government functions to Japan, and decisions
about which military facilities and many non-military
facilities would be retained by the United States and
which given over to the Japanese (and on what financial
basis).There were also byzantine legal questions about
past Okinawan claims against the United States Government, the status of American investments, and so on.[74]

The negotiations culminated in an agreement signed
by their principal overseers: Secretary of State Rogers
with the Japanese ambassador in Washington and Foreign
Minister Aichi with the American ambassador in Tokyo in
mid-June of 1971. Late that fall, the United States Senate, after a pro forma hearing, gave its consent on the
treaty's ratification by an overwhelming vote. A month
later, after considerably more debate, the Japanese Diet
also approved the treaty. There was real Japanese reluctance about and opposition to certain aspects of the
document, however, including the relatively free hand the

United States was allowed to maintain in keeping its
base facilities in the islands. The bases would, it
should be noted, take on the same status as other military installations in Japan under the 1960 Security
Treaty. The United States would thus be pledged to
"prior consultation" before effecting any major changes
in the base network. Japanese critics had charged in
1969 that the wording on prior consultation in the communique was so vague that it could be plausibly interpreted as extending the right to introduce nuclear weapons into Japan (i.e., after consultation) in certain
emergency situations, effectively widening American military latitude and violating Japan's long standing non-
nuclear policy.[75] Denials by the United States and Japanese treaty supporters had little effect.

During the first week of 1972, Prime Minister Sato
and President Nixon met at San Clemente, California, for
the last "adjustment" of reversion plans. In a move clearly aimed at helping the Japanese leader appease domestic
political opposition to the Okinawa reversion terms, the
President agreed to change the official date of the islands' return from July 1, as originally planned, to May
15 (although the Prime Minister had requested April 1).
Nixon also promised careful consideration of formal Japanese requests that the United States undertake "reduction or re-alignment" of bases near urban centers in the
Ryukyus. Advancing the deadline, to be sure, would cause
additional pressures and difficulties for USCAR authorities already working rapidly to make arrangements for
transfers of jurisdiction, physical plants, records--
quite literally packing up to go home. The concession on
the date of transfer can be viewed as a politically as-
tute (and deliberately staged) gesture at a time when Ja-
panese/American relations were especially tender on a
variety of issues. When the ceremonies for the long a-
waited return of the Ryukyus took place in Tokyo and Naha
in mid-May of 1972, there could be little doubt that the
Nixon White House had played to a fault the final scene
in a twenty three year series of conciliatory acts, beginning with residual sovereignty and the Amami reversion.
Such concessions were felt necessary to insure the larger strategic imperative of guaranteeing the military
use of the islands.

NOTES

1
The name "Okinawa" can be poetically, but accurately, rendered from the Japanese as "a rope thrown out on the water."

2
Kerr, op. cit., p. xvii.

3
Robert Sakai, "The Ryukyus as a Fief of Satsuma," in The Chinese World Order (ed.) John K. Fairbank, (Cambridge, Massachusetts: Harvard University Press, 1968) p. 112.

4
One can also argue, of course, that the seizure of Okinawa by the rulers of the four big islands was also motivated by late nineteenth century expansionism for its own sake.

5
M.D. Morris, op. cit., passim. For an even more skeptical view of the Japanese contribution to Okinawan development see Kerr, op. cit., pp. 448-449.

6
American and Japanese casualty statistics are rounded off from official American statistics, as cited in Appleman, op. cit., and elsewhere. Okinawan civilian casualty statistics are fragmentary and consist mostly of rough estimates revised upward over the years.

7
Daniel Karasik, "Okinawa: A Problem of Administration and Reconstruction," Far Eastern Quarterly, Vol. II No. 3, (May, 1948), p. 258.

8
See for example Leonard Weiss, "United States Military Government on Okinawa," in Far Eastern Survey,Vol. 15, (July, 1946). For a consideration of problems of national interest (and by implication national character) see Paul Seabury, Power Freedom, and Diplomacy, (New York: Random House, Inc., 1963) p. 86.

9
Some of the worst raids took place during the so-called
"ten-ten"(October 10) air raids of 1944. These exercises,
militarily described with the delightfully sardonic eu-
phemism of "softening-up missions," were referred to by
Okinawans as the "steel typhoon." Together with the artillery exchanges of March-June, 1945 they obliterated
the artifacts and architecture of an entire culture in
a fashion rarely equalled since Carthage's destruction
in Roman times.

10
Cordell Hull in Diplomatic Papers: The Conferences at
Cairo and Tehran, (Washington: United States Govern-
ment Printing Office, 1961), p. 324.

11Chiang Kai-shek, China's Destiny, (New York: Roy Publishers, 1947), p. 36.

12Official text given in Hull, op. cit.

13A. Doak Barnett, Communist China and Asia, (New York:
Harper Brothers, 1960), p. 79.

14For further record of Chinese claims, consult the New
York Times Index, 1969-1979, under the heading "Senkaku Islands."

15
State-War-Navy Coordinating Committee Paper No. 38/20,
declassified October 17, 1972, National Archives.

16Ibid., pp. 65-66. In a brief for the President dated
July 3, 1945 General George C. Marshall had stated:

    "..the Ryukyus and Bonins should be demili-
    tarized except for suitable U.S. bases...
    Since the United States has a continuing mil-
    itary commitment in the Far East and this
    can most effectively and economically be dis-
    charged in peace-time by primary reliance
    upon air power complemented by naval surface
    power, we should retain or acquire rights in
    areas around the perimeter of the Pacific de-
    signed to control the approaches thereto and

to prevent surprise attacks on vital strategic areas such as the Philippines, the
Marianas, or Hawaii...
"The mere possession by the U.S. of positions within range of troubled areas should
be a useful influence for peace and stability. Among the areas of potential trouble after the war is that bordering the Yellow Sea.
A base in the Ryukyus, therefore, is particularly desirable, with the remainder of those
islands demilitarized and in friendly hands.."

[17] Potsdam Proclamation, 1945.

[18] Dated October 11, 1945, p. 2. Declassified March 22,
1976.

[19] Ibid. p. 6.

[20] Ibid., p. 5.

[21] Document dated November 3, 1945. Declassified August 13,
1975, National Archives.

[22] JCS 570/40, October 25, 1945, pp. 204-205. Declassified October 10, 1974, National Archives.

[23] Ibid., p. 206.

[24] Regarding the third point: such outposts have usually
been the home, originally, of marginal populations
closely related to much larger groups of somewhat
more advanced kinsmen in the nearby region, e.g., Cy-
prus/Greece or Djibouti/Somalia. The phenomenon of
local populations wanting to reunite with their "coun-
trymen" only after occupation by an outsider-- whether
it be called enosis, reversion, or whatever-- is a predictable one if not completely understood.

[25] CINCPAC message cited in Weiss, op. cit., p. 235.

26
Ibid., p. 236

27Clellan Ford, "Occupation Experience on Okinawa," in
the Annals of the American Academy of Social and Political Sciences, Vol. 267, (January, 1950), pp. 177-
178.

28Ibid., passim.

29New York Times, April 6, 1945, p. 5.

30New York Times, February 14, 1946, p. 6.

31Views of the State Department were quoted in JCS
1619/5 dated September 16, 1946 (State Department
position dated in that document as June 27, 1946).

32Not to be confused with the later Okinawa Socialist
Party, the sister organization of the Japan Socialist
Party; see Higa Mikio, op. cit., p. 27.

33New York Times, February 26, 1947, p. 1.

34Ibid.

35FECOM, Ryukyus Military Government Section, Memorandum dated March 30, 1949.

36Frederick S. Dunn, Peace-Making and the Settlement
With Japan, (Princeton, New Jersey: Princeton University Press, 1962), pp. 54-56. MacArthur had himself
gone part of the way toward such a separation by issuing an administrative instruction, SCAPIN-677, on
January 29, 1946, which for administrative purposes,
did separate the Ryukyus and certain other areas from
Japan.

37
Army Memorandum submitted by Royall to Secretary of Defense Forrestal, designated as JCS 1380/48, p. 381.

[38]Ibid., p. 385.

[39]NSC 13/3, dated May 6, 1949, p. 3. (declassified July 23, 1975).

[40]Central Intelligence Agency report "The Ryukyu Islands and Their Significance," dated August 6, 1948. Declassified February 6, 1976, p. 3.

[41]Ibid., p. 2.

[42]Ibid., p. 1.

[43]Morris, op. cit., pp. 80-82.

[44]Ibid.

[45]Declassified 1975, National Archives.

[46]Watanabe, op. cit., p. 21.

[47]Department of State Bulletin (January 23, 1950), pp. 115-118.

[48]Joint Chiefs of Staff Directive, October 4, 1950.

[49]Watanabe, op. cit., pp. 24-30.

[50]In 1952 the Japanese government established a liaison office in Naha, the Naha Nihon Seifu Nampo Renraku Jimusho (Nanren), for limited consular-type business. Important Okinawans traveled to Tokyo more and more frequently in the 1950's, especially those connected

with the quasi-official Japanese <u>Nampo</u> <u>Doho</u> <u>Engokai</u>
(Relief Association for Southern Areas).

[51]Following is an excerpt from Dulles' statement at the
San Francisco Conference, in response to charges from
Poland that the United States was seeking territorial
expansion in the Ryukyus:

> As regards the Ryukyu and Bonin Islands, the treaty
> does not remove these from Japanese sovereignty; it
> provides for a continuance of United States admini-
> stration over the Ryukyu Islands south of 29º North
> latitude; that is to say that those islands nearest
> to Japan itself are to remain not only under Japan-
> ese sovereignty but under Japanese administration as
> well. This is in marked contrast to the provision for
> the complete renunciation of Japanese sovereignty over
> the Kurile Islands, but we think that this comparison
> should be born in mind by those who criticize the pro-
> visions relating to the more southerly of the Ryukyus,
> and to the Bonin Islands.

United States Department of State, <u>Conference</u> <u>for</u> <u>the</u>
<u>Conclusion</u> and <u>Signature</u> <u>of</u> <u>the</u> <u>Treaty</u> <u>of</u> <u>Peace</u> <u>With</u>
<u>Japan,</u> Record of the Proceedings (Washington: U.S.
Government Printing Office, 1951) pp. 93-94.

[52]For a discussion of Japanese scholarship and specific
arguments on the Ryukyus-Kuriles comparison see Hiroo
Kawaguchi, <u>The</u> <u>Japanese</u> <u>Views</u> <u>on</u> <u>the</u> <u>Reversion</u> <u>of</u> <u>Oki-</u>
<u>nawa</u> (Unpublished Master's Thesis, Charlottesville,
Virginia: The University of Virginia, 1969) pp. 90-91.

Also instructive is an exchange in an interview of
former Japanese Prime Minister Kishi Nobusuke (October 2, 1964 by Spencer Davis of the Dulles Oral History Project, Princeton University) in which Kishi
analyzes the comparisons made between the Soviets
in the Kuriles and Americans in Okinawa:

> ..The islands of the South and the North are
> entirely different in character-- the north-
> ern islands were taken over by Russia without
> any agreement with Japan and have not been re-
> turned. But the southern islands have been
> (taken over as part of an agreement in which
> the Japanese participated). The Japanese have
> agreed to it in the Peace Treaty.

A major line of Japanese argument has always been
that the Americans, as allies, owed them far more
reasonable treatment regarding Okinawa than the
Russians did regarding the Kuriles.

53
New York Times, August 9, 1953, p. 1.

54
Department of State Bulletin, January 4, 1954. p. 17.

One other concession to the Japanese, this one in
1952 before the departure of the Truman administration, was the establishment in the Tokyo Prime Minister's Office of a liaison secretariat with the office in Naha mentioned in note #50. Ostensibly just
for purposes of trade and technical consultation,
the secretariat was an important communications link
with the Ryukyus at a time when such contacts were
rare.

Also regarding concessions it should be pointed out
that during the pre-war years the Amamis had been
more closely linked with Kagoshima prefecture in
southern Kyushu than with Okinawa.

55
In a minor historical irony, it was Mr. Nixon who
later as President was to decide that the Communist
threat did no longer exist-- at least to the extent
that retention of administrative control of the island would be necessary.

56
New York Times, January 8, 1954, p. 1.

57
Higa op. cit., pp. 40-56.

58
Mark Selden, "Okinawa and American Colonialism,"
Bulletin of Concerned Asian Scholars (Spring, 1971),
p. 56.

In my own research, of the twenty-eight Japanese and
Okinawan foreign policy elite members interviewed,
7 were willing to characterize the United States involvement in the Ryukyus as "imperialistic" or "expansionist," but of these only 3 were willing to attribute consciously imperialistic intentions to the
Americans. The others qualified their characterizations

with modifiers such as "defensive" or "containment" oriented expansionism or "economic" and "non-territorial" imperialism. Those who attributed real expansionist motivations to the United States were Japan Socialist Party foreign policy expert Warashina Hiroto, Japan Communist Party foreign policy expert Nihara Shoji, and Marxist historian Makise Shoji. Seven interviewees stressed that the United States policy was <u>not</u> imperialist but "defense minded;" not surprisingly these were mostly Foreign Office officials or LDP members.

[59] Interview with Stephen Ailes, Washington, D.C. February 6, 1976.

[60] Joseph W. Ballantine, "The Future of the Ryukyus," in <u>Foreign Affairs</u> (July, 1953), pp. 663-674.

[61] Ralph Braibanti, "The Ryukyu Islands: Pawn of the Pacific," <u>American Political Science Review</u> (December, 1954), pp. 972-998.

[62] Watanabe, <u>op. cit.</u>, p. 158.

[63] Interview with Edward O. Freimuth, formerly head of the Liaison Office of USCAR, July 11, 1972, Washington D.C.

[64] Conlon Associates, Ltd., <u>Report to the United States Senate Committee on Foreign Relations-- Asia</u>, November, 1959, pp. 501-505.

[65] Higa, <u>op. cit.</u>, p. 15.

[66] Freimuth interview, <u>cit.</u>

[67] Watanabe, <u>op. cit.</u>, pp. 56-57.

[68] <u>Ibid.</u>

69

Priscilla Clapp, "Bureaucratic Interaction in Washington, 1966-69," Hakone Conference Paper 1975, mimeo.

70New York Times, November 16, 1967, p. 1.

71

Yara Chobyo, "Okinawa," in Pacific Community, (January, 1971), pp. 282-296.

72

See Binnendijk in Henderson, op. cit., p. 151.

73

New York Times, July 7, 1969, p. 19.

74

Final Report of the High Commissioner to the Ryukyu Islands, United States Civil Administration of the Ryukyu Islands, May 14, 1972, pp. 22-25.

75

Johannes Binnendijk, "The Political-Military Aspects of Okinawa Reversion," mimeo, pp. 49-53.

CHAPTER THREE: THE 1948-49 COMMITMENT
TO BUILD UP OKINAWA

The United States intends to retain on a long-term basis the facilities at Okinawa and such other facilities as are deemed by the Joint Chiefs of Staff to be necessary in the Ryukyu Islands south of 29°N., Marcus Island and the Nanpo Shoto south of Sofu Gan. The military bases at or near Okinawa should be developed accordingly. The United States agencies responsible for administering the above-mentioned islands should promptly formulate and carry out a program on a long-term basis for the economic and social well-being and, to the extent practicable, for the eventual reduction to a minimum of the deficit in the economy of the natives. At the proper time, international sanction should be obtained by the means then most feasible for United States long-term strategic control of the Ryukyu Islands south of latitude 29°N., Marcus Island and the Nanpo Shoto south of Sofu Gan.

The United States has determined that it is now in the United States national interest to alleviate the burden now borne by those of the Ryukyu Islands south of latitude 29°N. incident to their contribution to occupation costs, to the extent necessary to establish political and economic security. While it would not be in the interest of the United States to make announcement on this matter, and while it is not believed appropriate to obtain international sanction of this intent at this time, the United States national policy toward the Ryukyu Islands south of latitude 29°N. requires that United States Armed Forces and other Government agencies stationed therein pay their way to the extent necessary to carry out the above-mentioned program for the economic and social well-being and towards eventual reduction to a minimum of the deficit in the economy of the natives in this area beginning sixty days after this date, and that these islands must no longer be financially dependent upon or obligated to any other occupied area.

National Security Council Report 13/3,
Section 5.

93

The adoption of NSC 13/3 in May of 1949 as the definitive American policy statement on Japan and Okinawa
put the official seal of the United States government
on a signal change of orientation in this part of the
world. Reform and self-cleansing in Japan were to give
way to national responsibility and economic self-sufficiency. Okinawa would be developed in part to insure
that there was no outside interference with this process. Because the Okinawa section represented only one
part of this highly secret and important document and
because the deliberations leading to its approval were
both decentralized and out of the public eye, the decision is probably the most difficult of the five to analyze.[1] NSC 13/3 is also the most general policy statement in our five cases: in effect it was the sanction
and codification of a number of interrelated policies
which were under-way or would be soon.

Before re-constructing the setting and decision-
making which produced paragraph 5 (the Okinawa statement) of the NSC report, a brief look at the most salient related events of the preceding three postwar years
will be helpful. This "deep background" has been
touched on in the historical introduction; what we do
here is highlight relevant points for our in-depth investigation of the NSC's decision.

In 1944-45 postwar planners had already designated
the Ryukyus as a base of supreme importance. In January 1946 Secretary of State Byrnes received on his desk
State-War-Navy-Coordinating Committee paper 249/1, recommending that the United States assume sovereignty
over several sets of islands captured or recaptured in
the Pacific campaigns (i.e., the Marianas, Marshalls,
and Carolines) and strategic trusteeships for Okinawa
and the Bonins.[2] The State Department's own recommendation was that the Ryukyus should be returned to Japan: not to do so would be to court international dis-
favor and accusations of neo-colonialism especially
dangerous for the United States.

These opposing viewpoints epitomized the two-
pronged controversy-plagued "policy" of the United
States in the archipelago. There was no question about
the geopolitical value of the Ryukyus: it was simply
one of the two or three most strategically versatile
spots on the globe. What was in doubt was just what
course the Americans were willing to take to secure exclusive rights there, or at a minimum to deny it to
potential aggressors. Some policy directives in 1946,

94

mirroring the controversy, urged conservative measures, implying that Okinawa was to be treated as part of occupied Japan.[3] Others like a Feb. 26 Washington-to-CINCAFPAC* (Tokyo) instruction made a more liberal interpretation of "The Policy" with orders to: "regard Okinawa not repeat not as occupied enemy territory for purposes of planning for provisional housing for dependents."[4]

Late in 1946 the JCS fired another round in this fierce bureaucratic debate, saying they viewed "with grave concern that the Ryukyus Islands should be returned to Japan," characterizing the islands as the "best hope for a bastion against Soviet expansion to the southward which could in two decades extend to the Malay barrier by war or even by means short of war."[5] They specified a role for Okinawa which went beyond merely defending Japan (and which may have been among the reasons for State Department uneasiness about remaining there): "...a springboard from which to exercise some stabilizing influence over the area around the Yellow Sea."[6] A year later, in September of 1947, still troubled by the lack of a high level commitment to building permanent bases, the Chiefs issued paper 1619/24, reiterating the need for the Ryukyus to "be retained under strategic trusteeship."[7]

The unsettled status of Okinawa caused the most difficulty not at the rarified level of strategic theory, but in mundane matters like the construction of facilities to house men and equipment, especially important in this area of capricious and often violent weather conditions. Indicative of just how serious this problem was and the makeshift lengths to which the military were prepared to go, was a proposal reported by Brig. Gen. C.V.R. Schuyler in April, 1948, that since construction costs were viewed as so prohibitively high, some sort of amphibious rotation of units between the Marianas and the Ryukyus with men living "largely in the field under canvas" was desirable.[8] This was never officially adopted, although something not unlike it had actually been the situation in the Ryukyus, so flimsy was the construction of what housing facilities existed - mainly quonset huts. The decision-making on "what to do about the Ryukyus" is thus set against this landscape.

---

*Commander-in-Chief Armed Forces in the Pacific

Background

What follows is a reconstruction of the decision
environment of NSC 13/3 using the Snyder classification
system introduced earlier:[9]

   Internal Setting - Because the decisions leading
up to NSC 13/3[10] were taken so secretly, with very
little domestic input and equally scanty press coverage
and outside analysis, the determination of factors of
internal setting that may have influenced the princi-
pals is in large part educated guess-work. There are
enough clues, however, in the official memoranda and in
a careful, objective look at the domestic political
situation to make this guesswork reasonably well informed. Non-human factors, which refers to the material, physical needs of the United States itself, had
very little to do with this decision.[11] There is not
much evidence pointing to any resource or market-protection motivations in the minds of those planning Japan policy for this early period. Certainly the Ryukyus had no intrinsic short or long term political
value for the United States, and Japan itself had
little short term potential value. Rather, both areas
represented a drain on the American budget. As has
been the case for most of its history, Okinawa was valuable for its location rather than what it had to offer
materially: more resources were introduced into the islands than taken out.

   What societal factors might have had some bit of
influence on the deliberations of those involved in
NSC 13/3? Common values to be accounted for would have
to include American self-confidence following the Second World War and the feeling that America could not
allow this kind of conflict to occur again. Isolationist and pro-demobilization sentiments were strong, but
unlike in the post-World War I years there was a powerful counter-current of feeling that detachment and
"vigilance-from-a-distance" was no longer a satisfactory role for the United States.[12] More immediate was
the widespread concern, mostly press and foreign policy
elite-generated, that the Soviet Union, especially once
dominant in a Communist-controlled China, was posing an
increasingly serious threat to the United States (not
to mention Japan). Institutions and social structures
relevant to this kind of decision must be selected

somewhat arbitrarily, but as an example, the tremendous
rise in the prestige and scope of activity of the armed
services during the war by no means abated to the extent that it had in the 1919-1920's period. The victory over Japan had been "America's war" in a sense not
found in the 1917-1918 and 1942-45 European campaigns.
If Eisenhower, Patton and other vanquishers of the
European Axis were heroes, MacArthur as the Pacific
commander was a kind of "super-hero." Public opinion
polls during the war had shown Americans in favor of
retaining naval bases (although not territorial acqui-
sitions).[13] The most important early poll we have on
Okinawa, a Roper sampling taken in 1947, indicated 44%
favoring American possession of the Ryukyus, 38% U.S.
control but not ownership, 18% shared control with the
United Nations, and 5% "don't know".[14] What Snyder
calls human environmental categories, including cultural factors, are closely related: these include the complex and sometimes contradictory mix of historical factors: westward and Pacific expansion, naval exploration and fascination with Asian trade, and of course
the anti-colonial, anti-internationalist provincialism
that characterized American foreign policy until the
mid-19th century and influenced it considerably, if
sporadically, after that.

External setting - Here we are concerned with the
variables outside the domestic polity and society which
affect foreign policy and in the normally elitist world
of international affairs are likely to affect it more
directly than domestic ones. Our interest here is what
we previously described, following the Sprouts' distinction, as the operational environment, i.e., the relatively objective factors in the environment of those
entrusted with directing the fate of the Ryukyus.
Psychological environmental factors -- perceptions of
individuals or groups which are observably more limited or different from those which appear from historical research to be objective -- are identified as such
at relevant points in the discussion of the actual decision-making. The most obviously germane non-human
factors within the external setting include the location of Okinawa itself and the marginal economy of the
island. The age-old paucity of resources in the Ryukyus of course impeded a full recovery there; however,
there may have been a paradoxical advantage to this in
that the people were accustomed to natural disasters
and a meagre material existence. They functioned remarkably well at first on the barest of essentials provided by American relief efforts. The recuperation of
the Ryukyus was slowed by the difficulty of access to

materials which could be procured in Japan but not in Okinawa, because of an unfortunate policy technicality that prevented the United States from purchasing materials from one region in an occupied area to benefit another region. It was felt that local self-sufficiency even at the cost of some deprivation must be encouraged and that although the United States could supply emergency assistance, she could not spend scarce resources in Japan for transfer to another area technically part of Japan for purposes of building economic infra-structure. This maddening state of affairs was the subject of consultation and correspondence between Army Under Secretary William Draper and Assistant Secretary of State Charles E. Saltzman, especially during the period August-October 1948.[15] Both were anxious that the NSC 13 should be approved as quickly as possible, officially detaching Okinawa from Japan for eventual placement under a trusteeship and allowing materials and skilled labor to be purchased from Japan for Ryukyuan development. It should be remembered that the destruction in Okinawa, an area formerly heavily dependent on Japan for capital equipment and technical skills, was much more complete than in Japan. To have brought any but the most needed materials and personnel from the United States in large quantities in a time of high inflation and shortages would not have been feasible.

External cultural factors influencing NSC 13/3 are the general ones already alluded to, i.e., the State Department named ones of cultural affinity and close historical ties between the main islands and Okinawa, the fact that Okinawa was annexed-but-not violently--by Japan long before the recent imperialist surge. Within the Ryukyus themselves the people were, with few exceptions during the period, cooperative and very much dependent on the occupying Americans for a great many things. In spite of incipient reversion movements and the recent formation of political parties they could not be described as restive or dissatisfied in the sense that they would be during later periods (periods of far greater American assistance and more local autonomy, ironically.) The "other societies" category under external setting is closely related to other cultures. Within the category it might be good to mention Japanese society as a whole, of which Okinawa had recently been a part. The society of the Japanese state had been characterized by a number of features which Americans and American governments had found attractive, especially during the 75-year period between the "opening of Japan" by the Americans in 1853 and the rise of militarism around 1930. These included an intense dedication to modernization and industrialization which resulted in increased contacts between Japanese and Americans, a rapidly growing maritime trade, and a very gradual but observable spreading of wealth and economic opportunity accompanying dramatic rises in the standard of living. If the complexities of the emperorship, feudal and other ancient relationships of obligation were baffling and sometimes repugnant to Americans, the Japanese society's special brand of eclecticism and openness to change fascinated them.

The final category of external setting, foreign governments, is easily the most salient, especially for the sort of subtle esoteric high-strategy decision-making involved in NSC 13/3. Only four foreign governments appear to have figured in the decision-making of this period-and these in very different ways. They were (and it comes as no surprise) Japan, the USSR, China and Britain. The influence of Japan was considerable and unique; some attention has already been devoted to it. The controversial Ashida statement of 1947 was the first indication that Japan intended to offer some resistance to the separation of the Ryukyus from her; she could not agree that these were illegally seized territories. The assumption of the Japanese and indeed, the Americans was that a permanent arrangement could be worked out for the Ryukyus pursuant to a peace treaty but that there were likely to be differences as to what that arrangement should be. The Soviet Union figured into the calculations in two largely negative ways. The first was straightforward: Russia was regarded, we have seen, as a threat to Japan--as a worldwide threat for that matter. The Pentagon tended to view the threat as physically aggressive and the State Department viewed it more as "subversive", but by 1948 these became questions of emphasis. The departments were unified in the view that there was a real danger. NSC 7, dated March 30, 1948 put the matter bluntly:

Already Soviet directed world communism has achieved alarming success in its drive toward world conquest. Today Stalin has come close to achieving what Hitler attempted in vain. The Soviet world extends from the Elbe River and the Adriatic Sea on the West to Manchuria on the east, and embraces 1/5 of the

TABLE III-Snyder Framework
Applied to NSC 13/3 Decision

INTERNAL SETTING:
Non-Human Environment   Distance of United States from
areas of concern in Asia; eco-
nomic consideration largely
irrelevant

Society-
Social Structures   Marked rise in prestige of
military as result of Second
World War and Cold War; public
opinion favors base system but
not expansion of territory

Values   Countervailing values of isolationism and pro-demobiliza-
tion feelings versus need to
be vigilant against new enemies

Human Environment-
Culture   Interplay of historical factors: Pacific expansion,naval
exploration, Asian trade, provincialism

EXTERNAL SETTING:
Non-Human Environment: Economic helplessness of Ryukyus and need for American as-
sistance; strategic location

Other Cultures   Dependency of Okinawans on A-
mericans, but traditional ties
to Japan very strong

Other Societies   Admiration for Japanese society conflicts with uncertainty
about Japanese authority patterns

Other Governments   Consideration of Japanese seriousness about regaining Ryu-
kyus versus fear of Asian ambitions of USSR and China

INDIVIDUAL ACTORS:
                         Pres. Harry Truman; Sec. State
(Personality, Back-   George Marshall; Policy Plan-
ground, Values of   ning Head George Kennan; Sec.
interest)   Defense James Forrestal; SCAP

Douglas MacArthur; Army Under Sec. William Draper; Army Sec. Kenneth Royall; Joint Chiefs of Staff; NSC Exec. Sec. Sidney Souers

ORGANIZATIONS: Departments of State and Defense; SCAP; JCS; NSC

SITUATIONAL PROPERTIES: Decision neither routine nor crisis; anticipated rather than unanticipated; value magnitude high if viewed as part of Far East security

land surface of the world.[16]

The second potential area for negative Moscow impact on Okinawa-Japan policy was a more subtle one. The Soviets could and did charge the United States with high-handed policies and questionable intentions in meetings of the Allied Council of the FEC beginning in 1946 and were later to exploit America's plans for the Ryukyus in the international forum, charging neo-colonialism and aggressive designs.[17]

The impact of China on Ryukyus policy by 1948 was that of a persistent phantom: the increasingly likely prospect that the country would soon be ruled by the Communists and allied with the USSR. The CIA study of August 1948 quoted from earlier was typical in its concern and stated that any nod to the claims on the islands by Chiang Kai-shek would benefit not Chiang, but Mao Tse-tung in all likelihood. British influence, as far as we can tell, was comparatively slight. It was to become clearer during the peace treaty drafting of 1951, three years later, when the British urged that the U.S. get Japan to renounce sovereignty over the Ryukyus and the Bonins. Their pre-treaty policy was always a bit tougher on the question of separating Okinawa from Japan than that of the United States herself.

We move next to the third major heading within Snyder's analytic schema, individual actors involved in the decision. Unlike some of the later decisions we will be investigating, in which personal interviews with a number of the participants confirmed or corrected our estimates of the dramatis personae, for the 1948-49 decision we had to rely heavily on documents, memoirs, and secondary accounts.[18] The complete list of major participants is found in Table III, a summary of the Snyder framework as applied to this decision. What follows is a capsule characterization of each guided by Snyder's own categorization system: personality, social background-experience, and personal values.

Harry Truman

It was President Truman who gave NSC 13/3 a high degree of authoritativeness as an American policy statement with his signature. Not all such NSC papers were treated this way, but the statement of policy on Japan was considered important enough to warrant his endorsement. To our best knowledge the President became involved in the concerns of the document at a rather late stage and in a formal and almost perfunctory way, substance-wise.[20]

George C. Marshall

The Secretary of State was a strong asset to the Truman administration during a difficult period set in the middle of other difficult periods; his contacts with the military were obvious and his prestige with Congress high. He was cautious by nature, favored quiet diplomacy backed by unchallengable military strength and preparedness. An early strong advocate of a Pacific base system with the Ryukyus as its most important component, Marshall had become concerned that the unsettled status of the islands was nullifying their usefulness. Although the documentation is scanty it appears that he initiated a series of talks with the Defense Department in October, 1947 regarding Okinawa, under the auspices of SANACC, but these were discontinued on the advice of Forrestal. Influenced by Kennan of the Policy Planning Staff in the direction of delaying any treaty with Japan until that country got back on its feet, he dispatched Kennan to Tokyo in February 1948 to survey the situation.

George Kennan

The head of the Policy Planning Staff appears to have had considerable--perhaps even decisive-influence on the outcome of the NSC 13/3 recommendations. As a result of his trip to Japan in February-March 1948 and consultations with MacArthur he became a strong advocate of a key role for Okinawa. He probably influenced MacArthur at least as much in the direction of a reorientation away from reformist-for-reform's-sake programs to stabilization and economic re-emergence policies designed to equip Japan for the perilous conditions developing in Asia. Insightful and persuasive, Kennan served as the brains and the canny spokesman for the Containment Policy. Kennan in this period was at the height of his influence.

James Forrestal

The Secretary of Defense was known as a superb manager and given credit for much of the successful integration of planning for the services under the reorganization of the defense establishment in 1947. Taciturn and tough, he was also an extremely intelligent man who was articulate in his memoranda and a relentless modernizer and means-ends analyzer. He was never sanguine about dealing with the Soviets, and was apparently impressed with Kennan's arguments that economic and social reform in Japan had to give way to at least a partial re-surfacing of the pre-war and wartime managerial classes.[21]

Douglas MacArthur

An independently powerful military leader whose like has not been witnessed since his forced retirement 28 years ago, the Supreme Commander of Allied Forces in the Pacific was very important in the development of the commitment to the permanent garrison of Okinawa sanctioned by NSC 13/3. When Army Under Secretary Draper visited in 1948, MacArthur had "strongly urged," according to a State Department report, "that we devote adequate funds at once to the necessary construction for a permanent garrison."[22] Imperious and a zealous guardian of American prerogatives in ruling postwar Japan, it remains the subject of debate whether his firm refusal to let the Soviets extend their influence in the Far Eastern Commission created more destabilizing friction in the Far East than it preempted.

William Draper

The Under Secretary of the Army conducted his own investigation of the Japanese situation in April, 1948 and in the fall of that year was the major point of contact with the State Department on trying to resolve problems resulting from the unsettled status of Okinawa. He appears to have been more concerned about Asian matters than his superior, Army Secretary Kenneth Royall.

Kenneth Royall

It has been noted that the Secretary of the Army felt that Europe rather than the Orient was the area of greatest danger in 1948-49. He believed that American interests could be adequately defended from Okinawa and the Philippines, apparently, but that in the case of a

large-scale Soviet offensive on Japan, the United
States simply did not have the forces to resist successfully and should not divert men there from Europe.
His proposals in January 1948 that Japan be economically revitalized along something closer to the pre-
war lines than had been planned originally helped trigger a flurry of fact-finding and study missions to
Tokyo in 1948. These resulted in the turn-around of
occupation policy embodied in NSC 13/3 and other documents.

The Joint Chiefs

The Chiefs - Gen. Bradley, Admiral Denfeld, Gen.
Vandenberg - appear to have followed the lead of their
predecessors, Marshall and Nimitz - in recognizing the
tremendous value of the Ryukyus. In fact they were on
record as cognizant of the desire of the State Department to get a strategic trusteeship for Okinawa, but
felt that the Ryukyus should be secured whether or not
such a decision could be effected.[23]

Sidney Souers

The Executive Secretary of the National Security
Council, Mr. Souers, a former Rear Admiral, had a role
which has had no real equivalent in more recent years.
After December, 1948, he replaced Admiral Leahy in
briefing the President (on Leahy's advice and retirement). It was he who guided the Japan study through
the NSC 13/2 and 13/3 stages, and although his substantive input is not known to us, his role in coordinating
interdepartmental position papers and memoranda related
to the final policy statement appears to have been substantial.

Organizational factors - This category embraces
major organizational elements with input into the decision as organizations and helped shape the flow of
communications which resulted in the final policy
statement. The President did not have to rely on an
inner staff of experts as became prevalent in the
1960's; he had close working relationships with his
Secretary of State and Secretary of Defense, and relied
heavily on them, although he was certainly capable of
making his own decisions. The National Security Council at this early juncture has been described as more
a vehicle for information and organization for the

President than a consultative body with collegial decision-making power.[24] What consulting Mr. Truman did with its members he did with them in their capacities as officers in his Cabinet or members of the JCS.

The State Department was well represented in the decisions reflected in the NSC document; in fact Kennan himself was responsible for much of its content. The paper was in effect the final victory of the Policy Planning Staff over elements in the State Department which in late 1947 and early 1948 had favored a treaty with Japan which would have neutralized, demilitarized and placed her under international supervision: in other words a solution more geared to a Japanese militarist resurgence than a Japan threatened in a Cold War. The Army Department, and specifically Under Secretary Draper, had primary responsibility and interest within the Department of Defense; Draper's spring mission to Tokyo and his report bolstered and paralleled Kennan's of several weeks earlier. Forrestal and Royall, Secretaries of Defense and Army respectively, seem to have been pre-occupied during the decision-making on Japan with European concerns, the Berlin crisis especially, as well as the problem of American armed manpower and the battle over Universal Military Training. The Joint Chiefs of Staff input has already been extensively treated; suffice it to say here that their concern for the fortified position on Okinawa was the major reason-for-being of NSC 13/3. Kennan, Marshall, and ultimately Truman were essentially endorsing what the JCS had been pushing for months. Whether or not the Military Government on Okinawa had any influence on the high level policy statement in the NSC report we have not been able to determine: it seems doubtful. Even if they did, their views were completely filtered through the Headquarters of SCAP in Tokyo, whose unique and obviously important role in shaping the final commitment will be further elaborated as we proceed.

Situational properties - Here we have the immediate contextual factors of the decision-making surrounding NSC 13/3, following Snyder's formula. Unfortunately, the decision was taken in a fractionated way, really the composite of a number of decisions rather than a centrally directed process (i.e., coordinated yes, directed no). Our background chapter and previous sections of this chapter supply much of what we need here: the visits to Japan by Kennan and - shortly after - Draper (the latter accompanied by an

106

advisory committee of businessmen under the chairman-
ship of banker Percy Johnston); the tense situation in
Europe with the sealing off of Berlin and the collapse
of non-Communist resistance in the Czech coalition
government; threatened strikes and economic upheaval
in Japan; and finally the austere conditions and slap-
dash aspects of managing an island base that might
conceivably in a few months be a prefecture of Japan
again. The development of the Okinawa section of the
NSC paper is best seen as the culmination of a long
process; insofar as there was any triggering event for
the decision-making it could probably be said to be the
Kennan-MacArthur consultations early in 1948. Kennan
himself apparently has quite an opinion of the weight
which those meetings carried:

> ...my own visit, the talk with General
> MacArthur, and the directives that finally
> emanated from Washington represented in their
> entirety a major contribution to the change
> in occupation policy that was carried out in
> late 1948 and 1949; and I consider my part in
> bringing about this change to have been, after
> the Marshall Plan, the most significant con-
> structive contribution I was ever able to make
> in government.[25]

Turning finally to Snyder's suggested variables
pertinent to the analysis of the core-context of decisions, he and Robinson first distinguished between
anticipated and unanticipated decisions: which applies? NSC 13/3 was no routine decision-making exercise,
but here it is safe to place it in the "anticipated"
box because it was an issue which had been under scrutiny for months. By 1948 the unsettled nature of the
Okinawa situation had become more than just a problem
for strategic theory: it was causing countless administrative headaches with no end in sight. (e.g., no
treaty). Thus we have an anticipated action which, if
not routine, was not "crisis-like" either. Snyder's
value-magnitudes distinction is a difficult one to apply" compared with armed intervention, say, the values
of maintaining a commitment to Okinawa's fortification
and administration by the United States was small. As
part of a total strategic policy, that of containment,
however, its salience was high.

Alternative Explanatory Models

If the Snyder-Bruck-Sapin analysis helps us to create a giant tableau with which to view our decision, the contrasting models of Graham Allison provide an organized means of setting the tableau in motion. In order to determine the relevance of his bureaucratic politics explanation for our analysis of the NSC 13/3 decision, we first endeavor to portray the decision in the light of the rational actor and organizational models. What Allison depicts as the conventional or classical approach, analyzing national decision-making as rational action, would see the process something like this:[26]

Section 5 of NSC 13/3 committing the United States to a long-term investment in the Ryukyus was the outcome of a logical, if somewhat belated evaluation process, in which the goals of American foreign policy were coordinated with the actions proposed and that policy was well-served. During the State and Defense conversations on the Ryukyus in the fall of 1947, two major figures, Kennan and Marshall, in the State Department, determined that a high-level State Department investigation of the potential of the Ryukyus as a permanent military outpost should be made as part of a general exchange with the Supreme Commander in Tokyo. Thus did Mr. Kennan depart for Tokyo at the end of February, 1948 to consult with General MacArthur, and provide a basis for an independent State Department position on the Occupation and related security issues.

On Mr. Kennan's return he reported to the Secretary of State that Okinawa was a base of great potential value to the United States and needed far more attention than it had been getting - economically, socially, and otherwise conditions were not good. A solid commitment by Washington not only to a permanent presence in Okinawa, but also to an augmentation of efforts to restore economic stability and "normal political conditions" was needed. (This recom-

108

mendation was one among several from the Kennan
mission, the others related to such areas as the
Japanese economy, the purges, and -- of great related relevance - the reinforcement of the Japanese national police establishment).[27]

Kennan's recommendations were passed on to
the Far Eastern Office at State and finally to
the three armed services through the National
Security Council, where they were reviewed and
modified as part of the process of creating
NSC 13/2, the document on overall Japan policy.
Meanwhile, Kennan took every opportunity to
push the Okinawa build-up, speaking on the
issue more than once at the National War College
in the spring of 1948.

The final outcome of this activity did not
occur until May 6, 1949 when the President
signed NSC 13/3. The most crucial provisions
of Section 5 included: a. the announced U.S.
intention of retaining the facilities in the
Ryukyus and seeking "international sanction"
for the maintenance of "long-term strategic
control," b. initiation of a program specifically designed to enhance the economic and
social well-being of the inhabitants and reduce the burden on the United States, and
c. that the islands should no longer be dependent upon or obligated to (read "linked to")
any other occupied area (read "Japan").

It was felt that the fortification of the
Ryukyus would give Washington much greater
flexibility with her Japan policy: Japan could
be protected even after a treaty and although
it was being recommended that she build up her
internal defense capabilities, the strong bases
at Okinawa could help insure that Japanese
strength could still be kept at an acceptibly
modest level without jeopardizing her security.
Part and parcel of this whole plan was the reduction of troops of the Occupation to the
minimum possible level in Japan itself, a low-
ering of the American profile there and the
diminution of all Occupation manifestations
that could be diminished.[28]

It must be noted that the authors of the
document regarded it as an internal memorandum,

not for public consumption. Newsweek Magazine, however, had published a detailed and for the most part accurate summary of its contents back in late November of 1948, causing consternation in Japan and annoyance, but no confirmations or denials, from the United States government.[29] On May 7, 1949, the State Department issued a release which conveyed only the general sense of NSC 13/3, namely that Japan was being encouraged to become more self-reliant and develop her own role in international affairs.

The rational model characterization stresses 1. the perception of a problem, 2., consultations aimed at producing a solution, 3. coordination of the Okinawa policy with what the United States wanted to accomplish in Japan proper, and 4. a succinct policy statement calling for implementation beginning "within 60 days" of the President's signature. In accord with Allison's depiction of the rational paradigm, the description emphasizes a national actor, the United States, making policy on the basis of value-maximization, namely American security in the Far East (at reduced cost if possible!). Notable is the absence of attention to organizational goals or motivations and bureaucratic politics as characterized in earlier discussions of Model II and Model III. The organizational model analyst can be depended on to see deficiencies in the Model I account:

> The fact that the output represented in NSC 13/3 section 5 can plausibly be what the rational actor analyst describes as "United States policy" is the result of organizational process - not simply by reasonable discussions of alternatives and value-maximization. The problem itself, that of irresolution and paralyzing indecision on what to do about and with the Ryukyus was caused by organizational determinants in the first place. The State Department in 1946 and 1947 felt that after shearing Japan of her 1931-42 accumulated Co-Prosperity Sphere, there would be no particular advantage to detaching the Ryukyus from her. There might very possibly be negative repercussions. The Army and Navy Departments and particularly the Joint Chiefs of Staff (with the exception of Admiral Leahy) had argued that the United States should make clear its intention to retain control of the Ryukyus with or without

110

international sanction,[30] and strongly opposed talk of returning them to Japan.

In the fall of 1947 Secretary of State Marshall encouraged Secretary of Defense Forrestal to send representatives to meet with members of the State Department under the auspices of SANAAC to hammer out a coherent Ryukyus policy. For reasons of which we are not sure, these talks were suspended early in 1948, possibly because the State Department had not developed proposals for Okinawa which were substantial enough to serve as the basis for policy revisions. Policy Planning Staff Chief Kennan's Far East trip in February and March appears to have turned this around and returned the initiative on Ryukyus policy to the State Department. Convinced by MacArthur that Okinawa was a necessary adjunct to any practical Japanese policy, Kennan in turn seems to have demonstrated to MacArthur that an early treaty with Japan involved too much risk. A new emphasis would soon have to be placed on Japan's economic growth and stability, inevitably at some cost to the reform program. Whatever MacArthur's doubts about the wisdom of what Kennan was suggesting, SCAP did not interfere with or register serious objections to most of the substance of what was to become NSC 13/3.[31]

Under the supervision of Secretary of State Marshall and Mr. Souers of the National Security Council, the Kennan recommendations worked their way through the bureaucracy and were superficially amended by the Far Eastern Office of the State Department and then by the Joint Chiefs of Staff. Other points besides the Okinawa paragraphs underwent important revisions; Section 5, however, did not. The report signed by the President in May of 1949 represented a major organizational compromise of a small but salient strategic issue over a two year period. The State Department, under Kennan's leadership, had come around to an acceptance of the high strategic premium placed on the Ryukyus and the need to guard American options there. The Defense Department in turn accepted the necessity of an American commitment to try to secure the Ryukyus under United Nations auspices and to markedly reduce the visibility of the occupation in Japan,

111

including troop reductions and increased Japanese autonomy.

Note that there is not necessarily a profound cleavage between the Model I and Model II explanations of this decision. Logical organizational inference patterns and procedures produced some differences that had to be resolved, but they were resolved intelligently and through compromise spearheaded by sophisticated individuals. Allison does not pay enough heed to the fact that prestigious individuals - for example, the Kennans and MacArthurs of any bureaucracy can without prejudicing the position of their own organizations work to modify not only the perspective of the organization on specific substantive issues, but can to some extent redefine organizational self-interest to conform to new situations and the need for compromise. Sometimes compromise itself comes to be seen as the paramount objective, "rationally" and in forms of organizational health, but we have a third version of the story:

> The organizational explanation of NSC 13/3 was correct in its criticism of the simple means-ends analysis and unified actor approach of Model I; implicit in its own account, however, are the weaknesses of a purely organizational description. The fact that the State Department did a 180° turn on the Okinawa question and the Defense Department/JCS agreed to some rather drastic and experimental shifts in its policy bespeaks some powerful forces at work not linked clearly to organizational self interest. In a sense the answer to this contradiction may be found closer to the rational point of focus than the organizational.

> To determine whether this is so we need to zero in on the key "swing" component in this decision sequence, the State Department policy planning staff. Kennan, working with Secretary Marshall had developed a sophisticated and decidedly unsanguine view of the motivations of the Soviet Union and made a number of lengthy recommendations for "containing" Stalin beginning in 1947. He was a globalist, and not particularly in sympathy with those like Gen. MacArthur and a number of old Far East/Japan hands in the State Department who felt that the primary interest of the United States in the area was

112

the nurturing of a neutral, democratized re-
deemed Japan. Rather Kennan, and Marshall --
another globalist -- urged that it was time to
link Japanese policy to a global policy of
securing friendly countries against the incursions of the Russians. The United States
could not possibly afford to do this without
substantial help from regional friends; thus
Japan must be made to stand on her own feet.
A strong base on Okinawa would aid this process by permitting the United States to lower
her military posture on the main islands.

It could be argued that the Kennan position,
which eventually won the day, was based on the
man's rational calculations of the need for the
policy he was recommending, and his ability to
persuade others - others who already agreed with
important, but differing parts of his plan.
State Department Japanists, for example, supported his insistence on having any permanent
arrangement for Okinawa internationally sanctioned; the Joint Chiefs were pleased with his
recognition that bases in Okinawa alone were
not enough, that there must be American administration for an indefinite period. However
credible the rational interpretation, and however
enlightened his objectives may have been, there
is a clear element of the promotion of a strategic doctrine and a career at work here. His
own evaluation of his performance, cited earlier
in this chapter, clearly indicates a strong
personal stake in the outcome.

There is more evidence that the Kennan-
engineered compromise may have involved something besides overwhelming the military with
the force of persuasion, and the logic of
arming Okinawa to the teeth so that the shadow
of American troops occupying the main islands
in great masses could be diminished. Kennan
offers this account of what he saw as the
logical outcome of a skillful implementation
of NSC 13/3:

> Once internal conditions in Japan had
> been stabilized and once the country
> was equipped with an adequate police
> establishment, and particularly with
> a smart, effective maritime police

113

force that could prevent infiltration
from the mainland, we would be able to
afford, it seemed to me, to offer the
Russians in effect the withdrawal of
our armed forces from the Japanese
archipelago (about Okinawa I was not
so sure) in return for some settlement
that would give us assurance against
the communization of all Korea.[32]

Kennan thus saw the build-up on Okinawa as
ideally leading to a major reduction in American troops, and ultimately, coupled with an
agreement with the Soviets, an   insurance policy that would allow for the more or less
complete withdrawal of troops from Japan.

But the military evidently saw things from
a quite different perspective. If Kennan were
hopeful that the build-up on Okinawa might
allow for something more than NSC 13/3 called
for, i.e., the eventual complete withdrawal
of American armed forces from Japan, the military were convinced that Okinawa would not be
sufficient protection in the case of removal
of the bases from the Japanese main islands.
A month after NSC 13/3 was signed, Forrestal
submitted a document to the National Security
Council-NSC 49--which contained this paragraph
of warning:

> If it should be impracticable or impossible
> to obtain bases on the Japanese main is-
> lands, bases on Okinawa or other islands
> of the Ryukyus along with other U.S. bases
> in or near the Pacific would not meet
> our essential needs.[33]

The memorandum goes on to recommend against
a peace treaty at that time because of the
likelihood of insufficient guarantees for Japan's security. What the Department of Defense
document does when examined alongside of Kennan's statement of his own hopes and intentions is to cast doubt that a very deep mutual
understanding of what the various NSC 13/3
participants saw as the probable outcomes of
their actions. Indeed, such an understanding
might have precluded the agreement. But there
was a high premium on some kind of unified

114

statement, after months of ambiguity and in light of the growing threat seen on the Asian mainland. A rational actor explanation carries with it the expectation that if agreement is produced, it is on the basis of a mutual understanding of the issues and implications of the policy agreed upon. This does not seem to be the case with the NSC 13/3 decision.

The major purpose of presenting accounts of the 1948-1949 decision sequence in the three variations suggested by the Allison models is to get a sense of the relevance of his distinctions (can they improve our understanding?) and, especially, to search for the presence of the game-like, non-rational, (but not purely organizational) factors in the process. I think it can be said that in the case of this decision, the different perspectives provided by his competing paradigms very clearly aids in the total quality of explanation. The organizational model alerts one to organizational difference-splitting that might wrongly be seen as a sort of rational dialectic if it were only the premises of Model I that were operative (i.e., that the Defense Department and SCAP were somehow intellectually persuaded that a substantial troop reduction in Japan was for the best and that Okinawa could be a hedge against risks related to such an action). The bureaucratic politics model brings out some of the personal and sub-organizational factors that help build a stake into certain solutions in a way that goes beyond the mere sifting among alternatives. What might be seen as "intellectual spiritual conversions" within Model I or "difference-splitting" among powerful organizational actors in Model II, becomes more credible when Model III factors like personal ambition (even in pursuit of a rationally powerful doctrine) and the agreement-imperative of organizations and individuals wanting simply to keep things moving, are brought into play.

The Decision: Rational-Comprehensive or Incremental?

An analysis of the NSC-13 story in terms of Lindblom's rational-comprehensive versus incrementalist schema is greatly aided by the consideration of Allison's perspectives. One might well expect, for example, that a decision sequence in which organizational compromise and intra-bureaucratic bargaining were commonplace would be far more likely to be "disjointed and incremental" as Lindblom would phrase it - than ration-

115

al-comprehensive. It is clear from reading the background documents available on NSC 13/3, Section 5 that three major alternatives for Okinawa were being considered between 1946 and 1948: 1. return to Japan, 2. annexation as U.S.territory, and 3. some sort of arrangement falling between these extremes, but one that would guarantee the relatively unrestricted use of the islands - perhaps trusteeship. By the spring of 1948, although all of these options were still theoretically open, it seemed unlikely that the United States would try to annex the islands. That would leave Washington open to charges of neo-colonialism and be offensive to Japan, which was coming to be seen as a potential ally rather than as an international parolee for whom the United States had responsibility. Yet equally improbable was an outright return of the Ryukyus, given their value to the military and the generally dwindling sense of security felt by American strategic planners. This left the middle option, and by the time Mr. Kennan's plane left Washington for Tokyo in February, there was every probability that "trusteeship" or some sort of "indefinite leasehold" arrangement would be the outcome. If the decision-sequence is defined as beginning with the Marshall-Kennan talks of late 1947, then incremental decision-making is an adequate construction of what followed. Some sort of borrowing arrangement would be arrived at when a peace treaty was being negotiated, but no major changes in the status quo were contemplated for the interim.

Here the analysis becomes tricky. Although the Kennan-Marshall and Kennan-MacArthur talks led to a decision outcome that amounted to a top-level confirmation of the existing state of affairs regarding Okinawa's legal ownership, at the same time a bold program of military construction and local development was heralded. On top of that it must be remembered that what appeared to be a no-change (no-return) policy for Okinawa was, in NSC 13/3, one component of a truly profound change in overall United States Japanese policy. This change, i.e., the move toward scaling down the Occupation and giving more access to political and economic power to those from whom it had been taken in 1945 resulted from several studies and missions (Draper-Johnston, Kennan, Dodge)[34] which, if "disjointed" and overlapping in their execution, had results which were hardly incremental. It is this dual nature of NSC 13/3 Section 5 that we want to take careful account of: a confirmation of the status quo which indirectly

116

permitted one set of profound changes (on Japan) and directly entailed substantial changes through the Okinawa build-up. We are left with a paradox which Lindblom's theory has difficulty accounting for but which is by no means uncommon in state policy-making: a decision not to alter things which might have once been expected to be altered, the "status quo decision" then having big consequences.

The question of rationality in policy construction is a central one for Lindblom and one we should pause to consider more directly. At its core rationality involves: A. means which are consistent with ends, B. means which furnish a relatively efficient path to those ends (i.e., a minimum of time and resources spent for maximum gain), and C. ends which are demonstrably connected to the broad interests of the actor, be it an individual, group, state, or whatever. If a crazed national leader wished to get revenge against a population up in arms against him and did so by drawing his country into a nuclear clash with a neighbor, he might be acting rationally given his ends, but the ends themselves would not be rational by our definition.

In the case of NSC 13/3 the ends are clearly stated (see document appendix) and include "not to press for a peace treaty at this time," "a minimum psychological impact of the presence of occupational forces on the Japanese population" and so on. The statements about Okinawa are less clear in their delineation of ends, but one has the strong impression that they are linked closely to the goals expressed elsewhere in the report. The mention of reducing the economic burdens on "the natives" and encouraging economic growth and self-sufficiency as soon as possible to avoid outside dependence is indicative of a desire to have an economic sub-structure conducive to an orderly, stable environment for the contemplated expanded military garrison. Another goal, implicitly, is international approval of the whole project, but there seems to be no hurry about getting this and few hints about how it might be done. Given the rational, if not necessarily "prudent" or "realistic" goals of Pacific security for the United States and the contribution to be made to that by the resurrection of Japan, the Okinawa section of NSC 13/3 is a rational, if very general statement. It conforms to Lindblom's description of many decision-making processes as operating with the assumption of rather limited options (e.g., a substantially reduced American presence in the western Pacific

117

was not an option) and failing to make broad, comprehensive re-assessments. It does not always resemble his model of uncoordinated, tentative policy-change at the margins, however. It may prove necessary to develop a new model which is neither synoptic nor incrementalist, but which may be closer to the former than Lindblom would have us believe corresponds to many real-world cases.

Conclusion

In this first application of our composite foreign policy analytical framework, the Snyder-Bruck-Sapin schema was used to order the historical data of Part II as it applied to the NSC paper of May, 1949. More specifically, organizational and individual actors were identified and placed in an internal setting (i.e., domestic political milieu) and the external setting (international milieu aspects which had identifiable impact or probable impact on some or all of the participants). After discussing the anatomy of the decision in the Snyder group context, we proceded to view its physiology by applying an analysis based on the three models of international decision advanced by Allison. In relating the events of the decision sequence in this way, it became clear that while the latter phase of the discussion had certain coordinated, structured elements essentially this was a decentralized decision which evolved out of the compromise of both organizational positions and bureaucratic bargaining maneuvers. The decision also can be said to have evolved incrementally, for the most part, rather than in a well-planned coordinated fashion following the contrast in styles posited by Lindblom for governmental decision strategies. There certainly were rational aspects to the 1948-49 sequence, however, and the sequence conforms imperfectly to the Lindblom disjointed-incremental model. In spite of plural and competitive centers of policy-directing power, there were careful evaluations and an ultimate drawing together of recommendations regarding the Ryukyus which might incline some observers more in the direction of the synoptic evaluation. My conclusion, however, is that the incremental vision of the unfolding of policy decisions is the more reliable of the two.

NOTES

[1] See methodological appendix. The few currently active men who participated in NSC 13/3, such as Kennan, I found unavailable for interviewing or discovered to be so far out on the edges of the decision process that their insights, while interesting, would not have been comparable to those used in the subsequent decision case-studies.

[2] From SWNCC chairman, H. Freeman Matthews to Byrnes, January 22, 1946. Declassified excerpt obtained March 22, 1976.

[3] War Department memorandum from Brig. Gen. George A. Lincoln, Plans and Operations Division, Army, dated April 15, 1946.

[4] Dispatch from Maj. Gen. H.A. Craig to CINCAFPAC, Tokyo dated February 25, 1946. Declassified March 22, 1976.

[5] JCS memorandum on JCS 1619, September 16, 1946.

[6] Ibid.

[7] Declassified excerpt obtained March 23, 1976.

[8] Memorandum from Schuyler dated April 10, 1948, declassified March 22, 1976.

[9] Terms actually employed in the Snyder-Bruck-Sapin schema are underlined here. (Refer to Figure B, Ch.1)

[10] For convenience we refer to the May 6, 1949 NSC 13/3 Report, Section #5 on Okinawa simply as NSC 13/3. The reader should bear in mind that the document contained several other equally important policy statements having nothing to do with Okinawa.

[11]It is worthwhile noting that although non-human environmental factors appear to have had very indirect impact on NSC 13/3 Section 5, the part played by such factors in the implementation of Section 5 was considerable. I refer here to a natural disaster, Typhoon Gloria, which ravaged the Ryukyus in the summer of 1949, a few months after the promulgation of the Truman-approved policy statement. As noted in Chapter Two, the amount of damage caused by the storm led to an extensive investigation and upgrading of the facilities in the archipelago. This coincided with the build-up envisioned (in the most general way) in the NSC paper.

[12]For one discussion of this generally accepted interpretation of Post-World War II domestic attitudes see Thomas A. Bailey, A Diplomatic History of the American People, (New York: Appleton-Century-Crofts,1969), 8th ed., pp. 768-772; also Wendell Willkie's role in bringing isolationist Republicans around to a more cosmopolitan position is detailed in D.B.Johnson, The Republican Party and Wendell Willkie, (Urbana, Illinois, 1960).

[13]Opinion News, Sept. 4, 1945, p.1, cited in Bailey, op.cit.,p.770.

[14]Cited in Binnendijk, in Henderson, op.cit., p.153.

[15]Draper-Saltzman correspondence in Army Plans and Operations decimal file #104.1 TS, National Archives, Washington, D.C., declassified March 22, 1976.

[16]NSC 7, p. 2.

[17]The best source on USSR-American disagreements regarding Japan policy in the period is Herbert Feis, Contest Over Japan, (New York: W.W.Norton & Co.,1967).

[18]To some extent, having access to formerly highly classified and in some cases detailed memoranda and papers may offset the handicap of having most of their authors either dead or too old for personal interviews to be ethically attempted or justified.

[19]This technique of character-sketching according to the Snyder formula and criteria worked well for Glenn D. Paige in The Korean Decision, op.cit.

[20]This is based on a general reading of the memoranda and documents for the period of the decision (no personal interest from the President was indicated until late 1948).

[21]James Forrestal, The Forrestal Diaries (ed.) Walter Millis, (New York: The Viking Press, 1951) pp.328-29.

[22]SCAP CONVERSATIONS, Recommendations With Respect to U.S.Policy Toward Japan, "Views of General of the Army Douglas MacArthur," April 16, 1948.(published in JCS 1380/48).

[23]JCS 2078, dated November 21, 1949 (but developing a position worked out much earlier).

[24]Keith Clark and Laurence Legere, The President and the Management of National Security (Institute for Defense Analysis), (New York: Praeger, 1969)pp.58-59.

[25]George F. Kennan, Memoirs: 1925-1950, (Boston:Little, Brown and Company), 1967. p. 393.

[26]The hypothetical account of a rational-model analyst which follows conforms to the format we shall be using in all of the case-study chapters. Essentially it employs the component assumptions, spirit, and style of presentation used by Allison in his analogous descriptions of the Cuban crisis. Since I am describing Okinawa decisions based on my own use of the Allison method, however, it should be noted that I alone have responsibility for the decision reconstructions.

[27]Kennan, op.cit., pp. 391-393.

[28]Note other sections of NSC 13/3 in Document Appendix.

[29]Newsweek, October 25, 1948, p. 52.

[30] JCS 570/48, January 17, 1946. Declassified May 3, 1972.

[31] Frederick Dunn has pointed out that at the time of Kennan's visit, MacArthur had apparently been "stung" by charges that some of his reforms were playing into the hands of the Communists., Dunn, op.cit.,p. 74.

[32] Dated June 15, 1949. Declassified November 25, 1975.

[33] Kennan, op.cit., p. 392

[34] These were the major investigatory missions to Japan in 1948-49; all essentially recommended changes in policy which would promote Japanese economic self-sufficiency and growth, as well as more rapid indus-trialization. Joseph Dodge and Percy Johnston, in particular, as financial experts, were responsible for advocating austerity (anti-inflationary) measures for Japan.

CHAPTER FOUR: DULLES AND THE

RESIDUAL SOVEREIGNTY FORMULA, 1950-51

Even a superficial reading of the development of the residual sovereignty formula for the "territorial question" in the 1951 treaty negotiations established it as a decision markedly different from the one just analyzed. In the preceeding chapter it was seen that the national security managers grappling with what to do about Okinawa were confronted over many months with a fast-changing geo-political and psychological situation through which they had to grope their way. Mr. Dulles, on the other hand, was presented with a fairly traditional and well-defined diplomatic problem -- reaching a peace accord with a defeated power -- and given broad latitude in constructing a solution. His solution as regards Okinawa was one which embodied compromise not only between different viewpoints within the American government, but also took into consideration the preferences of Japanese and other potential Pacific allies. It allowed the U.S. to maintain a position of unquestioned pre-eminence in the Ryukyus, while leaving open the possibility of international trusteeship and not prejudicing the long-term legal claim of Japan to the archipelago.

The deep background against which I will be reconstructing the Dulles-led decision in this chapter has three principal components: 1. the implementation of NSC 13/3 (discussed in the preceding chapter) during 1949-50, 2. the outbreak of war in Korea in June,1950, and 3. the general strategic context of the actual treaty preparations in late 1950 and 1951. As indicated in previous chapters, the fulfillment of the provisions of NSC 13/3, combined with the increased construction funding that became available in the wake of the calamitous typhoon season of 1949, was responsible for a considerable improvement in the physical conditions of buildings and transportation infrastructure on Okinawa.[1]   And although the NSC paper did not end the improvisational quality of the administration of the Ryukyus, it made virtually certain that, barring unforeseen circumstances, the United States would hold on to the bases in the islands as part of any peace agreement with Japan.

By the end of 1949 several studies assessing the American strategic position in the Far East and making recommendations relevant to peace agreements with the Japanese emerged. A JCS paper "Current Strategic Evaluation of U.S. Security Needs in Japan", noting that "...the spreading chaos on the mainland of Asia heightens the importance of Japan to the U.S.", warned that "too much emphasis cannot be placed on the unhealthy psychological effect of a peace treaty followed immediately by a substantial withdrawal of military force from Japan."[2] Interestingly, Japan was seen, militarily, as contributing to the security of <u>Okinawa's</u> bases, <u>i.e.</u>, the Japanese facilities were <u>supportive</u> of the Ryukyuan.[3]

A somewhat more general and broadly coordinated statement of government policy was NSC 48/2, "The Position of the United States With Respect to Asia," which was actually assertive rather than simply defense-minded in its recommendations. It concluded that a basic security objective of the United States in Asia was:

> Gradual reduction and eventual elimination of the preponderant power and influence of the USSR in Asia to such a degree that the Soviet Union will not be capable of threatening from that area the security of the United States or its friends and that the Soviet Union would encounter serious obstacles should it attempt to threaten the peace, national independence and stability of the Asiatic nations.[4]

The effect of such position papers -- even when one considers that they were general policy statements rather than specific commitments -- was to underscore the national security establishment's support for a tough, resolute position in Asia generally and in the Okinawa bastion in particular.

The Korean War is the second historical factor salient for analyzing this decision. It was the first major use of Okinawa as an active staging ground for[5] military action rather than merely a deterrent base. As such the island was an extremely useful supplement to the facilities in Japan and a graphic demonstration for Dulles, who had begun working on the treaty just over a month before hostilities began, of the practical usefulness of the Ryukyus and the concern of the military to maintain options there.

Dulles' appointment as chief draftsman of the treaty with Japan in May, 1950 thus followed closely a hardening of the American position in Asia, manifested in statements like NSC-48, as well as a general, global strategy of greater vigilence and assertiveness than had been anticipated by many observers a few years earlier. The development of NSC-68 as the most authoritative and widely discussed internal guideline as the 1950's dawned is further evidence of the sort of increasingly sophisticated and ambitious global policy line which had taken hold.[6] The attribution of influence and guidance on the part of the Russians in North Korea, compounded by the active intervention of the Communist Chinese in the conflict late in November of 1950 seemed to vindicate the efforts of military planners since 1948 to bolster the position of smaller Asian states in the shadow of Communist giants with such positions as Okinawa.

Background

Internal setting -- Dulles' planning and bargaining over Okinawa must be seen as one series of maneuvers within the larger drama of putting together the multi-lateral treaty with Japan. Here we explore the domestic American factors that may plausibly be expected to have some impact on his handling of his assignment between May, 1950 and September, 1951, mostly as regards the particular parts of the treaty dealing with territorial issues, but with the treaty-as-a-whole on occasion. The Snyder-Bruck-Sapin category of non-human factors, as was the case in the 1948-49 decision, is a difficult one to apply precisely because it entails economic factors like resources and geographic location of the united States which are either quite general (American physical distance from Asia and need to maintain forward positions) or irrelevant (e.g., need for vital minerals). What about institutional and social structure factors? Since NSC 13/3 decision-making period the role of the military had continued to grow in foreign affairs decision-making, although it was at times anxiously watched and dramatically checked by the civilian authorities, the landmark example of this being the removal of General MacArthur from his commands in March of 1951. I have not been able to find data that enlarges the perception of American public opinion on maintaining the American position in the Ryukyus after the 1947 poll cited in the preceding chapter but Bernard Cohen has presented extensive data analysis on

125

public opinion regarding Japan generally in his 1957 study The Political Process and Foreign Policy. A general pattern emerges of an American public increasingly tolerant of and friendly toward the Japanese by the early 1950's.[7] It seems safe to assume, then, that if the public continued to favor holding the Ryukyus to the extent reflected in the 1947 survey, they did so for reasons other than animosity or suspicion toward the Japanese.

In the institutional context, a word should be said about partisan political considerations, which appear generally to have affected the Okinawa and Japanese Peace treaty decision more than the others I analyze in this study. Dulles' selection as treaty maker has been widely attributed to the desire of Democrats Acheson and Truman to revitalize bipartisan foreign policy with a key role for the most prominent foreign affairs spokesman of the opposition party. As the Republican party as a whole wavered between a position of disinclination toward foreign involvements and a harder anti-communist line than the Democrats, it seems safe to assume that Dulles had at least as much latitude and probably more in working out the peace terms than most Democrats would have. With respect to Okinawa specifically this may have afforded him a bit more elbow room in making the concessions and guarantees to the Japanese about the sovereignty of the islands that were the outcome of his labours.

The common values category under societal factors and the cultural factors under the human environmental classificatory label are closely related for the purpose of analyzing the residual sovereignty solution. Societal values of Americans which influenced John Foster Dulles and those who advised and supervised him included the disinclination to engage in territorial aggrandizement which has made every expansion of this country the subject of controversy since the closing of the frontier late in the last century (e.g., the Hawaiian, Philippine, and Puerto Rican annexation controversies). Americans had a history, moreover, of sponsoring lenient and somewhat naive peace settlements, reflecting idealistic rather than realist perceptions. Culturally one can point to this country's traditional interest in the Pacific and peculiar westward orientation that had made Japan, China, and the South Pacific areas of American foreign policy activism (e.g., Roosevelt's intercession in the Russo-Japanese conflict, Hay's China policy, etc.) in contrast to the

126

habitual United States reluctance to become enmeshed in European affairs where, until 1919 and Versailles at least, it could not play as distinctive a role.

External setting - What relatively objective factors can we point to which appear to have affected the external environment faced by those responsible for getting a satisfactory settlement with Japan on the disposition of the Ryukyus? In the non-human variables category of the Snyder framework one has economic-resource and geographic considerations. While there has never been much question about the strategic value of Okinawa -- the very name in Japanese means "a rope out on the water" connoting a sort of slender bridge to China and the rest of Asia -- the natural resources there have been almost negligible. It would be an over-statement to say that Tokyo did not press Dulles harder because of a complete lack of economic interest in Okinawa; but it is accurate to describe Japan's desire for the archipelago's return as far more culturally and emotionally motivated. And one must assume that had Okinawa been blessed by rich mineral deposits or some other lucrative resource, the economic shakiness of Japan would have forced a more assertive posture on the part of Yoshida.[8]

In the analytic category of external cultural factors, the same sorts of historical ties between the Ryukyus and Japan mentioned in Chapter 3 are active, and were undoubtedly called to Dulles' attention many times in the course of his discussions with the Japanese, (see pp. 63 & 98). His own statement on residual sovereignty in testimony before Congress in 1952, coupled with previously cited observations by his principal aide, John Allison, reflect an awareness of the sensitive nature of the problem. As for other societies, we again have the strong attraction between the different-but-compatible Japanese and the American decision-making elites (i.e., the Dulleses, MacArthurs, and Allisons of the earlier years, and the Reischauers and Kennedy's later on). Beyond this very general use of that particular analytic category of the Snyder group, there seems to be very little helpful connection between the structure of Japanese and Okinawan society and the specific outcome of the peace settlement as regards Okinawa.

The fourth area of external setting, and the crucial one for most of the decisions in this study, is that of societies-organized-as-states, or more simply

"foreign governments". With the Japanese peace treaty
interlinked in complicated ways not only to the global
power balance between the United States and Russia,
but also to the varying strategies of American allies
and Pacific states such as those of the British Commonwealth, Dulles had quite a large number of foreign government considerations to keep account of. The most
obvious and pervasive of these were those of the Japanese; but so much space is devoted to Tokyo's interest
in the territorial question elsewhere in this monograph that only a brief mention of it is needed here.
As noted in the strategic analysis of preceding chapters, China caused additional headaches for those
charting the American peace treaty strategy in the late
1940's because of the upheaval on the Chinese mainland
and the chaotic transition to Communist control there.
The fact of Mao Tse-tung's supremecy by mid-1949 and
the British government's recognition of his government
made Chinese participation in the treaty-making of
1950-51 highly problematic. More specifically relevant
to the Okinawa issue, America's continued recognition
of Chiang as spokesman for China, balanced against
British and Russian acknowledgment of Mao's claim to
that role made any further input -- and especially
claims -- on Okinawa unlikely.

The Soviet Union, as a member of the Far Eastern
Commission, was to present Dulles with many problems
in the engineering of a multilateral pact generally and
the territorial question specifically. In May, 1950
as he was beginning his diplomatic assignment, the Russians on the Allied Council for Japan had demanded a
report from the Americans on their administration of
the Ryukyus. This demand was turned down flatly by
MacArthur, who insisted that matters pertaining to Okinawa affairs were not within the scope of FEC or
Allied Council concerns.[9] Sensing the ever more con-
frontational nature of American-Soviet relations late
in 1949, the State Department had issued a memorandum
advising that an ordinary, rather than a strategic,
United Nations trusteeship be sought for the Ryukyus,
because the latter type required Security Council approval and would therefore be subject to a Moscow
veto.[10] In spite of the conscientious, if reluctant,
support of the United States for honoring the Yalta
commitments to the cession of the Kuriles and Southern
Sakhalin to the USSR as part of a peace treaty with
Japan, the Soviets were to object strenuously and consistently to American plans for retaining control of
the Ryukyus (see discussion on pp. 71 &72)[11] As plans
for the San Francisco Conference proceeded in 1951, it

became apparent that the territorial question was one of several peace-treaty-related areas of contention between the two super-powers which would not be resolved. The major concern of Dulles, according to our best information, was to develop the American position on the Okinawan matter which would be the least vulnerable to Soviet and other countries' accusations of American neo-colonialism.

The influence of Britain and the Commonwealth countries on this external setting of decision making is worthy of some consideration. To begin with, it was highly diverse. As we have noted, Great Britain's draft of a peace treaty in the spring of 1951 called for renunciation of Japanese sovereignty over the Ryukyus and Bonins. At the opposite end of the spectrum, India supported the outright return of the islands to Japan as part of any settlement. Although they were to have misgivings about many aspects of the final treaty and were insistent upon an American protective partnership (which eventuated in the ANZUS pact of 1951), Australia and New Zealand did accept the American line of thinking on Okinawa. Undoubtedly, the concerns of these states over a possible resurgence of Japanese militarism helped stiffen American determination to remain in the Ryukyus and carefully separate the terms related to base use there from those regarding Japanese bases.[12]

The third large category in the Snyder decision analysis checklist is that of individual actors involved in the policy making processes, with special attention to their personalities, social background - experience, and personal values. As was the case with the 1948-49 decision, I was not able to interview enough people close to the center of action on the residual sovereignty question to be certain that all of the participants characterized here were in fact the most important ones or that I have not omitted a few.[13] From documentary, academic, and a limited number of personal interview sources, however, I am confident of reasonable accuracy in this regard.

John Foster Dulles

Mr. Dulles was, of course, the chief drafter of early versions of the Japanese peace treaty and formally named negotiator with the rank of Ambassador in January of 1951. From every indicator I have been able

129

to find, the decision to resolve the Okinawa question
through the residual sovereignty formula was more completely Dulles' than was any other decision-case in
this study the work of a single individual. This is
not to say, however, that he did not operate within
certain constraints. His major challenge was to hand-
craft a settlement which would protect American freedom in the Ryukyus and re-assure both the United States
defense establishment and its Pacific Allies without
hurting Japan badly and fueling Soviet and Third World
charges of expansionism any more than necessary. Dulles
was noted as a hard-line anti-Communist, although his
performance during the Japanese treaty negotiations reflected a more pragmatic and less doctrinaire approach
than was to become manifest during his years as Secretary of State. He was a leading proponent of an international network of anti-Communist security pacts and
effected agreements with the Philippines and Australia
-- New Zealand while working on the Japanese treaty.
He was a man of exceptional intelligence and articu-
lateness who, nevertheless, was highly orthodox in his
capitalism and political conservatism. A number of
biographical and autobiographical writings about Dulles
are available; relatively few of these, unfortunately,
are objective by any standard.

Dean Acheson

Secretary of State Acheson was formally Dulles'
superior during the period of decision-making on the
Japanese treaty drafting, and in this role he did have
the final word as to what the American position could
and could not be. In practice, however, the Republican negotiator had a virtually free hand and very little interference from Mr. Acheson. Acheson was a
Europeanist by background and while far from uninter-
ested in Far Eastern affairs, had given Dulles the assignment with the specific stipulation that he would
have considerable flexibility to work out the details
of the Japanese and related security arrangements (although within the generally accepted American negotiating framework, which Dulles was unlikely to want to
depart from in any case). As indicated earlier,
Acheson was fully sympathetic to the idea of America's
holding the Ryukyus as part of the "Defensive perimeter".[14] Although the desires of the Japanese for the
return of the southern islands had been made increasingly clear, Acheson -- faced with the conflict in
Korea six months after his January speech declaring

130

American intentions to remain in Okinawa -- was unlikely to subordinate global power considerations to alliance pressures. The available documentation on the internal governmental correspondence and other communications for the peace treaty development is even scanter than that for the NSC 13/3 sequence, however, so these impressions are largely educated extrapolations based on public statements and secondary source accounts.

Harry Truman

As was the case with NSC 13/3, President Truman's impact on the peace and related security settlements of 1951 was in the nature of broad guideline-setting and approval of final drafts, more than ongoing supervision. He was flexible and believed in giving his negotiators leeway, as exemplified in his acceptance of the cluster of bilateral pacts negotiated with Japan, the Philippines and Australia/New Zealand in 1951. He would have preferred a regional multi-lateral pact, but acquiesced to the latter states' antipathy to being party to any security arrangement of which Japan -- the recent enemy -- was a part. The President is known to have been reluctant to appoint Dulles to handle the negotiations at first, considering him an overly partisan Republican, but deferred to the judgment of Acheson and other advisors that Dulles was the man for the job and could best restore the sense of bipartisanship the President desired.

Douglas MacArthur

I include Gen. MacArthur as an important individual for this decision-sequence even though he had been removed as Supreme Commander (because of his refusal to submit to White House control of Korean War strategy) six months before the Japanese peace treaty came to fruition in September, 1951. MacArthur was consulted on a number of occasions by Dulles and is known to have impressed the latter, who was much affected and concerned by the General's firing during the final stages of the treaty work. More than any other single individual, MacArthur may be credited with the conception of Okinawa as a Pacific strategic trump-card in case of difficulties in Japan or pressure from the Soviets or Chinese in the area.

131

TABLE IV - Snyder Framework Applied To
             Residual Sovereignty Decision

INTERNAL SETTING:
Non-Human Environment - Geographic importance con-
                        trasted with economic unim-
                        portance to American economy

Society -
            Values - Waning American expansionism
                     and general reluctance in the
                     twentieth century to acquire
                     new territory

    Social Structure - American friendliness toward
                       Japan on the increase (public
                       opinion factor); re-assertion
                       of civil dominance over mili-
                       tary

Human Environment

            Culture - Interest in Pacific affairs;
                      feeling that America has a
                      special and distinctive role
                      in the Pacific unlike Europe

EXTERNAL SETTING:
Non-Human Environment - Strategic location of Okinawa
                        alleviating problem of Amer-
                        ican distance from Asia

    Other Cultures - Perceptions regarding the
                     feelings of Japanese and Oki-
                     nawans that the two areas
                     should be united

    Other Societies - Mutual attraction of American
                      and Japanese socio-economic
                      elites

    Other Governments - Japanese territorial interest;
                        Communist supremecy in China
                        making Chinese influence neg-
                        ligible; Soviet interference
                        and resistance within FEC;
                        Australia and New Zealand
                        fear of Japan and refusal to
                        participate in security
                        treaty which included her
INDIVIDUAL ACTORS:

    Personality   Negotiator John Foster Dulles;
    Background   Secretary of State Dean Ache-
    Values   son; President Harry Truman;
                         SCAP Douglas MacArthur; The

                         132

ORGANIZATIONAL NETWORK:

SITUATIONAL PROPERTIES:

Joint Chiefs of Staff;
Principally Dulles and his
own staff; The State Department; National Security Council; Joint Chiefs of Staff;
SCAP headquarters

Anticipated; neither routine
nor "crisis"; value magnitude
of Okinawa settlement marginal, but of treaty great

The Joint Chiefs of Staff

The most prominent individual members on the JCS for the Japanese peace treaty were Gen. Omar Bradley, Chairman, and his Army colleague, Gen. J. Lawton Collins, Chief of Staff of that service branch. Bradley was an excellent team player and a strong advocate of the treaty once it was being guided through the Senate hearings in 1952, although he had initially been reluctant to push a treaty that might lessen the flexibility of the American position. Collins was known to favor a hard position of American strength (i.e., tougher than MacArthur's) in the Far East, calling for a substantial build-up of forces in Japan in February, 1949. Although his individual input on the peace treaty terms and the Okinawa settlement in particular was unavailable in the archives we examined, he almost certainly favored a strong United States position there and probably disapproved of any guarantee of residual rights to Japan.[15]

Organizational factors - Because of the paucity of unclassified information available on inner-decision-making for the 1951 treaties, organizational positions are better known in many respects than individual ones. Because of the detailed elaborations of the development of the State and Defense Department thinking between 1945 and 1949 in the two preceding chapters, it is necessary here to summarize only the positions of these and related elements of the foreign affairs bureaucracy at the time of the actual negotiations in 1950 and 1951. The White House, it has been noted, did not play an active supervisory role in the negotiating process.

While the details are not readily available, there is reason to believe that Dulles was forced by the military to specify in his Seven-Point Memorandum of fall, 1950 that the United States should be the sole administrator of Okinawa under any trusteeship arrangement.[16] (Dulles' original paper had proposed simply that Japan be required to "accept any decision of the United Nations which extends the trusteeship system to all or part of the Ryukyus and Bonin Islands.") The State Department, which had originally favored the return of the Ryukyus and was much more interested in obtaining international sanctions for the United States position there, nevertheless by 1951 fully agreed with the nec-

134

essity for guaranteeing an undisturbed American military presence in the archipelago.

Situational properties - Of all of the decision cases being studied here, the residual sovereignty formula decision was probably the most anticipated (in terms of the Snyder-Robinson category criteria). Once NSC 13/3 had been signed and the build-up of Okinawa's garrisons assured, it was clear that a solution which would protect that investment would be necessary when it became time to negotiate a treaty. Position papers arguing the merits of various arrangements for the Ryukyus and Bonins had flowed among various bureaucratic components and key individuals since before the surrender of Japan. As with NSC 13/3 section 5 the decision was hardly "routine" in the accepted sense of the word, yet it was not a crisis decision in any sense. The time demands were not great, although the principal individual actor had set the goal of one year for himself (it was hardly a rushed time-limit in spite of the formidable number of issues to be resolved when compared with the frequently much more constricting time-frames faced by decision-makers involved in equally challenging issues.) As for magnitude and scope of values involved, the third Snyder-Robinson sub-category, the residual sovereignty solution was relatively minor in the total scheme of the peace treaty, a way of finessing a somewhat humiliating arrangement in a way that would be at least minimally acceptable to the Japanese.

Alternative Explanatory Models

In the Allison lexicon, the classical or Model I approach to explaining the residual sovereignty solution would focus heavily on the role of John Foster Dulles, who, while operating with a certain amount of guidance, can be equated with the "rational actor" determining the American position. Thus in Model I terms the story might run as follows:

The residual sovereignty formula represents an almost perfect textbook case of rational diplomatic problem solving by a master strategist. In the spring of 1950 Secretary of State Acheson had responded to Dulles' suggestion that a single individual be given one year to negotiate a workable multilateral treaty with Japan with the full backing of the United States

135

government. If he succeeded in his task, the
Dulles reasoning supposedly went, great prestige would be his, the initial prospect of
which would provide great incentives for whom-
ever was given the assignment. Not surprisingly, Dulles himself was appointed to the task
in May. One of his most intricate challenges
would be to work out a satisfactory way for the
United States to retain control of Okinawa without causing disgrace to Japan.

Because Dulles was given such wide authority,
the analogy between the state-as-actor and the
individual rational human actor is especially
applicable in this case. If Allison's own territorial question involved value maximization
in its answers: the selection from among alternatives carefully considered to bring about the
best possible combination of results. What were
the values to be maximized? Certainly security
and stability in the Far East generally, and secure protective positions in the Western Pacific
-- including Okinawa -- ranked high. But the
desires of the Japanese (now clearly seen as
soon-to-be-allies) and even the Okinawans, could
not be overlooked. Nor could the preferences of
friendly small powers in the southwest Pacific
like Australia, New Zealand, and the Philippines
-- or for that matter the Soviet Union's. Between the drafting of his first memorandum on
the peace treaty in June of 1950 and the Seven
Point Memorandum (the initial basis for negotiations with the Japanese) Dulles received a
certain amount of prodding from the Defense Department to specify United States control over
Okinawa rather than merely United Nations trusteeship as the terms for settlement of the Ryukyu question.

In his meetings with Prime Minister Yoshida
and other prominent Japanese political figures
in January of 1951, however, it became apparent that the Japanese were very much concerned
to retain the maximum possible hold in the Ryukyus, that they regarded the archipelago as Japanese in a sense quite different from the ac-
quisitions of the Co-Prosperity Sphere era, and
that the loss of sovereignty over the islands
would be a blow to relations between two friendly countries. At least one close associate of

136

Yoshida's believes that the Prime Minister
very strongly encouraged Dulles to come up
with a solution that did not interfere with
the Japanese nationality of Ryukyuans, regardless of how complete American administration control was to be and for what length
of time.[17] Dulles was apparently thus encouraged to put his wits to work engineering a
compromise. He did balk, however, at the Japanese request in a statement on January 30,
1951 that any reference to Okinawa in the
peace treaty be accompanied by an American
declaration of intention to return control of
the islands to Tokyo as soon as the international situation permitted.

The final text of the treaty published in
San Francisco at the conclusion of the San
Francisco conference made no specific reference to residual sovereignty; but a Dulles
statement at the conference put the United
States on record as fully acknowledging that
the islands were legally, if not practically,
Japanese. Because Article II of the treaty
involved Japanese renunciation of rights to
the Kuriles and South Sakhalin (a virtual
cession of these areas to the Soviets, who
had physically occupied them), it was somewhat more difficult for the Russians to make
a credible case for superior American territorial advantages being derived from the settlement.

While it would be difficult for the intelligent
organizational model analyst to deny that there were an
impressive number of "rational actor" features in a
treaty negotiation process in which a specially appointed non-career diplomat was given wide negotiating
latitude, he could still point to some impressive organizational determinants of the outcome:

The creative imagination and national value-
maximizing diplomacy used by John Foster Dulles
to strike the compromise embodied in Article III
of the treaty was merely a reflection of the
needs and priorities of the great organizations
with a stake in the outcome. Dulles, far from
being an independent agent, was in the employ
of the State Department, which by 1948 had largely

137

come around to the position that the United
States would have to hold on to Okinawa regardless of the peace settlement finally arrived at.

The Defense Department's reasons for wanting to have the most exclusive rights possible
in the Ryukyus were relatively straightforward:
the islands were strategically highly desirable
and physically more easily defended than Japan.
In the event of a peace treaty, which the Defense Department was generally in no hurry to
see come about, Japan, with a population ex-
ceeding 90 million, would be a less domesti-
cally stable and controllable environment than
Okinawa. The State Department's reasoning for
holding the Ryukyus was more subtle: being generally disposed toward the normalization of the
United States -- Japan relationship and anxious
to be rid of the burden of being an "occupying
power", it viewed Okinawa as the key to getting
Defense Department (and especially JCS) support.

Seen in terms of organizational theory, the
military had every reason to resist not only
the return of Okinawa to Japan with bases equivalent to Japanese bases, but also any trusteeship arrangement in which American power was
shared with the United Nations. Army control of
the Ryukyus had created a base complex there
with very few restraints, much like the great
base complexes in the United States (e.g., comparable to those in Hawaii and the metropolitan
Washington, D.C. area). Substantial allotments
of military financial and technical resources
had been directed to the Ryukyus; thus the only
kind of Japanese claim over the islands acceptable to the defense establishment was the formal, nominal one which they hoped was meant by
residual sovereignty.

The bureaucratic politics model developed by
Graham Allison and (later) Morton Halperin represents
a return of emphasis on the individual present in the
rational actor model but largely missing from the organizational model. The crucial difference between
Model III and Model I, however, lies in the former's
vision of decision-making as an arena where perceptions, values, and techniques of action are often dis-
orderly, inconsistent and uncoordinated. In the present decision case, the image of predictable or even

138

definable organizational positions on the details of the Japanese settlement is as subject to question as the notion of one or a group of intelligent, thinking men setting down and reasoning-through a series of alternatives. Instead the process of decision is better depicted this way:

Organizational compromise -- a splitting of the differences in approach of the State or Defense Departments, principally -- is hardly an adequate summary description of the solution of residual sovereignty. The Defense Department and the uniformed military certainly never proposed a solution which in effect recognized the Japanese nationality of Okinawans; in fact several important military spokesmen who played key roles in the development of Okinawa policy have raised serious questions about the legality and propriety of Dulles' formula.[18] The formula came to be regarded more and more as a millstone around the necks of the administrators of the Ryukyus: a pretext for disruptive elements in Japan and Okinawa to consolidate their energies and undermine the United States position.

Residual sovereignty cannot be termed a State Department innovation either. An international legal curiosity, unprecedented, it was difficult for the Japanese to understand and not much easier for State Department spokesmen to handle. The Japanese and Yoshida's Liberal Party in particular problems had a more direct impact on Dulles' thinking on the subject than his consultations with American foreign policy strategists.

While it may be tempting to interpret Dulles' handling of the Ryukyus question as brilliant compromise or diplomatic rationality in its profoundest sense, there is ample evidence to indicate that that would be an oversimplification. His appointment in the first place was exactly the sort of bureaucratic maneuver or "political resultant" that Allison has spotlighted as center-stage in many foreign affairs dramas. As an establishment Republican with good connections, Dulles was handed a complex assignment to bolster bipartisanism in foreign policy making, and if he failed -- well, the Democrats could hardly be blamed in the partisan way they were taken to task for their handling of the China problem.

There were clear indications for Dulles when he was negotiating with Yoshida (notably the January 30, 1951 note on the Ryukyuan question) that a settlement which separated the archipelago from Japan in any definitive way would be unsatisfactory and, by implication, very difficult to sell to the Japanese people. Because Dulles himself had suggested that a single individual be allowed to match his wits against the complexities of a multilateral Japanese peace treaty and because he had become that individual, it was all the more important that he succeed. As the probable heir to the Secretaryship of State should the Republicans gain the White House the following year, it was essential that he not fail to get a satisfactory settlement. To do this he had to neutralize the Joint Chiefs of Staff, who were all the more suspicious of "international sanction" for United States control of Okinawa because Russia seemed to be getting the Northern Islands outright. Dulles' final achievements were: 1. to convince the military that American rights in the archipelago would be unfettered, 2. to persuade the Japanese that they were not really losing the Ryukyus, and 3. to assure the State Department and the President that, while vague and non-committal, Article III could give American Far East strategists a bit of breathing space, cutting losses to America's international reputation for anti-colonialism without actually hampering military activity in the Ryukyus. For some this was a truly brilliant diplomatic achievement, for others sophistry; for the bureaucratic political analyst, however, it was simply the practice of the craft of Model III.

How does one go about critically evaluating such different interpretations of the same decision-sequence? In rebutting the interpretation of the bureaucratic politics analyst, the classical foreign affairs commentator would be likely to note that whatever parochial or career-enhancing considerations which might have stimulated Dulles' efforts at finding a workable answer to the territorial question, these surely paled in significance compared with the substantive achievement of the residual sovereignty scheme. For this Model I critic, Dulles was unencumbered by intrabureaucratic biases. In any event he had a highly suc-

140

cessful career outside the government and was far more likely to advance his position by continuing to polish his reputation within his own party as a man who could rise above Washington intrigue and tie the loose ends of policy together in the interests of American strategy as a whole.

The bureaucratic politics theorist would beg to differ. He would point to evidence, which does exist, that the basic contours of consensus for the United States position were visible well before Dulles entered the picture, worked out through the NSC system and inter-departmental conversations. Dulles' real accomplishment, then, was to get the authority to take this position, make small modifications in it as became necessary, and use it as the basis for discussions with the Japanese.

Frederick Dunn, known primarily as a scholar of world affairs in the classical model tradition, came very close to the Model III perspective in characterizing Dulles' performance:

> It should be noted that the conception and many of the details of the pre-Dulles October 13, 1949 draft were very similar to the treaty finally negotiated by Dulles and signed at San Francisco in 1951. The only important divergence between the two situations was that in 1951 the ground had been cleared for a security pact with Japan, whereas in 1949 the Far East Section of the State Department envisaged such a pact but did not have sufficient influence within the United States government to carry out its conceptions. It is therefore perhaps not accurate to refer to Mr. Dulles as "the architect of the Japanese peace treaty", as has often been done, but rather as the one who successfully negotiated and carried out, albeit with various improvisations and innovations, a previous blueprint.[19]

On balance, however, it appears to me that the contribution of the Allison Model II perspective to an understanding of the decision to grant the Japanese residual sovereignty is not impressive. Granted the organizational procedural structuring of much of Dulles' range of choices and the career gamesmanship and domestic political incentives that may have been operating, all of this does not detract from an explanation

141

which stresses a thoughtful man consulting with a number of interested parties, exploring alternatives and acting in what he believes to be the broadest interest of his "clients". Decisions are never taken in a vacuum, there are always these internal and external givens within which the actor must operate. Yet in a sense rarely duplicated in American diplomatic history, Dulles was conducting a free and lofty diplomacy unconstricted if not untouched by organizational demands and energized but not heavily colored by his personal ambition.

The Decision: Rational-Comprehensive or Incremental?

How useful might a comparison between the rational-comprehensive and disjointed-incremental models of Lindblom and Braybrooke be for analyzing a decision of this type? We know, for example, that the residual sovereignty formula represented a way of making the status quo (American rule in the Ryukyus) tolerable, if not pleasant, for the Japanese; as such it represented a rather small change over the pre-treaty state of affairs. Certainly the deep-background policy making on Okinawa which relates to this decision (i.e., departmental positions developed between 1946 and 1949) had many of the attributes of incremental action, with cautions, limited-alternative evaluations and bureaucratic inertia precluding a definitive stand on the base question until NSC 13/3. Yet as the assessment of the Allison models makes clear, negotiator Dulles had a remarkable degree of freedom in considering solutions to the territorial question within the context of the larger treaty negotiations. If it was unlikely that he would opt for the extreme courses of pushing for American annexation of the Ryukyus, or recommend their unconditional return to the Japanese, he otherwise had a number of possibilities before him as he considered the question in the spring of 1950. One alternative was to avoid annexing Okinawa, but to make Japan renounce sovereignty over the islands just as she was to do in the case of the Northern territories. This option, as has been noted, was originally the one favored by the British, and certainly would have been the preferred solution of at least some important elements of the United States military. A second choice was to return the Ryukyus to Japan in deference to the strongly expressed wishes of the Prime Minister and the Japanese Foreign Office, but at the same time to give America a degree of freedom in operating bases there that she

would not enjoy as part of the security pact to accompany the peace treaty. This solution might please
the Japanese, but it would certainly not be to the lik-
ing of the Pentagon, and might well interfere with a
satisfactory security agreement with Tokyo. By signing
away rights to Okinawa for the foreseeable future, Japan probably gained more leverage and say-so regarding
security arrangements for the four main Japanese islands. A third possibility, and the closest to what
Dulles eventually decided on, was to have the Japanese
stop short of a renunciation of rights to the archipelago, but instead to obtain a pledge from them not
to interfere with American administration or international trusteeship. The final solution at the San
Francisco Conference departed from this third option
only in that there was an American declaration recognizing latent Japanese sovereignty over the islands but
making no specific pledge to a time-table for their return:

> Several of the Allied Powers urged that the
> treaty should require Japan to renounce its
> sovereignty over these islands in favor of
> United States sovereignty. Others suggested
> that these islands be restored completely to
> Japan.
>
> In the face of this division of Allied op-
> inion, the United States felt that the best
> formula would be to permit Japan to retain
> residual sovereignty, while making it possible
> for these islands to be brought into the
> United Nations trusteeship system, with the
> United States as administering authority.[20]

Thus, the question of synoptic versus incremental
problem solving in the present decision case boils
down to a question of definition. While there was considerable central coordination and control over the
process of drafting the treaty, and a host of alternatives were considered, the outcome was one which on
the surface represented very little advancement over
the mysterious status quo in which the Americans preserved their options without settling any of the specific issues of territorial rights and nationality.
Yet a decision which is exhaustively researched and
carefully monitored by those in positions of considerable authority, need not be a dramatic departure from
the status quo to conform to the synoptic model (refer
to the previous decision analyzed). The available evi-

dence indicates that such a model comes far closer than disjointed incrementalism to explaining Article III of the treaty. If in Dulles' frenzied schedule during the 1950-51 negotiations he did not have time and resources to study all possible implications of the various possible compromises on the Ryukyus, neither did he follow the path of least resistance.[21]

Conclusion

The enumeration of individual actors through the Snyder framework helps dramatize the far more focused and centralized nature of the residual sovereignty decision when compared with the National Security Council decision of 1948-49. With the historical chapters and supporting research as background, the Allison foreign policy models were applied to the Dulles decision-sequence with the result that the rational-actor model fared remarkably well (at least in my reading of Allison). The reason is not far to seek: the Special Negotiator had virtually total responsibility for the treaty entrusted to him. Models of organizational process and bureaucratic politics are certainly capable of enlarging our understanding of the decision sequence but they are by no means sufficient to replace the traditional classical style explanation. In other words, what Allison calls Model I best reflects the decision style of this particular episode. One might suspect that an implication of this successful instance of the rational actor model might be the validation of the synoptic characterization of decision-making which Lindblom holds is an ideal and an exception rather than the norm. This investigation reveals that the action of the 1950-51 decision sequence was very much centralized under Dulles and that he and his staff considered a number of alternative solutions, although admittedly the practical options were few. If the episode was an example of highly imperfect synoptic decision-making, it still comes closer to this descriptive device than to disjointed incrementalism.

144

[1]There is evidence that NSC 13/3 section 5 did not put an end to the uncertainties about the United States presence in Okinawa and immediately resolve all of the administrative problems which led to the study in the first place. A memorandum from Maj. Gen. Joseph Smith, an Air Force member of the Joint Strategic Plans Committee, dated December 7, 1949, lays out troop levels and construction requirements for an effective strategic role for the Air Force in Okinawa, but questions how it might be implemented because of the still-unresolved issue of the obtaining of international sanction for the American occupation (to cite only one example).

[2]Document dated June 15, 1949 and declassified November 25, 1975. The JCS position on the prospect of an immediate peace treaty with Japan is summarized in section 9, which reads:

"...the Joint Chiefs of Staff are of the opinion that, from the military point of view, a peace treaty would, at the present time, be premature since the continuing Soviet policy of aggressive communist expansion makes it essential that Japan's democracy and western orientation first be established beyond all question, and since global developments are in such a state of flux that measures leading to the risk of loss of control of any area might seriously affect our national security."

[3]From points 4 and 6 of the Army Plans and Operations study, "United States Post-Treaty Requirements -- Japan" dated December 20, 1949, declassified June 8, 1976. Point 4 reads in part:

"...Retention of Japan would assist in blocking Soviet expansion in the Far East and would strengthen our position in that area. In addition it would contribute to the security of Okinawa."

[4]Dated December 30, 1949 and declassified August 20, 1975.

[5]Binnendijk has made the interesting observation that "The Korean War shattered hopes that continued U.S. presence on the islands might deter conflict in Asia." It should be noted, however, that the deterrent value of Okinawa in preventing such conflicts was never as important to military leaders as the potential value of the island as a flexible multi-purpose base once hostilities had begun. "Political Military Aspects.." op.cit., p. 6.

[6]The study which made up the bulk of NSC-68 was engineered by Paul Nitze, head of the Policy Planning Staff at the State Department.

[7]See the analysis of data on American public opinion regarding Japan in Bernard C. Cohen, The Political Process and Foreign Policy: The Making of the Japanese Peace Settlement, (Princeton, New Jersey: The Princeton University Press, 1957), Ch. 3.

[8]Watanabe cites Asahi Shimbun of June 7, 1947 as quoting Foreign Minister Ashida Hitoshi as saying Japan's interest in regaining Okinawa was sentimental, not economic. Watanabe, op. cit., p.23.

[9]Reported in Asahi, May 4,5, 1950, cited in Watanabe, op. cit., p. 174.

[10]State Department Memorandum dated December 20, 1949. Declassified March 22, 1976.

[11]Soviet objections to an unchallenged American position in the Ryukyus were based on strategic as well as political considerations. T.B. Millar offers this explanation of general Russian naval-strategy limitations: "Except during the few weeks of high summer, maritime movements between the eastern and western Soviet Union have to be around the Cape of Good Hope and through the Indian Ocean unless the Panama Canal is used. The Sea of Japan and (to a lesser extent) the Sea of Okhotsk came close to being inland seas. All the ice-free Soviet Pacific ports and bases are on the Sea of Japan, with exits through only one of the four narrow straits..." Millar goes on to explain that these straits are fairly easy for Japan to control, which is why the Soviet Union is very reluctant to discuss the return of the Northern Territor-

146

11 (Cont.)
ies. See T.B. Millar, "Naval Armaments in the Far East", in George Quester, (ed.), Sea Power in the 1970's, (New York: Dunellen, 1975), pp. 159-177.

[12]This is the opinion of Mr. Kitazawa, personal secretary to the late Prime Minister Yoshida, whom I interviewed in Tokyo on August 7, 1975. See also the discussion in Watanabe, op. cit., p. 28.

[13]We were fortunate enough to interview some individuals close to the principal participants, however, these including Kitazawa (see note 12), Yoshida's secretary and a key aide of John Foster Dulles, Robert Fearey, who later became Civil Administrator of the Ryukyu Islands (1969-72).

[14]Acheson speech before the National Press Club, January 23, 1950 Department of State Bulletin.

[15]Both General Lyman Lemnitzer and General James E. Moore, former heads of the American military administration of the Ryukyus in the 1950's expressed doubts about the authority of Dulles to commit the United States to the residual sovereignty formula in interviews with the author (see interview listings in appendix).

[16]See Dunn, op. cit., 138. It is essential to note that the Japanese always hoped that the United States would not carry out its option to place the Ryukyus under international trusteeship, which they regarded as an affront to their national dignity. In an interview with the author in Tokyo on July 30, 1975, Dr. Ohama Nobumoto, former President of Nampo Doho Engokai, revealed that he had written Dulles to request (as a distinguished Japanese legal scholar) that the trusteeship plan be dropped, as it would be insulting to both Japan and Okinawa.

[17]Kitazawa interview, cited.

[18]Lemnitzer and Moore interviews cited in note 15.

[19]Dunn, op. cit., pp. 85-86.

147

20
 Dulles' statement before the San Francisco Conference
 on September 5, 1951, as recorded in the Conference
 Proceedings, op. cit., p. 78.

21
 One of the triumphs of Dulles' peace treaty diplomacy
 was his ability, through the extraordinary nature of
 his appointment by the President through the Secretary
 of State, to devote full time and energy to innovative
 solutions which the frozen gears of the State and Defense Department bureuacracies were unable to handle.
 This is the solution to the perennial problem of bureaucratic disfunctionalism closest to the heart of
 Henry Kissinger and at the center of his own person-
 alist diplomacy in the 1970's. See his "Domestic Structure and Foreign Policy," in Daedalus (Spring 1966),
 pp. 503-529.

CHAPTER FIVE: THE KENNEDY- KAYSEN INNOVATIONS
OF 1961-1962

Three events of the late 1950's are especially important as "deep background" for the Kennedy changes in
Okinawa policy during the first fifteen months of the
administration: Executive Order 10713, the land problem settlement, and the release of the Conlon Report.
All of these have been described at some length in the
historical chapter;   the focus here is their impact on
the policy environment regarding Japan/Okinawa problems
when President Kennedy took office.

Executive Order 10713 in 1957 was both a clarification of previous directives, orders, and guidelines
on the administration of the Ryukyus and a more explicit centralizing of that administration under the Secretaries of Defense and the Army through their representative in the field, thenceforth to be called the High
Commissioner.   The High Commissionership replaced the
Deputy Governorship; the chain of command, which before
had run through Tokyo and Honolulu, now went only
through Honolulu and officially the High Commissioner
had direct communication access to Washington.   Before,
the selection process for the post had been strictly a
military one; now that process was to be civilianized
through Section 4 of the executive order, which read in
part:

...The High Commissioner a)   shall be designated
by the Secretary of Defense, after consultation
with the Secretary of State and with the approval
of the President, from among the active duty
members of the Armed Forces of the United States,
b)   shall have the powers and perform the duties
assigned to him by the terms of this Order,
c)   may delegate any function vested in him to
such officials of the Civil Administration as
he may designate, and d)   shall carry out any
powers or duties delegated or assigned to him
by the Secretary of Defense pursuant to this
Order.[1]

Although the executive order guaranteed the Okinawans
certain rights and a degree of participation in their

own governance, it had the rather unfortunate side-effect of appearing to formalize and harden the United States position in the Ryukyus and aggregate even more power to top military figures there. Not that the Japanese or Okinawans expected American loosening up in the archipelago in the immediate future, but neither did they anticipate a full blown, Presidentially sanctified reaffirmation of the United States' intention to stay and rule as long as necessary. It is certainly true that as much depended on the temperament of the man serving as High Commissioner as on the formal body of rules given him to operate within. After the first High Commissioner, Lt. Gen. James Moore (who had held the last Deputy Governorship also) left in 1958, he was replaced by the mild-mannered Lt. Gen. Donald Booth, who gardened and fished alongside the Okinawans and generally won their respect. Booth in turn was followed in February of 1961 by Lt. Gen. Caraway, who represented the high water mark of High Commissioner power and whose administration helped trigger the events which are discussed in this chapter.

The settlement of the land problem by August of 1958 had rather the opposite affect of the executive order, giving Okinawan activists some evidence of United States pliability under pressure and more liberality than had been expected. If tempers had been frayed and bad feelings created by the Price Act aid ceiling and by the protracted nature of the haggling over the land policy, the solution of the land dispute with more rental options for Okinawan farmers and a virtual doubling of rental rates restored some confidence in the reasonableness of the occupying power.

I have discussed the Conlon Report at some length; here it need only be noted in passing that its effect on the political ambience greeting the incoming Democratic administration was an Okinawan elite which believed there were powerful forces in the United States willing to consider the return of the Ryukyus to Japan. They felt it significant that the Senate Foreign Relations Committee had ordered the study, and that a prestigious (and by no means left-wing) scholar of Asia, Robert Scalapino, assisted by a talented Okinawan named Higa Mikio, had authored the recommendations. Whatever spiritual uplift was generated in the Ryukyus by a high-level study urging a conciliatory policy, it would be fully two years before an indication of concrete policy re-evaluation emerged.

TABLE V-A - Growth of Asian Importance to
U.S. Foreign Trade (Source:
U.S. Commerce Dept., Historical
Statistics of the United States,
Vol. II, 1976, pp. 903, 905.)

Exports to Asia as Percentage of Total U.S. Exports

1950 - 15%   ($1.539 bil. of $10.275 bil. total)
1955 - 16.5% ($2.581 bil. of $15.547 bil. total)
1960 - 20%   ($4.186 bil. of $20.575 bil. total)

Imports from Asia as Percentage of Total U.S. Imports

1950 - 18%   ($1.638 bil. of $8.852 bil. total)
1955 - 16%   ($1.876 bil. of $11.384 bil. total)
1960 - 18%   ($2.271 bil. of $14.654 bil. total)

151

The more immediate background of the Kennedy decision, which I explore in greater detail under the "situational properties" section below, included the increasing dissatisfaction of both Okinawans and the American administrators with the level of developmental
funding providable within the six million dollar annual ceiling of the Price Act and the magnification of
those irritations because of the expressed willingness
of the Japanese to contribute more aid and the hesitan-
cy on the part of the Americans to allow this. Another
sensitive issue was the 1960 Security Treaty, which had
caused the LDP a great deal of domestic political grief
and seemed to some Japanese to imply a certain obligation on the part of the United States to reward that
sacrifice.

Background

Internal setting - As has been the case with the
two previous decisions I have analyzed, the internal
setting appears to be of limited direct relevance to
the 1961-62 decision background because of the small
group of elite decision-makers involved and the isolated, non-public nature of the Okinawa problem itself.
The first task is to determine which factors in the non
human or physical environment could plausibly be assumed to have had an effect on the decision. This is not
an easy question. If one broadens the definition of
non-human environment to include general economic needs:
access to Asian markets and resources (or what some
have called economic imperialism vis a vis Asia) one
can marshal statistics to show that the Asian region
was becoming relatively more important to American capitalism. It was in fact the region of the fastest
growing markets for United States exports in the world
between 1950 and 1960 (with the exception of the tiny
but rapidly increasing segment of trade with Australia)
-- though not as a source of American imports (see
Table V-A). The imperatives of protecting American
military facilities could, then, be linked to trade
and resource factors or even more purely non-human
variables of the internal setting like the almost too
obvious one of the physical distance of the mainland
United States from these interests in Asia.

The societal determinants of the internal setting
were also fairly stable. Major common values relevant
to foreign policy are not easy to pinpoint precisely,
but interpreting the 1960 election results and public

opinion polls during the early Kennedy months, a sense
of heightened competitiveness and belief in the imperative of accelerated American achievement against the
Communist World and in the eyes of the under-developed
world, were prominent themes.[2] Judging from the bipartisan support in Washington for a stepped up space
program, aid programs, the Peace Corps, and -- notably
-- an augmented defense budget, elite values were sensitive to achievement and superiority over the Soviet
Union above all else.

Institutional patterns relevant to any decision on
Okinawa or Japan policy generally would include the
burgeoning prestige and influence of the defense establishment and their access to increasing resource
allotments enhanced by newly felt pressures in Asia --
Laos and Vietnam especially. The social structure and
organizational determinants of the internal decision
setting are complex; beyond the expansion of military
scope and sophistication which have been emphasized at
length, the influence of American society on foreign
policy makers must be traced through the political
system and especially the installation of the new Democrat regime. It was this administration which, while
presiding over the expansion of the military and the
military-related economic sub-sectors, also challenged
the judgment of those in uniform to a degree almost
never witnessed in the Eisenhower years, evidenced in
the civilianizing of control in the McNamara Defense
Department and the penetration of non-military experts
into areas of national security and foreign policy
which had been the near-exclusive domain of the armed
services.[3] The part of the electorate and thus society
which put Kennedy into office had a strong component
of younger, idealistic and increasingly activist voters. The elites of this group were relatively more
concerned with civil rights and international development problems than the half-generation-older group of
voters who were their 1950's counterparts and who were
more orthodox, business-oriented, and deferential to
their elders as decision-makers. Under Snyder's human
environment category, including culture and population,
one can place the interplay of historical factors such
as "Manifest Destiny" and Pacific expansionism counter-
poised against anti-colonial and isolationist strains,
as with the two previous decisions. Unquestionably
the traditionally vigorous skepticism about the superior wisdom and competence of the military must be figured into calculations of socio-cultural forces which
led to the Kennedy-Kaysen modifications of military

control. Talking about influence of course is quite different from talking about causality; it seems desirable to steer clear of the latter. Otherwise one would be in the anomalous position of "explaining" the modest curtailment of unquestioned military decision-making power on Okinawa by the traditional civilian brakes on soldiers, and then having to use some other intellectual device to account for the greatly expanded military role in planning America's Southeast Asia policy.

As in the two preceding chapters I limit my investigation of the external setting of decision-making at this point to the so-called operational -- rather than psychological -- setting. There are of course hundreds of variables which could be subsumed under external setting; tens of important ones. It is necessary to be selective. Aspects of the non-human environment which impinged on United States decision-makers necessarily included the tiny size and sparse resources of Okinawa. The island's unmatched strategic location acted to underscore the need for a solution that did not jeopardize the military base operations.

External cultural factors would include consideration of Okinawa's traditional aversion to military activity, intensified during the mauling it received as a result of hosting the greatest Japanese-American land confrontation of the war.[4] The most obvious cultural variable is the strong historical link with Japan, although, as we have pointed out, this is a tricky matter, in view of Okinawan resentment at partial Japanese (Satsuma) subjugation of the Ryukyus in the early 1600's and the end of the Okinawan semi-autonomy in 1879, followed by a period of Japanization but also neglect. The fact of the quite consistent claims of Japanese affinities and loyalty made by the great part of Okinawan articulate opinion over most of the twenty-seven years of American rule can be taken as a sufficient indicator for our purposes, however. Related and relevant was the irredentist sentiment in Japan, a feeling readily exploitable by the Japanese left who could convincingly claim that the Ryukyus were a kind of occupation never never land -- neither Japanese nor American, nor self-ruling. Other societies as part of the external setting of the decision means most importantly Japanese Society, one pictured as pronouncedly friendly, capitalistic, and open to America's role as Pacific leader and protector of Japan. A certain wariness and mildly suspicious quality was oc-

154

casionally displayed in the interviews of American Oki-
nawa-policy-makers about Japanese proclivities for
authoritarianism and perhaps even latent militarism.[5]
There was also a recognition of the Japanese voting
public's potential impact on the Japanese government,
especially if the Okinawa issue ever caught fire in the
rough winds of Japanese domestic politics.[6] This
brings us to the fourth factor of external setting,
"Societies organized as states" i.e., foreign governments. Although the opinion about Okinawa expressed
by the governments of Korea, Taiwan, Communist China,
and the USSR have carried weight at various times, the
Japanese government, understandably, was the most
directly influential on American policy. As mentioned,
the punishment taken by the LDP leadership as a result
of the 1960 Security Treaty and Japan's reputation as
a trustworthy ally among American officials appears to
have played a strong role in United States wishes --
especially in the State Department/Tokyo Embassy -- to
accommodate the Japanese to the maximum extent possible
without jeopardizing the American base positions.[7]

The next task in reconstructing the decision background using the Snyder framework is the identification
and characterization of the major individual decision-
makers themselves. Based on interviews with men reported to have been directly involved (by Clapp and by
Watanabe, op. cit., the principal secondary sources on
the occupation) I was able to assemble a list of those
regarded as having participated importantly in the
Kennedy-Kaysen decision. Extensive interviewing and
document checks did not change this list. Occasionally one individual would mention the name of someone
he recalled as having played a role in identifying the
problem or acting on it, but unless the name came up
more than once it was relegated to a minor position,
sufficiently described by the original mentioner and
not considered to warrant a separate interview (refer
to methodological appendix). From this procedure I
can offer brief sketches of individuals in their roles
as they and their colleagues described them. I was
aided here by Snyder's descriptive categories of personality characteristics, social background-experience,
and personal values. Of the eleven individual participants in the decision-sequence occurring between
July, 1961 and March, 1962, I was able to interview
seven. Of the four major actors who were not interviewed, two -- the President and his brother, the
Attorney General, were dead; the two others, former
Defense Secretary Robert McNamara and former Deputy

Under Secretary of State George Ball were not available.[8] The roles of those not interviewed have been reconstructed in considerable detail from others' accounts, but I cannot claim that this method gives the same picture that a personal interview would.

John F. Kennedy

The President was directly involved in the Okinawa decision-making and personally interested in obtaining a satisfactory result. He had listened to the earnest concerns of an early distinguished visitor to the White House, Prime Minister Ikeda Hayato, regarding the future of the Ryukyus and was apparently quite receptive to the suggestion of Ball and Bundy that a study-group headed by a member of his inner staff look into the administration of the archipelago. Hardnosed on defense matters, the Chief Executive was also sensitive to diplomatic problems, as evidenced by his appointment of Edwin O. Reischauer as ambassador and his enthusiastic backing of Reischauer's performance.

Edwin O. Reischauer

A pivotal figure and continuing force in Okinawa-related policy-making, Reischauer was the earliest strong advocate of substantial concessions to the Japanese regarding Okinawa. He believed that the issue affected every other matter between Tokyo and Washington, coloring the relationship subtly but increasingly distastefully.[9] Reischauer appears to have been a strong influence on Carl Kaysen.[10] The ambassador had been a distinguished Japan scholar for a number of years and was widely viewed even by admirers as being strongly sympathetic to Japanese interests on most questions. He was not particularly tolerant of the military viewpoint regarding Okinawa and found himself at odds with the High Commissioner, Caraway, on several occasions during the three years of Caraway's service in Naha.[11]

Paul W. Caraway

Lt. Gen. Caraway was the bete noir of Ambassador Reischauer as described above and the foremost proponent of a tough and assertive American position re-

156

garding the running of the Ryukyus. There are some indications that he may have encouraged the appointment of the Kaysen task force with the hope that more funds might be appropriated so that he could carry out his programs, designed to strengthen the American position and reduce the relative attractiveness of Japan.[12] After the visit of the Kaysen group, however, and the initial less than favorable reports from his Army colleagues in Washington regarding the progress of the Kaysen report late in the fall of 1961, Caraway developed a distaste for the enterprise. Many of the recommendations proposed by the Task Force, he felt, would hinder his own efforts there. Through the Under Secretary of the Army, Stephen Ailes, he succeeded in watering down some of the recommendations made by the Kaysen group to the President.

Stephen Ailes

Under Secretary of the Army Ailes was the chief trouble-shooter for Army Secretary Elvis Stahr; by all accounts Stahr delegated almost complete responsibility for the problem to Ailes. Because the Department of Defense tended to let Army handle Okinawa without interference, at least until about 1965, Ailes was the major spokesman for the Pentagon position among its non-uniformed top managers. He was moderate by nature, but a strong backer of Caraway and USCAR in the battles over the Task Force recommendations.

Gen. Lyman Lemnitzer and the Joint Chiefs of Staff

Gen. Lemnitzer was Chairman of the JCS at the time of the Kaysen-Kennedy decision sequence and can be considered the embodiment of the input of that group, whose opinions were put forth formally and collectively most of the time. Lemnitzer's major contribution was made at the initial briefing for Kaysen, at which time he urged caution regarding any changes in Ryukyus administration that might have adverse indirect effects on the security of the bases. He rightfully considered himself unusually qualified to represent Pentagon interests in the Okinawa facilities because he had been Governor of the archipelago over Deputy Governor Moore from 1955-57 while serving as Far East Commander in Tokyo. He apparently did not interfere with the Kaysen group's work, however, even when it became obvious that some of the suggestions in their report were not

157

at all in accord with the JCS preferences.

McGeorge Bundy

Bundy played an essentially passive role in the 1961-62 decisions once he had assigned the job of researching the Okinawa problem to Carl Kaysen. He was, however, the initial sparkplug of the issue, having been disturbed by the reports from George Ball and an evaluation of the Ikeda meeting that the Okinawa problem was the number one issue between the United States and Japan.

Carl Kaysen

As Bundy's deputy on the White House Staff, Kaysen's training was in economics (he was a Harvard professor of that subject) and his more recent forte had been European strategy. In August of 1961 and from that time until he wrote the draft of the executive order finally issued in March, 1962, he was completely in charge of the problem with direct access to the President. Influenced by Reischauer, he was sympathetic to the Japanese position without displaying a strong predisposition in that direction. In fact, he was cautious and conservative about doing anything which might unnecessarily antagonize the military. He deliberately painted the issue as a United States adjustment of its own national security affairs rather than allowing the Japanese to be drawn in too visibly, which would antagonize the Army.

Dean Rusk

Secretary of State Rusk had been an early State Department advocate of the return of Okinawa to Japan in the late 1940's. Prudent and non-committal by nature, he recognized the potential for friction in the Ryukyus problem of the early 1960's and, while apparently in no way hindering the reassessment of that policy, was no leader in its review either. This can be attributed not only to the fact of Kaysen's competent, methodical handling of the matter, but also to Rusk's own increasing preoccupation with both Soviet and Southeast Asian matters in 1961.

158

Robert McNamara

As stated earlier, McNamara was a willing backer of the review of Okinawa's administration but, like Rusk, left the initiative to Kaysen and Ailes, and appears to have assumed that Lemnitzer and the military would protect their own interests satisfactorily. Documentary and secondary source accounts and the writer's consultation with Paul Nitze, McNamara's first Assistant Secretary for International Security Affairs, reveal a personal openness (in McNamara) on the issue but an official position of support for his generals and High Commissioner and their perception of the potential de-stabilizing effects of overhauling the administration of the Ryukyus.

George Ball

The fast-rising Deputy Under-Secretary of State was an enigmatic influence in this decision-case -- all the more, in retrospect, because of his refusal to be interviewed. It is known that he stopped off in Okinawa after an Organization for European Economic Development (OEEC -- now OECD) meeting in Tokyo during the summer of 1961 and was upset by what he saw. He reportedly made the observation back in Washington a short while later that the United States had "a military dictatorship" in the Ryukyus which bore investigating.[13] His role was not mentioned as having extended beyond this by anyone involved in the decision at high levels with whom we consulted, but his initial influence has been established as considerable. This is especially noteworthy since he tended to be a tough pragmatist with a European orientation and not likely to be swayed by the sorts of considerations which motivated Reischauer.

Robert Kennedy

The Attorney General occupies a unique place in the decision-sequence; he did not even take part in it, as far as we can tell, until February, 1962. In that month he made a trip to Japan on behalf of the President and, according to others in the decision sequence was very much impressed by the depth and breadth of concern over Okinawa on the part of the Japanese. Several persons whom we interviewed, including Ambassador Reischauer, were of the opinion that Mr. Kennedy significantly contributed to the President's resolve in getting a satisfactory interim solution to the US/Japan/ Ryukyus problem.

Organization factors - The governmental organizations involved in the re-evaluation of Okinawa policy in 1961 reflect the influence and participation patterns of the individuals just described roughly rather than precisely. The Department of State participated actively on the Kaysen task force assembled in September; it was State (along with the Labor Department) which took a tough line on the need for extensive revamping of Okinawa policy. The embassy in Tokyo functioned principally as a source of information on Japanese desires and as an influence on people like Kaysen who were not initially aware of the seriousness with which the Japanese regarded the problem. The Defense Department had several factions, some more sympathetic than others to the idea of having a civilian number two man on the island or to increased Japanese participation in Ryukyus development. The most important organizational elements were within Army itself. The day to day administration of Okinawa was the domain of USCAR, which had considerable advantages in informational access and tended to operate within the bilateral perspective more than any other single bureaucratic component. It was USCAR, including some of the civilians working within it, which tended to be most skeptical about the real political value of a civilian Civil Administrator and the most uneasy about increased Japanese aid and the effect that it might have on the American position and its own position. At the Washington end the component managing the more routine administrative and policy supervisory matters was the Civil Affairs Division of the Office of the Deputy Chief of Staff for Operations (DCSOPS), which tended to work closely with USCAR and sympathized strongly with its needs. Participation at higher levels centered on the Under Secretary's office, the involvement of which grew out of the delegation of the Okinawa problem from Defense Secretary McNamara to Army Secretary Stahr and in turn to Stephen Ailes, who took a direct personal interest in the matter and saw to the creation of a Deputy Under Secretaryship for International Affairs to be concerned with the Ryukyus as a matter of top priority. At the top of the uniformed hierarchy, the JCS were concerned about Okinawa, but confident that mili-

160

tary interests would be served by High Commissioner
Caraway and his opposite number in DCSOPS and, they
hoped, by Under Secretary Ailes as well.

The impact of other groups was more transitory in
terms of the ongoing making of Okinawa policy. The
White House Staff of course played a key role in this
decision. The determinations about what changes if
any would be made in Okinawa policy were the President's to make and kept close to his attention by virtue of Kaysen's access to Bundy. The Department of
Labor and the Agency for International Development
(AID) had representatives on the Task Force, but their
input was of a lesser order of magnitude than State's
and Defense's by all accounts. Congress played a shad-
owy role, but one underemphasized in most published accounts. The Price Act had created the increasingly
constrained aid situation, which was an important background factor for administrators watching Okinawa lose
ground to Japanese prefectures the economic growth of
which it had formerly outpaced. Congressman Otto Passman (Dem.,La.) was the actual holder of the purse
strings as Chairman of the House Appropriations Subcommittee on Foreign Operations. Passman's subcommittee
was an exacting taskmaster at the annual appropriations
hearings, willing to part with money for the Ryukyus,
but severe in its questioning and insistent upon evidence of the Executive Branch's dedication to a long-
term, serious strategic commitment to Okinawa.

This brings us to the situational properties --
the core context of the decision. Here we draw on
several factors introduced in the course of the narra-
tive of this chapter. One immediately relevant aspect
of the situation was the newness of the Kennedy administration, only seven months old when the Okinawa
problems began to materialize in the psychological environments of those in the positions of highest foreign
policy-making responsibility working for Kennedy. This
gave people like Kaysen and Bundy a certain flexibility; lines of communication and precedents of policy
could be more easily changed. This was compounded by
the tendency of any incoming administration,especially
one of a different party, to be suspicious of all
"Standard Operating Procedures" even if the changes
actually effected are mostly confined to organization charts and style rather than substance. A corollary effect of this revamping imperative is the ab-
rasive effect it has on the entrenched bureaucracy -
military and civilian -- who are understandably sus-

161

TABLE V-B - Snyder Framework Applied to
_____ Kennedy-Kaysen Decision

INTERNAL SETTING:

Non-Human Environment - Increasing importance of
                        Asian resources (and markets)
                        distance of mainland U.S.
                        from vital Asian economic and
Society   strategic areas
                Values - Need for more U.S. achieve-
                        ment vis a vis USSR;greater
                        defense and aid efforts

        Social Structure - Rise of the defense estab-
                        lishment; politically acti-
                        vist electorate elements
                        concerned with civil rights,
                        international development
Human Environment
        Culture - "Manifest Destiny" and Paci-
                        fic expansion v. Skepticism
                        about military and popular
                        isolationism

EXTERNAL SETTING:

Non-Human Environment - Strategic location of Oki-
                        nawa; Ryukyus poor economy
                        and need for resources from
                        without
        Other Cultures - Okinawa anti-militarism; Ja-
                        panese irredentism

        Other Societies - Japanese society essentially
                        pro-U.S., free enterprise;
                        some latent hostility on far
                        right and left
        Other Governments - USSR and Asian governments
                        other than Japan of little
                        importance re Okinawa policy;
                        Japan/LDP very influential

INDIVIDUAL ACTORS:
                        President John Kennedy; Am-
        Personality   bassador E.O.Reischauer;
        Background   High Commissioner Paul Cara-
        Values   way; Gen. Lyman Lemnitzer;

162

ORGANIZATIONAL
NETWORK:

Asst. to President for Nat.
Sec. Affairs McGeorge Bundy;
Task Force Head Carl Kaysen;
Sec.State Dean Rusk; Sec.Def.
Robert McNamara; Dept.Under
Sec. George Ball; Attorney
General Robert Kennedy

White House Staff; State
Department; Defense Depart-
ment: Secretary's Office,
Army Secretary's Office,
DCSOPS, USCAR; House Foreign
Operats. Subcommittee of Ap-
propriations Committee

SITUATIONAL
PROPERTIES:

Relatively High Value Magnitudes; Anticipated; Routine
Time Pressures

163

picious and resentful of "the new leaf" being turned over from above: assessments, reconsiderations, directives, etc.

Returning to Snyder's own categories under core-context we have first the anticipated v. unanticipated nature of the decision. Here we encounter the complexities of situations not easily compressed into neat analytic boxes. The final Kennedy decision, the Executive Order of March, 1962 was not actually anticipated until well after the initial investigation by Kaysen had begun, but some form of Presidential action was anticipated soon after Kaysen's mission. There was no crisis mentality either; the problem of Okinawa dissatisfaction and Japanese concern was rather viewed as worthy of immediate attention, but not great haste. It would be better to effect meaningful changes after careful study than make a dramatic gesture, because the stakes were high -- high for the Japanese and Okinawans, high for the Department of State, and high for the military. As indicated in Table V-B, then, the Okinawa decision was anticipated, routine in terms of time-demands and of a fairly high value-calibre, i.e., involving defense issues versus American administrative/political principles and considerations of an important alliance.

Alternative Explanatory Models

How valid a picture of the Kennedy innovations can we get through the three competing paradigms laid out by Allison? The rational-actor model would view the final product of the decision-sequence, i.e., the executive order and the changes it embodied, as the outcome of choosing from among a series of options determined during the investigative process. A rational model account of the process leading to this decision might, briefly, go as follows:

The changes enacted in Okinawa administration by the President were the outcome of a carefully orchestrated investigation. After his meeting with Ikeda in June, 1961 and after Mr. Ball reported to him and/or Bundy /we are not sure which7 a rather disturbing picture of Okinawa in July, it became clear that something had to be done to improve the situation there. The ends of the administration were clearly spelled out

164

in NSAM-68, which directed that a task force: "investigate the extent to which economic and social conditions contribute to the dissatisfaction of the Ryukyuans, what measures we can undertake to improve economic and social conditions, and what specific steps are needed to make such a program effective. In carrying out its task the group will bear in mind the importance to us of:
a. Okinawa as a military base, b. continued friendly relations with Japan, and c. our responsibility to the people of the Ryukyus under the peace treaty with Japan."[14]

The Task Force's Working Group arrived in the Ryukyus October 3rd for preliminary data collection, briefings, etc., and Mr. Kaysen followed a week later. Lengthy meetings were held with the High Commissioner and all branches of USCAR, with the GRI, and with various Ryukyuan groups. Kaysen and part of his staff then visited the American Ambassador in Tokyo, the Japanese Prime Minister, and the Foreign Minister, for consultation. The Task Force continued to meet in Washington after their return (as they had during the weeks prior to the Okinawa trip), preparing individual reports and recommendations based on departmental expertise and then working out compromise positions. The Task Force issued its confidential report to appropriate government agencies and to the President in December, 1961.

As USCAR and the High Commissioner received drafts of parts of the report they sent their comments; major points of controversy involved a. greater autonomy for the GRI and greater contact with the Japanese, and b. increased Japanese aid levels permitted. The Task Force recommended both of these changes; USCAR advised that there were dangers attached to each (lack of GRI readiness for expanded responsibility, the problem of curbing Japanese irredentist influence if aid greatly increased). Kaysen and top aides worked with the report during January and February of 1962 and presented a draft executive order to the President, which he approved with few modifications and announced officially on March 19th. Major recommendations included: a. a civilian Civil Administrator, b. expansion of the legislative

165

term from 2 to 3 years, c. nomination of the
GRI Chief Executive by the legislature instead of
simple appointment-with-consultation. Accompanying the executive order was a statement pledging
to increase American aid and to cooperate with
Japan in improving the living standards in the
archipelago (See document appendix for complete
text). Apparently the President's brother,
Attorney-General Robert Kennedy, helped assure
an Executive Order with significant changes, by
reporting the great interest in Okinawa manifested by the Japanese during his trip to Japan
one month before the order was signed.

If this is a largely accurate sketch of how the
decision sequence unfolded then an impressive example
of rational problem solving has occurred, even if not a
pure, ideal-type instance (which would not be possible
anyway). It certainly comes closer to this ideal-type
than the previous decisions we have looked at: the
1948-49 decision to harden the American position in the
Ryukyus and the Dulles residual sovereignty compromise.
Before commenting further, however, it seems advisable
to let an imaginary analyst of the Model II school, who
has examined the facts just as carefully, develop the
decision sequence as he reads it:

> While certain objectives appeared attrac-
> tive to top Kennedy advisors who had perceived
> the need for a change in policy by mid-summer
> of 1961, the objectives had to be reached --
> if they could be reached at all -- through
> careful organizational procedures, ones that
> would not damage the interests or routines
> of operation already established. The Presi-
> dent, after all, could have appointed a com-
> mission of extra-governmental policy elites,
> scholars, and others to examine the problem;
> this is the way many blue-ribbon investigatory
> groups are comprised. As this was largely a
> government and administrative evaluation, how-
> ever, it was imperative that all organizations
> -- especially within State and Defense -- be
> brought in on "the action."
> Kaysen's group consisted of nothing more
> than an interdepartmental-panel for the exam-
> ination of a functional problem, a decision
> strategem with venerable roots in Depression-
> era bodies, World War II coordinating commit-
> tees, and, subsequently, in the 1960's, in

Senior Interdepartmental Groups (SIG), etc. USCAR, the Army Secretary's Office, and State Department representatives on the Task Force consistently supported positions that would reduce the risks to normal patterns of operation and allow them to continue carrying out their goals or enhance the carrying out of these goals. Thus USCAR was reluctant to have increased Japanese aid coming in in many cases because its own aid funds from Washington were so limited that Japanese resources were thought to have the potential of undermining the American image as "benevolent developer" (already eroding).

The State Department was highly critical of certain aspects of military rule and felt that by maximizing concessions to Japan (including greater autonomy for Okinawa) its alliance-minded-goals would be enhanced (the Tokyo embassy played an important supportive and informational role here).

The Task Force report of December, 1961 represented something of an inter-organizational compromise, although departmental reports and background papers allowed special organizational concerns and emphasis to remain in tact for the record. In early 1962 at the White House staff level, Kaysen worked out a draft of the most urgent but bureaucratically practicable recommendations to be embodied in the final policy statement.

Here we are told that more is at stake for the participants than simply the confrontation of the problems laid out in NSAM 68 and their healthy resolution in the interests of "the U.S.government", or "American policy". While problem-solving individuals looking at issues (like Japanese sensitivities, Okinawan grievances about self-government and about their standard of living relative to Japan--lower than that of most prefectures) could have based their recommendations on their own coldly rational "for the good of U.S.policy as a whole" conclusions, in many cases these conclusions bore the strong imprint of organizational needs and priorities. But the third account remains to be presented, that of the bureaucratic politics analyst:

Neither of the foregoing accounts is satisfactory. As our organizationalist critic pointed out, had Kennedy and his staff wanted a fully objective assessment of the situation in Okinawa they could have assembled an investigatory body composed at least in part of outsiders and also imposed the changes which appeared appropriate and seemed to satisfy the political needs of the administration (after an investigation and a hearing-out of the military point of view at the Pentagon and on Okinawa). The Model II observer argues that this did not happen because those concerned with Okinawa were in the government -- there was no real outside constituency. Because these organizations would have to administer whatever "reforms" took place, they had to have a voice in the decision; their recommendations had to be heard.

What in fact took place was more complex than rational choice-making or organizational problem-solving. To begin with, one cannot account for the fact that many of the recommendations embodied in the executive agreement and the supporting Presidential statement favored State Department arguments purely on the basis of the State Department's position. That department had been an advocate of Okinawa's return to Japan in the late 1940's and had been trying to get more influence over Ryukyus policy for years with little success. The Army was graced with the most strong-willed and articulate High Commissioner of the entire occupation in General Caraway, who argued against many of the innovations which the Task Force appeared to be moving toward.

With the Army on record as highly skeptical of the value of a civilian Civil Administrator, unimpressed with arguments that the advantage of increased Japanese aid would outweigh the drawbacks of increased Japanese influence by raising Okinawan living standards it is noteworthy that both of these changes were successfully pushed through. So were the increased terms for Ryukyuan legislators and the change of the Chief Executive designation procedure-- against Army preferences.

The explanation lies in large part in the roles of three pivotal individuals: Reischauer, Kaysen, and Ailes. Reischauer was keenly attuned to Japanese sensitivities and had had no direct experience with the attempts of State

168

to get a softening of the DOD/Army position.
His advocacy of reform was based on a sincere
assessment of the need for this sort of gesture to the Japanese, also a desire to enhance
his own position as a diplomat that could get
things done for Japan and the United States.[15]
Kaysen was something of a blank slate on the
issue, but was impressed by Reischauer's arguments and was not by temperament pro-military.[16]
He had very little incentive in his first major
White House assignment to develop either a set
of recommendations which supported the status
quo with only trivially cosmetic changes or to
propose such a sweeping overhaul of policy that
a full-scale Pentagon revolt would ensue, in all
probability setting back the cause of "reform"
on Okinawa. Ailes was a compromiser and acted
to defend most of the counter-recommendations
from Caraway's USCAR, but with a soft, persuasive voice. His crucial position between the
JCS, USCAR and the task force allowed moderated
versions of the Kaysen group's recommendations
to go through.

In evaluating these three accounts it should be
made plain that none of them, to the very best of my
knowledge (based on interviews, repeated checks of documents, and other assessments of United States Japan/
Okinawa policy) contains any statement which is false
or even misleading. The divergences come in interpretation and evaluation of which facts are most salient. This may reflect a pitfall of Allison's technique of "trichotomizing" his explanations. As in the
case of his Cuban missiles analysis, an integration of
the three perspectives, at least after presenting them
separately initially, may be advisable with the Kennedy
innovations in Ryukyus policy. It would also appear
that there is a stronger element of rationality and
choice-making even within organizational and bureaucratic politics decision evolution than might have been
expected. Kaysen, for example, was able to enhance his
personal stature and influence by making recommendations which pleased the State Department without raising the ire of the military -- or at least not sufficiently to provoke a showdown. Yet his recommendations
were based on exhaustive research, interviews, and
many, many hours of briefings. If the final recommendations in the executive order were to some extent the
outcome of personal and sub-organizational game-playing
as well as organizational routines and imperatives,

TABLE V-C - Indication of Rapidly Increasing
Japanese Share of Aid Funds to
GRI after the 1962 Kennedy Policy Changes. Source: Akio Watanabe, The Okinawa Problem,(Melbourne Australia: Melbourne University Press, 1970) p. 55.
(Adaptation).

Share of Japanese, U.S. and Ryukyuan Funds in the
General Account of the Government of the Ryukyu
Islands

Fiscal Year	Japan $000	%	U.S. $000	%	GRI $000	%	Total $000
1958	⎯		817	3.3	23778	96.7	24595
1959	⎯		2316	9.8	21655	90.2	24016
1960	⎯		2456	9.6	22996	90.4	25454
1961	⎯		3105	11.2	24509	88.8	27614
1962	55	0.2	4821	13.6	30434	86.2	35310
1963	417	1.2	6621	14.9	37400	83.9	44438
1964	2664	5.2	5220	10.1	43585	84.7	51469
1965	4258	7.7	5801	10.5	45377	81.8	55436
1966	5890	8.9	7091	10.7	53424	80.4	66405
1967	15375	17.1	10265	11.4	64386	71.5	90026
1968	23715	19.8	16668	13.9	79369	66.3	119752

SOURCE: Sorifu, Okinawa sanko shiryo (mimeo January 1966); Ryukyu Seifu, Okinawa yoran, 1967,
p. 147; Okinawa Nenkan, 1968, p. 598.

they also embodied choice and responsiveness to long-outstanding problems which would have been very difficult to resolve without "change from above" and the concern of a President with achieving certain ends.

The Decision: Rational-Comprehensive or Incremental?

Before contrasting the rational and incremental approaches and determining which appears better to fit this decision-sequence, it will be helpful to examine the nature of the changes called for in the outcome of the decision, i.e., the President's policy statement and Executive Order 11010. Do they represent marginal, limited considerations of options or dramatic departures from past policy? First, consider the alterations in the way the Ryukyus were to be governed as an outcome of the Kennedy executive order: 1. High Commissioner veto powers would be curtailed somewhat and a civilian deputy to the High Commissioner designated, 2. extended legislative terms were prescribed, and 3. a more democratic selection process for the Chief Executive was approved, by providing that the High Commissioner either accept or reject the Legislature's own nominee instead of merely consulting with them. All of these changes were basically marginal; the desire of the Okinawans for the popular election of the Chief Executive, vehemently opposed by USCAR although considered by the Task Force, was not decreed. Even Gen. Caraway did not express much concern over having a civilian Civil Administrator, as long as that person was clearly subordinate.[17]

The other major set of changes related to the proposed lifting of the Price Act ceiling to allow for more United States developmental aid to the archipelago annually thereafter which in fact resulted -- although with some time-lag -- in substantially increased revenues for the Ryukyus and increased Japanese developmental assistance being permitted, (the latter occurring with considerably greater time-lag; see Table V-C). Whether or not the American increase in appropriated funds represented a comprehensive or incremental change depends on an essentially arbitrary difinition of the terms, but if the increase in aid during the two Fiscal Years prior to the Kennedy statement (34%) is compared with that of the two years following (63%) it is evident that a fairly dramatic change took place.

The history of the Kaysen investigation and the Kennedy policy re-direction contains many rational-comprehensive features, if one is willing to ease Lindblom's requirements even slightly. The policy ends were clearly stated in NSAM-68, the Task Force was required to establish a detailed research agenda well before it went out to Okinawa, with its investigatory techniques pegged to the instructions in the NSC directive. The evolution of the decision-sequence was "controlled" and centrally coordinated in the sense that Kaysen and the White House staff directed the study and effectively determined the amount of military input which took place.[18]

There is no doubt that there were certain constraints on the breadth of options being considered by the Task Force for recommendation to the President. Kaysen noted in retrospect that even if eventual reversion was implicitly in his mind and those of others conducting the investigation, there was little question of this being among the short-term alternatives proposed (the military would have been too antagonized).[19] As Kaysen describes it, his strategy was to get modest but constructive reforms accomplished -- probably more than simply marginal -- without arousing full-blown JCS, USCAR, or other opposition.[20]

How do the arguments of Allison and Lindblom come out in the light of this decision experience? For Allison's work, impressively many indicators from the decision favor a rational-actor paradigm-style explanation. No careful appraiser would attempt to deny that organizational procedures and bureaucratic politics helped shape and limit the decision-sequence leading from the Kennedy-Ikeda conference and Ball's report and the Reischauer recommendations, but neither could he deny that the procedures of the inquiry conformed rather remarkably with any reasonable real-life expectation of the rational model. Even with the demands on rational decision-making imposed by Lindblom, synoptic decision-making in this case fares relatively well. By making a distinction between investigatory procedures, (which were aided in their rationality by an abundance of time, staffing, and funding) and the actual breadth of change contemplated which was modest with the exception of the United States/Japanese aid increase, we can give him a split decision, regarding the "fit" of his model.

Conclusion

The background of the Kennedy executive order of 1962, altering the American method of administering the Ryukyus, was clearly one of favorable circumstances converting what had long been a stalemated situation into one calling for decisive action. From the middle-1950's until 1961 it was axiomatic in the military and international affairs planning of Washington that Okinawa had to be tightly controlled with a minimum of interference from Japan allowed. The new Democrat administration in 1961 sent a strongly pro-Japanese ambassador-scholar to Tokyo, who helped activate Japanese willingness to discuss Okinawa with high American officials (most importantly in the Ikeda-Kennedy talks of July of that year). The decision sequence formally got underway with the appointment of an investigatory commission under Mr. Kaysen in late summer. From the documents examined for this study and from related interviews, a convincing case for a rational-comprehensive model explanation of the 1962 decision can be made. Changes of policy may well have been incremental, in Lindblom's terms, until mid-1961, but after that the scope of participation in Okinawa policy by the White House and other formerly "outside" agencies broadened considerably and many possible innovations were discussed, especially by the Ryukyus Task Force. There was enough interagency bargaining however, to give weight to an Allison/Model III or bureaucratic politics explanation for the decision outcome. In spite of bureaucratic games -- e.g., the maneuvering for influence over the decision between the Tokyo embassy and USCAR -- there was enough central coordination and control of this particular decision (not to say Okinawa policy generally) for the rational-actor Model I explanation to be credible as well.

173

NOTES

[1] Executive Order 10713, June 5, 1967, USCAR File mimeo.

[2] See for example, James L. Sundquist , Politics and Policy: The Eisenhower, Kennedy, and Johnson Years, (Washington: The Brookings Institution, 1968), pp. 466-469. See also Frances Rourke, "The Domestic Scene," in Robert Osgood, et. al., America and the World, (Baltimore: The Johns Hopkins University Press, 1970), pp. 183-185.

[3] The Kaysen mission was itself an important early evidence of the Administration's willingness to move into "military territory" to effect changes.

[4] Any military activity which represented a qualitative change observable by the Okinawans themselves -- e.g., the visits of nuclear submarines to Naha port or the stationing of B-52 bombers -- was likely to trigger this profound and understandable anti-war-technology outpouring of sentiment. The project to stock Okinawa with MACE-B IRBM's, scheduled for completion in December, 1961, triggered protests which coincided with the Kaysen group's visit. Demonstrations had in fact been going on for several months. New York Times, April 1, 1961, p. 2.

[5] Former USCAR officials and defense people were the most frequent observers of the Japanese penchant for group solidarity and the possibility of protests being more cohesive and focused in Japan than was likely, say, in the United States; fears of revived militarism were largely confined to the early, uncertain post-war years, but not entirely so.

[6] The issue got quite warm, but never did actually catch fire.

[7] This was emphasized particularly in our interviews with John K. Emmerson and Edwin O. Reischauer.

[8]Mr. McNamara declined to be interviewed because of his present position as head of the International Bank for Reconstruction and Development and a personal policy of avoiding comment on U.S. policies, past and present, in most instances; Mr. Ball simply declined the interview on the basis of having too many such requests.

[9]Interview with Edwin O. Reischauer, Belmont, Massachusetts, June 13, 1975.

[10]Impression based on interview with Carl Kaysen, Princeton, New Jersey, January 19, 1976.

[11]Based on impressions from interviews with both Reischauer and Caraway (cit.) and from Clapp, op.cit., pp. 12-15.

[12]A memorandum for the Secretary of Defense from the Secretary of the Army (McNamara and Stahr respectively) undated because it was a draft (i.e., the document to which I had access) but undoubtedly composed during the period December, 1961 - January, 1962, stated the following: "The High Commissioner's concern over the economic welfare of the Ryukyus and rising Japanese influence and activity there gave rise to the Task Force Ryukyus (TFR)..." (Kaysen group). This is almost certainly an overstatement: while USCAR concern with the situation on Okinawa may have been an important factor in the creation of the task force, the Ball-Bundy-Kennedy interchange and the Kennedy-Ikeda meetings were at least as directly responsible. Gen. Caraway did confirm that he was an early instigator of an Okinawan study mission, although he had some reservations about the way in which the mission was ultimately carried out (personal communication, September, 1976).

[13]From the Kaysen interview, cit.

[14]Cited in the Report and Recommendations of the Task Force Ryukyus, December, 1961, p.i.

[15]Reischauer interview, cit.

175

[16]Kaysen interview, _cit._

[17]Caraway interview, _cit._

[18]Interview with General Lyman L. Lemnitzer, Ret.,
Washington, D.C., March 15, 1976. Kaysen himself
described the decision process as having incremental aspects, but as generally being as methodical
and wide-ranging an investigation as he could re-
member having participated in. Although he might
have been expected to say this on the basis of his
role, it should be borne in mind that he is a social
scientist and appeared to be fully aware of the limitations of his 1961-62 enterprise. Great amounts
of information were obtained and digested, but not
necessarily all of the most crucial information.

[19]Lemnitzer interview, _cit._

[20]Kaysen interview, _cit._ There was some opposition in
Congress. Rep. Leslie Arends (Rep., Ill.) stated:
"In view of the extremely important role of Okinawa
in the strategy of the Western Pacific, that Executive Order poses serious problems from the standpoint of U.S. security." 87th Congress (House)
April 12, 1962. _Congressional Record Appendix_ vol.
107 A2852-2853.

CHAPTER SIX: THE JOHNSON REVERSION PROMISE OF 1967

"Dear Lord, we earnestly pray that
peace may come quickly to our world
in order that our next High Commissioner
might be the last High Commissioner it
would be necessary to send us."

> --The Rev. Taira Osamu at the
> November, 1966 investiture of
> High Commissioner Ferdinand
> Unger

The 1967 policy statement by President Lyndon Johnson on the Ryukyus culminated the most complex and controversial decision sequence of our five decision-cases. In the November Joint Communique with visiting Prime Minister Sato, Johnson expressed American sympathy toward the idea of reversion "within a few years" and agreed to the immediate return of the Ogasawara Islands. For some the Johnson statement, taken together with the trend of thinking within the foreign affairs bureaucracy, was tantamount to a guarantee of the American intention to give back the Ryukyus in the near-rather than the indefinite-future, as had been the case in earlier communiques.[1] More skeptical interpretations, chiefly those of the Japanese opposition parties (and, ironically, the more hardline elements of the American military), have stressed that the Johnson statement was one of sentiment or intention but not commitment. Fortunately I have been able to draw on a wide range of sources of this investigation of the events leading to the 1967 statement; both Japanese and American public officials involved at high levels having made themselves available even if the secret memoranda are not.[2]

The discussion of the principal deep-background events for this decision-sequence can be abbreviated because most of the history has been covered in other chapters. Three important occurrences deserve further mention: 1. the transition from High Commissioner Paul

177

Caraway to High Commissioner Albert Watson in 1964, 2. the Sato-Johnson summit meeting of 1965, and 3. the 1965 strategic study of the potential difficulties of administrative reversion.

Many Japanese policymakers and Okinawan officials regarded the replacement of the outspoken Lt. Gen. Caraway, who retired in 1964, with Watson as highly significant and the result of a decisive victory of pro-Japan-trilateralist types in the U.S. foreign affairs establishment over military globalists. The prevailing assumption of Caraway's period was stated by the General in 1963 Congressional Testimony:

> President Eisenhower and President Kennedy have declared on a number of occasions that the Ryukyus Islands will be retained under American jurisdiction as long as conditions of threat and tension exist in the Far East. Knowledgeable observers realize that the United States must remain in the Ryukyus for a long time to come.[3]

Watson fully subscribed to this same thesis; his difference was one of style and emphasis rather than substance. He resented certain kinds of Japanese involvement (or "interference") in American operations in the Ryukyus, as he made clear to Prime Minister Sato in 1964 when the two met in Tokyo to lay out ground rules for the "post-Caraway era" in the Ryukyus.[4] He was, however, less prone than his predecessor to remind the Okinawans of their shortcomings and more willing to cooperate in limited displays of Japanese influence in the archipelago, e.g., the historic visit of the Prime Minister to Okinawa in August, 1965. Although he consistently repudiated the position that some administrative functions could be turned over to the Japanese without endangering American military security on Okinawa, through his own personality and his carrying out of policies from Washington he created the impression of a new United States openness about Okinawa policy.

The second deep-background factor, the Johnson-Sato 1965 summit, was as significant for what it did not accomplish as for what it did. Although there was a general agreement on expanding the functions of the United States-Japanese Consultative Committee on Okinawa to include the working out of administrative and political as well as economic-technical problems, the main outcome of the conference was the inability and

178

unwillingness of the President to make anything more than the general verbal commitment to Okinawa's eventually being returned that Kennedy had made nearly four years earlier. The impact of America's Vietnam involvement was already being felt; it was not the best time to talk of returning the Ryukyus.

Finally, there is evidence that the top military planners for the JCS were concerned that a liberalization of American policy in the Ryukyus might be in danger of going too far. About the same time as Ambassador Edwin O. Reischauer was recommending an interdepartmental study of the Okinawa matter, the Chiefs produced a policy paper pointing out the dangers of administrative reversion of the archipelago to the Japanese. The main argument -- and one made many times by High Commissioner Watson -- was that giving Okinawa back to the Japanese would represent a kind of zero-sum game: regaining an acceptable degree of autonomy over the islands by the Japanese would unacceptably hamper the military, while an arrangement acceptable to the military would probably be so full of "conditions" as to be offensive to the Japanese.

Background

Internal setting -- The domestic setting of events is particularly important for the 1967 decision on Okinawa because of the shifting weight of various interested parties in the international affairs bureaucracy and in the American polity itself. Non-human factors continue to depend on whether one takes an American-economic-imperialism-perspective in one's view of Asian policy, or whether one considers the primary reason for the American presence in Vietnam and influence in other Asian areas as psychological and more narrowly political. What is not a matter of dispute is that America's distance from the Vietnam battleground -- whatever its complex motives for being there -- made the physical location of Okinawa more valuable than ever in the mid-1960's.

Under Society and common values one can point to the declining -- but still existent -- majority of Americans who believed that most aspects of the United States involvement in Asia, including Vietnam, were deserving of support.[5] There was however both within and outside of the government an increased tendency to question the efficaciousness of military solutions to

179

"the Communist challenge" in the Third World. The competitive can-do hubris of the early 1960's was beginning to give way to a period of increased national self-doubt and discouragement with the turbulence and variously caused frustrations of the domestic reform movements at home. Foreign policy debates still did not take place along party lines, for the most part, but there were deepening cleavages between the center and large chunks of elite and mass opinion feeling that the United States was either overly ambitious and destructive in its role in the global arena or increasingly weak and ineffectual.

Institutional and structural patterns were closely related to these value trends. If the resources and talent available to the Pentagon in 1966-67 were unprecedented, there was an unmistakable trend within the public forum and the public press to question the way these energies were being put to use. Small scale but decisive American interventions in the Dominican Republic and the Congo, whatever their merits, had generated criticism from traditional friends as well as predictable enemies. Those like Reischauer in the State Department who seriously questioned the desirability of letting the making of a powerful point in Indochina dominate all of United States, Asian and even global policy had not won the day by any means, but their influence was increasingly felt. And the United States was increasingly on the defensive in international meetings with its presence in Okinawa, like Vietnam,[6] subject to criticism and resolutions of disapproval.

In the human environment, the Johnson Administration's 1967 Okinawa policy was caught up in the same welter of conflicting traditions as were the past decisions we have analyzed. On the one hand there was the feeling that the United States had a traditional role to play in the Pacific. But over-extension of financial and human resources has always made governments in this country highly vulnerable to criticism and flamed the smoldering embers of isolationist and provincialist spirit.

External setting - If the preceding paragraphs have, in a very general way, outlined the internal climate which the policy makers concerned with Okinawa in the mid-1960's had to consider, what more explicitly "outside" factors affected their thinking? Non-human environment, again, tends to complement that of the internal setting: i.e., presumably what the United States lacks and needs in Okinawa is what Okinawa can provide

180

-- mainly its convenient closeness to China and Indochina, in the mid-1960's the most relevant places. In terms of economic gain, the archipelago had no more value to the United States in 1966 than it did in 1945 or 1960, except perhaps in providing a cheap labor force for American base facilities.

External cultural factors include the usual ones of historical connections between Japan and the Ryukyus: highlighted during Sato's summer, 1965 visit to Okinawa by both hostile crowds (who felt Japan was not doing enough about reversion) and cheering crowds of Okinawan school children waving Japanese flags. By 1967 those Okinawans who still supported a policy of gradualism in returning to Japan were increasingly on the defensive: the following year an anti-American-presence candidate easily won the first popular election for Chief Executive of the Ryukyus.

External Societal factors relevant for this decision are inevitably arbitrary and difficult to isolate as for any decision, but among those that stand out are the increasing independence and self-defined self-interest of the Japanese both politically and economically. Without becoming side-tracked into the question of whether the increased self-sufficiency and economic competitiveness of Japan and the United States was an "inevitable outgrowth of capitalism," it is certainly true that the normally pro-American Liberal Democratic party faced increasing pressure on a variety of fronts, one of which was to encourage a more independent and assertive Japanese foreign policy. Beyond doubt, moreover, there were disagreements within the dominant party which worked against Sato's own preference for accommodating the Americans whenever possible.[7]

The fourth external setting category of the Snyder group, societies-organized-as-states or simply foreign governments can be efficiently limited to four: Japan, the USSR, Communist China, and a residual category which we might label "Third World opinion." The Japanese influence on all matters Okinawan is obvious and extensively treated enough elsewhere to warrant no detailed comment here. The Soviet Union had long ago ceased giving anything more than ritual criticism of American imperialism in the Ryukyus; it was obviously not in much position to do much while still occupying the Kuriles. Although it is unlikely that the Johnson administration's decision to give qualified approval to the idea of reversion within a few years was much af-

181

fected by the thought of any direct Soviet aggression
in the Far East, the fact that Moscow was instrumental
in sustaining the North Vietnamese war effort indirectly contributed to the extreme reluctance of the Joint
Chiefs of Staff to give much on Okinawa.

The Chinese factor in the equation has been briefly mentioned in an earlier chapter: it is very likely,
though I have no direct proof, that the instability of
the situation during the Cultural Revolution combined
with uncertainty about a possible Chinese intervention
in Vietnam made decision-makers, especially in the uniformed half of the Pentagon, even more reluctant to do
anything about Okinawa that might be interpreted as a
show of weakness.[8] Chinese criticism of American policy in the Ryukyus, while harsh and predictable, was
apparently never much of a bother to Washington and
with the exception of the tiny Senkaku Islands (thought
to contain valuable oil deposits) in the late 1960's
no territorial debates ever really materialized. Mao-
Tse-tung himself by the mid-1960's was as prone to
criticize the Soviet occupation of the Northern Territories as the American presence in the Ryukyus.[9]

Of perhaps greater concern to American policy-makers was adverse publicity over Okinawa generated at the
various international conferences of non-aligned
states.[10] While it would certainly be difficult to
argue that United States concessions to Okinawan demands or Japanese pressures for reversion was materially influenced by Third World criticism, there was always a concerted public relations effort within USCAR
to emphasize the democratic aspects of American rule.
And for understandable reasons liberalizations of
USCAR policies -- the granting of greater autonomy and
authority to the GRI in this or that decision-making
area -- were more and more frequently accompanied by
fanfare and maximum publicity.

Individual actors - What follows is a set of capsule portraits of the most active participants in the
total sequence which led to the Johnson statement on
Okinawa in 1967. By this sequence is meant the studies of the Okinawa problem engineered in the Interdepartmental Regional Group during 1966-67 and the
period immediately before the November 1967 summit
meeting when the American positions on the communique
were being drafted.

182

Lyndon Johnson

The President typically, did not become actively involved in the planning for Prime Minister Sato's second trip and what the United States was going to do about Okinawa until rather late in the game. From his autobiography Vantage Point there is no evidence of any interest in the Ryukyus nor is there any particular reason why there should have been, (he was so weighted down with Indochina and Middle East problems not to mention the domestic difficulties -- summer race riots, etc.). Those of his subordinates with whom I talked felt that his concerns about the islands were necessarily more colored by considerations of their being coveted by the military than by the exigencies of the Japanese alliance. By mid-1967 he was almost certainly open to some sort of concession for the Japanese Prime Minister, which turned out to be the handing back of the Bonin Islands. His consultation with Senator Richard Russell, the most prominent Senate spokesman for the military, shortly before Sato's visit however, was the most dramatic aspect of his role, limiting greatly the possibility of a concrete pledge to return Okinawa at a precisely specified time as the Japanese had hoped.

Dean Rusk

The Secretary of State, as has been noted, had a long-term interest in the Okinawa question, having recommended the islands' return during his service in the State Department during the Truman administration. As with the Kennedy decision in 1962, he gave his assistants free reign in studying the Okinawa problem in 1966-67, but according to Clapp was in favor of deferring a final decision on reversion until after the 1968 election.[11] He has described himself as taking an "all or nothing" position on Okinawa, wishing to either give it back or retain it fully, and discouraged formulas which would hand over responsibilities to the Japanese bit by bit. In my own communications with the former Secretary, he did not recall having played an active role in the 1967 Communique drafting, nor did he have any recollection of Senator Russell's role (he did say that Johnson's consultations with Senate friends on such matters were not rare occurrences).[12]

183

Robert McNamara

I was not able to interview the former Secretary of Defense, but the best information I could get from those who did discuss the Okinawa question with him was that he was sympathetic to the Ryukyus return in principle, but unwilling to make an issue over it with the generals. Clapp reports that the Secretary allowed his International Security Affairs (ISA) office, specifically Deputy Assistant Secretary Morton Halperin, [13] handle the problem for the greater part of the time. Reportedly when a three-option position paper on Okinawa circulated among the top intra-departmental echelons in 1967, McNamara was willing to back the option calling for the archipelago's return.[14] This paper, apparently did not make it to the President's desk, however, and whether the Secretary would have been willing to actively support quick action on Okinawa is purely a matter of speculation.[15]

Richard Sneider

Mr. Sneider became Country Director for Japan early in 1966 and in that capacity quickly set out to get machinery moving on the Okinawa question, which he perceived as inadequately attended to. He formally functioned as head of the Ryukyus Working Group headed by Assistant Secretary of State William Bundy, but by his own account (and Bundy's and everyone else's) he was the man most completely managing the review of Ryukyus affairs. A man with considerable experience in Japanese relations, he took the trilateralist view that the Okinawa question was one for the United States and Japan to work out jointly with the Okinawans, and that the international significance of the Ryukyus was only viable to the extent that Tokyo was happy with the arrangements there.

William Bundy

The Assistant Secretary of State for Far Eastern Affairs was less Japan-oriented and more "globalist" than his Japan Country Director, but deferred to the latter's judgement on Okinawa and had great admiration for Sneider's handling of the matter.[16] He was among those working closely on the communique draft during the weeks before Sato's arrival and was as nonplussed

184

as any of those backing a solid commitment to the Japanese when Senator Russell's intervention caused that commitment to be watered down.

Morton Halperin

Mr. Halperin labored closely with Richard Sneider on the Ryukyus Working Group and was in effect Sneider's opposite number within the Defense Department. If any single individual can be said to have been the "swing man" or crucial participant, it would have to be Halperin. In his capacity as Deputy Assistant Secretary of Defense for Policy Planning and Arms Control he might well have been expected to be protective of military prerogatives on Okinawa, but in fact he was not. Rather he took an open view of the matter and made it possible for continuous interdepartmental communication and study of the Okinawa issue to take place without a State Department versus Defense Department confrontation to occur during the studies of the Ryukyus requirements. The fact that ultimately some confrontations did occur at higher levels does not detract from the importance of his role.

Edwin O. Reischauer

For this decision sequence Reischauer served as a sort of eminence grise, his influence was always felt, even after his departure from Tokyo in late 1966. He had recommended a concerted study of the Okinawa question in 1965, and of course had much earlier advocated serious American attention to Japanese grievances on this territorial question. His influence on the military was not great, so dedicated an "alliance man" he was, but he certainly provided affirmative guidance to those like Sneider and Kaysen who worked -- in different periods -- in the interests of a new United States perspective on the Ryukyus issue.

Alexis Johnson

Mr. Johnson replaced Reischauer as Ambassador to Japan at the end of 1966 and was another very consequential figure in this decision-sequence. By mid-1967 he had been persuaded by Sneider and others of something he had suspected for a long time, that if Japan could be encouraged to make some specific proposals on the Okinawa question, the military and the Administration might well be more receptive than to the perennial blanket calls for their return. Johnson was unusual in that he was a Japan specialist of note who also had excellent connections with the American defense establishment (which Mr. Reischauer did not). He worked very closely with USCAR and the Pacific Command from the beginning of his tenure in Tokyo to assure that the military were aware that he understood their perspective but also to persuade them of the danger to the alliance and to the Okinawa bases themselves if a no-concessions-on-reversion policy were pursued much further. The ambassador was also instrumental in the intricate workings of the draft communique text and its coordination with the Japanese draft in the weeks immediately preceding the November summit.

Ferdinand Unger

High Commissioner Unger assumed his duties in November of 1966, succeeding Lt. Gen. Watson. As has been noted, Unger worked closely with Ambassador Johnson on the Tokyo-Washington coordination of the Okinawa problem; their relationship was the best between a High Commissioner and an Ambassador during the whole period of the occupation. Unger's input in this decision sequence is difficult to measure, but we include him as a central participant because of his frank reporting of local sentiments for return to Japan and his deft balancing act between Okinawan reversion forces and his military colleagues in Naha (who valued the island highly for its usefulness vis a vis Vietnam).

The Joint Chiefs of Staff

The roles of individual members of the JCS during 1966-67 are not well known; as a body they were certainly very much preoccupied with Vietnam, especially JCS Chairman Gen. Wheeler and the Army Chief of Staff Gen. Johnson. Discussion of their role is thus deferred until the next section (organizational actors).

James Siena

James V. Siena assumed his duties rather late in the decision period, June of 1967. The Army was the service branch in charge of day to day operations on Okinawa and the Deputy Under Secretary had the major

186

responsibility for coordination between USCAR and the Washington national security establishment, including State, Defense, and the JCS in particular. Siena succeeded Thaddeus Holt, who might easily have been included in this list of individual actors, but who was not a part of the final pre-Communique policy discussions. Army Secretary Stanley Resor is not included in this list even though he had formal authority to speak for the Army on Okinawan matters because in fact he delegated most of that authority to his Deputy Under Secretaries, who specialized in these problems and the analogous ones in the Panama Canal Zone.[17] Siena was important in a way similar to Halperin's importance; he was open and flexible on an issue in which he might easily have been expected to represent Army interests -- i.e., the uniformed Army -- as those of a constituency.

Richard Russell

The Chairman of the Senate Armed Services Committee must be considered a central participant in this decision because he was consulted late in the sequence and did alter the content of the decision. Whether or not he entered on behalf of the Joint Chiefs of Staff or purely on his own is the subject of speculation; it is clear, however, that his own instincts ran toward a tough defense posture and not doing anything which would possibly undermine the already strained United States position in Southeast Asia.

Organizational actors - Our treatment of the extensive cast of individual actors allows us to be brief in our account of organizational roles, because it is very difficult to spotlight the former without casting some light on the latter. As has been made clear, a special organizational set-up consisting of the Ryukyus Working Group within the Far Eastern Interdepartmental Regional Group was central in the consideration of the Okinawan problem prior to the Communique and wove together the interested elements of the State, Defense, and Army (considered here as separate from Defense) Departments. The important formal study of the problem was made in 1967, although the Group was fully active and consulting on Okinawa the previous year.

The State Department's position had traditionally and understandably been much more amenable to returning the Ryukyus and Bonins than the Defense Department's.

Although the military took a generally more liberal view of the matter as the 1960's progressed, the rise to prominence of Edwin O. Reischauer and Richard Sneider in Japanese policy-making pushed the State Department toward a position which even flexible military types had difficulty with, i.e.,active consideration of the reversion question. The Embassy in Tokyo under Reischauer and to a somewhat lesser degree under Alexis Johnson, was a sympathetic advocate of the most forthcoming practical position on Okinawa (i.e., not directly jeopardizing military interests) although it would be a gross oversimplification to say these men were merely advocates of the Japanese viewpoint.

The Army Department did not speak with one voice in this decision any more than did the other departments, but its most active component, the Office of the Deputy Under Secretary for International Affairs, took a direct interest in studying the reversion question and not considering military rule on Okinawa as sacred. As Clapp has pointed out, however, Mr. Siena and his staff did have an obligation to steer something of a middle course between the State Department and the Joint Chiefs.

The JCS role in the policy-making was as fascinating as it was enigmatic: many of the details are still not available. It appears that the generals gave tacit assent to the 1966-67 reviews of Ryukyuan problems but were disturbed about the option paper circulating in the fall of 1967 which seemed to indicate that the return of the archipelago was being more than just contemplated theoretically. Some accounts have linked the participation in the pre-Sato-visit American position-planning by Senator Russell, an intelligent and unquestionable friend of the armed services, to an actual request by the Joint Chiefs, although I could find no hard evidence of this. In any event the Senator's intervention appears to have been more directly occasioned by his personal rapport with both the President and the top military than by any overt role-playing as spokesman (and Chairman) of the Senate Committee on Armed Services.[18]

While the role of the President in determining finally what was to be given to the Japanese at the summit was crucial, the White House staff as such does not seem to have counted for much (unlike the 1961-62 decision sequence).

TABLE VI - The Snyder Framework Applied to the Johnson
Reversion Promise Decision

INTERNAL SETTING:

Non-Human Environment - America's physical distance
from point of involvement in
Asia; no economic need for
Okinawa per se, although island may help defend Asian
economic interests.

Society -

Values - Declining support for Vietnam involvement, increased
tendency to regard Indo-
china troop commitment as
mistake on part of U.S.pub-
lic; less internationalism.

Social Structure - Enormous resources available
to military establishment
increasingly offset by decline in public support for
government and other institutions; rise in societal
tensions.

Human Environment
Culture - Tradition of interest and involvement in Pacific affairs
coupled against even older
isolationist-provincialist
tendencies.

EXTERNAL SETTING:

Non-Human Environment - Prime strategic location of
Okinawa enabling U.S. to pro-
ject power conventionally;
lessened nuclear-strategic
value vis a vis Communist
China.

Other Societies - Increased Japanese economic
and political strength and
independence; growing pressure on Sato to get favorable settlement on Ryukyus.
(CONT.)

189

TABLE VI - (Cont.)

Other Cultures -   Increased Japanese irre-
                          dentism regarding Okinawa
                          and Okinawan demonstrations
                          of desire to return to Japan.

Other Governments -   Japanese interest as ally
                          and most involved "third
                          party;" USSR indirect influ-
                          ence thru Indo-china aid;
                          Chinese upheavals; some ele-
                          ments of Third World call
                          Okinawa "colony."

INDIVIDUAL ACTORS: President Lyndon Johnson; Sec.
                          of State Dean Rusk; Sec. De-
                          fense Robert McNamara; Japan
                          Country Dir. Richard Sneider;
                          Asst. Sec. State for F.E.
                          William Bundy; Dep.Asst.Sec.
                          Def. Morton Halperin; Amb.
                          Edwin Reischauer; Amb.Alexis
                          Johnson; Dep. Under Sec.
                          James Siena; JCS; High Comm.
                          Ferdinand Unger; Sen. Rich-
                          ard Russell.

ORGANIZATIONAL NETWORK: White House; State Department;
                          Defense Department; SIG-IRG;
                          Army; Embassy.

SITUATIONAL PROPERTIES: Decision anticipated, time-
                          frame not too restrictive;
                          value-magnitudes high, but
                          not of the highest variety.

Situational properties - What were the immediate characteristics of the situation surrounding the 1967 decision? To begin with, the making of a decision was something which had been anticipated well in advance; certainly as soon as it was known that Sato would be visiting Washington in November, a posture on the Okinawa matter had to be formulated. Okinawa would unquestionably be at the top of the Prime Minister's agenda. The applicability of the Snyder-Robinson variable of "routine" versus "crisis" decision-making is as questionable in its relevancy for this decision as for the others we have investigated so far: although definitely not of the crisis variety, it would be difficult to depict the decision as routine, involving as it did the major issue between the United States and its most important single ally. As for the magnitude of values related to the problem, they were much higher for the Japanese than for the United States, which was undoubtedly the cause of much misunderstanding about the issue in the first place. But if the American negotiating position on Okinawa is considered as bound up with the larger issues of Pacific security and support for operations in Vietnam (though it need not necessarily be), the value magnitudes for the United States on Ryukyuan policy could be said to be considerable.

Alternative Explanatory Models

Our technique of giving parallel renderings of the decision sequence in light of each of Graham Allison's policy-making models is by now familiar enough to proceed directly to the Model I perspective:

> President Johnson's decision to be very encouraging but to give no hard and fast commitment to the return of the Ryukyus to Japan when Prime Minister Sato visited in 1967 was based on substantive and rational considerations, if not necessarily the right ones. The fact that Mr. Johnson overrode the consensus of much of his policy-making bureaucracy at the last minute is dramatic evidence of the primacy of Model I -- the authoritative decision-maker acting on the basis of his perception of the best means for meeting the right ends.
> This decision-sequence is no more discreet and isolable as a historical incident than any other, but insofar as it can be said to have a

191

beginning, that probably came with the establishment of the Ryukyus Working Group in 1966. The group was staffed by bright and pragmatic bureaucrats under the direction of the State Department's new Japan Country Director, Richard Sneider. Sneider had been a long-time believer in the rightness and good sense of returning the Ryukyus and Ogasawara to the Japanese. With a Japanese Prime Minister in office intent on getting Okinawa back and High Commissioners who were somewhat more receptive to this broader vision of American interests than had previously been the case, the time was ripe for Sneider to act.

In the spring of 1966 a study had been completed within the SIG-IRG system which assumed that Okinawa would not be returned to Japan in the immediate future, in a sense deferring to the 1965 JCS paper which had argued that the administrative return of the Ryukyus would jeopardize the base system. The review of the first part of 1966 was designed to seek ways to mollify and reassure the Japanese and Okinawans short of actual reversion. It was undertaken without the active participation of the military.[19]

In 1967 the Working Group Study was at the same time more ambitious and more cautious than the earlier one. This time the assumption was that the Ryukyus would be returned to Japan; the object was to determine the effects of this on the base system there, assuming reasonable conditions. This time also the military were closely consulted at every stage of the review, and their positions were meticulously incorporated into each section of the report. The result was the beginning of a consensus that the military functioning on Okinawa would not necessarily be seriously impaired by the Ryukyus' being treated like any other Japanese base area under the 1960 security treaty.[20] The major base activity that could be limited was the use of airfields for bombing missions. (The question of the use of nuclear weapons was not taken up in the study).

The essentials of the study were incorporated into the aforementioned paper circulated at the top levels of the bureaucracy for approval (including the JCS, the Ambassador to Japan, the Assistant Secretary of State for Far East-

ern Affairs and the Secretary of Defense).
There is evidence, although not conclusive,
that all of the major reviewers of the paper
signed the option calling for further serious consideration of the reversion question
(i.e., the middle-of-the-road position), except for Secretary McNamara, who initialled
the more strongly pro-reversion option three.[21]
As we have pointed out, however, Secretary of
State Rusk used his authority to prevent the
paper from reaching the President. This was
apparently not because of any opposition to
an openminded view of the Okinawa question,
but because he felt that it was better for the
President to make up his own mind on the matter. Rusk's own opinion, according to Clapp,
was that the issue should be deferred until
after the 1968 election, i.e., for a year.
Rusk also discouraged the then-Foreign Minister Miki from expecting too much from the
up-coming summit talks during the latter's
visit in September.[22]

The working draft of the communique seems
to have had included a fairly explicit commitment to reversion within a clear time-
frame with the details to be worked out in
the interim. The President reversed judgment on this matter until consulting with
Senators whom he knew to be interested in
security affairs, Senator Russell was the only
man who objected to a commitment per se, but
this was enough to cause the draft to go back
to the drawing board and to upset the Japanese at the other and who, in spite of Rusk's
statement to Miki, expected something more
than they were apparently going to get.

The final wording of the communique contained
a far more subtle promise of American intentions to return Okinawa than the Japanese would
have liked. But given the President's perceptions of the need for flexibility in using
the Ryukyus military facilities and the fact
that there was no immediate end in sight for
the Vietnam War, his reluctance to make more
of a commitment was understandable. The fact
that he was influenced in this by key advisers
does not detract from the essential issue-ori-
ented and unified nature of the decision.[23]

The organizational-model critique of this account rests on the argument that the President himself was not really interested in the specifics of the Okinawa problem. Rather from the Model II perspective, clashing organizational interests determined the outcome when Mr. Johnson responded to that organizational component whose frustration and opposition he had the most to lose from:

The interests of the Joint Chiefs of Staff, as represented to the President by his trusted former colleague, the senior Senator from Georgia, appeared to have overruled not only the interests of other foreign affairs-involved organizations but also the reasoned foreign policy judgments of Mr. Johnson himself. Reports indicate that the President was prepared to accept the advice of the SIG-IRG structure, of which the Sneider-Halperin Working Group was the most active part, and was genuinely surprised when Senator Russell objected to the sort of very general commitment which was being recommended.

The Model I account is defective in other respects as well. The very fact that the military were happy to participate in the 1967 study, in which their views were methodically taken into account, even though this study was investigating a more far-reaching hypothetical situation [24] than the 1966 policy review which they had rejected, lends weight to the contention that cooperation is achieved by bringing all interested parties into the "action" rather than by the force of one group's reasoning over another's. Richard Sneider, an organization man par excellence, had learned his lesson well in 1966 and was determined from then on that no matter what the apparent merits of the general's case, they must be allowed to participate in these reviews and never feel ostracized.[25]

By bringing together able representatives of the three main bureaucratic components concerned with the Ryukyus -- State, Army, and Defense-ISA, the Working Group was able to present the Secretary of State with a reasonably coherent report of the risks of reversion, the desirability of certain concessions, and the minority opinions of the military (the latter usually on technical points). We say "reasonably" because at this stage the facts of the case become subject to real question. Clapp is of the opinion that although the Chiefs were willing to initial a memorandum option in effect endorsing the study of the reversion question, they balked sharply when it became apparent that their flexibility might lead to some quick concessions on Okinawa at the November summit.[26] This line of reasoning appears somewhat strained, however. It is difficult to imagine that the JCS would be so naive as to endorse a paper which had been in the mill for months and then turn around and resume their old hard line position, using Senator Russell as a front man. But I was not able to uncover the facts to resolve the paradox.

One must look to the total context of and follow-up on the Johnson Okinawa pronouncement of November to appreciate fully the importance of organizational factors. The compromise between the Ryukyus Working Group and the military was reflected in the return of the Ogasawara Islands, in the Japanese language version of the communique which was allowed to contain reference to anticipation of reversion in two or three years (rather than merely the "few years" of the English version), and in the administrative reforms of 1968, including the executive order permitting popular election of the Chief Executive. If the vast military network with the JCS at its apex won on the issue of a concrete commitment to reversion in November, 1967, they paid a price for it. It was to be the last time that the generals held sway over State Department and Pentagon civilian officials in alliance.

Organizational compromise and self-interest can explain many aspects of the 1967 Presidential decision which Model I cannot account for, but there are some important anomalies which remain. Insofar as they can be resolved at all, they must be by our recourse to the bureaucratic politics line of analysis:

The nature of President Johnson's final decision on "how much to commit on Okinawa" must be seen as as much political as simply rational/issue-oriented or organizational

195

compromise. Careers were at stake here and sometimes loyalty to and belief in a sub-organizational unit in which an official found himself actually contributed to his working against the normally expected interests of the organization as a whole. Of course the process we are talking about is rarely a conscious one: policy strategists often embrace positions and strategems helpful to them personally and to their small bureaucratic shops, wrapping these positions in the cloak of rationality and "the best option available."

To fully understand this decision-sequence it is essential to train our analytic zoom-lens on four key individuals -- men who made a difference -- Richard Sneider, Edwin Reischauer, Morton Halperin, and Richard Russell. The bureaucratic chess-games (one of Allison's favorite analogies) in which these men were players are the arenas where the President's decision was in effect determined for him.

Japan Country Director Sneider was the kind of man who played his chess very well. Allison has described a bureaucratic law of the game that he who hesitates loses the chance to play, and he who is unsure about his recommendation is outflanked by players who are sure. When it came to the Okinawa question Sneider was always very sure. He directed, orchestrated, and choreographed the 1967 study so well that an interdepartmental consensus emerged which many would shortly before have regarded as impossible.

Ambassador Reischauer, among others, claims that his own recommendations were the crucial trigger of the 1966 policy review, even though he had left his Tokyo assignment as the 1967 study-phase actually got under way. Sneider, by contrast, emphasizes his own role from the early 1960's in bringing attention to the Okinawa issue. As with many cases in which historians and political analysts ask "whose idea was it?" or "who was the moving force?" the answer may be simply that creative and previously undeveloped ideas occur simultaneously to perceptive men involved with the same subject matter. In any event if Reischauer was the most prominent early proponent of returning Okinawa, Sneider was the man who picked the idea up and brought it to fruition, enhancing

his own career considerably in the process.
Morton Halperin, who later became a prominent exponent of bureaucratic political analysis a la Allison, was a significant figure in the games played by the Ryukyus Working Group second in the degree of his contribution only to Sneider. In another sense he could be said to have been even more pivotal than Sneider: unlike the latter, Halperin might have been expected to defend his organization's interests, i.e., those of the Defense Department. Instead, he chose not to let organizational priorities dictate his position on Okinawa. Rather, he regarded the Okinawa dilemma as a challenging balancing act: appease the Japanese but at the same time not drive the military to despair or open opposition. Whatever rational components there may have been in the way he approached his job, in effect he contributed original thinking and a detached -- but not anti-military-interests-- posture which certainly enhanced his reputation as a skillful bureaucratic gamesman.

Senator Russell is our fourth difference-making individual. He was involved in a different game or set of games from the intra-departmental Working Group. His ties to the President were close and long-standing, his constituency obviously radically different from that of Sneider, Halperin and company. Presumably the President owed Russell a certain number of favors, or at least a certain kind of deference: it is difficult to be sure of the specifics (both men are dead, their staff-men claimed simply not to be aware of the details of the consultation). The one game in which Russell played against the bureaucracy, he won. But it was a short-term victory: President Johnson conceded less than he might have on the Ryukyus in 1967, but ended up owing the Japanese more. The next time the matter came up, in 1969, the Republicans were in the White House and checking reversion through Senator Russell was not really necessary.

Although it would be possible to account for the Okinawa clause in the Johnson-Sato joint communique by saying Johnson in effect rejected the advice of his experts and decided on the basis of a sixth sense (which said "avoid confrontations with the military at

this time on this issue"), thus dismissing much of the
bureaucratic politics-style explanation, it would be
very difficult to come to a real understanding of the
significance of the Johnson solution without Model III.
The consensus-building of the sub-cabinet bureaucratic
structure for a liberal and free-wheeling position on
reversion did not evaporate simply because of the Deus
ex machina of the Russell intervention: the very fact
that the Japanese version of the communique referred to
"two or three years" -- and that the Americans permitted this wording to stand -- is indicative that the
President was not simply setting aside the bureaucracy
and "ending the game."[27] The organizational paradigm
(Model II) is not terribly persuasive here because not
only did organizational lines get crossed many times
(e.g., Halperin's and Siena's advocacy of positions
not in line with the military's view of its interest),
but standard operating procedures tended to be less
relevant and central than innovative devices such as
the Working Group, and even less organizationally relevant personal contacts such as the close rapport
quickly established between Sneider and Halperin.

The Decision: Rational-Comprehensive or Incremental

     In evaluating the fit of the two distinctive deci-
sion-making models described by Lindblom and Braybrooke
to the 1967 Okinawa decision, we look first at the decision itself to see what sort of advance it appeared
to represent over how things were before the decision.
From the perspective of a number of the Japanese and
Okinawans interviewed and some of the scholars who have
written on the subject, the Johnson commitment was not
much of a commitment at all.[28] The return of Ogasawara
was significant, but it was not enough to satisfy the
political appetites of the Japanese opposition parties
or the political needs of the LDP. Consequently it
did not satisfy the pro-alliance trilateralists; nor
was the statement that the President "fully understood
the desire of the Japanese people for the return of
these islands" (in the watered down final version)
really satisfactory. Viewed in a narrow or literal
sense, then, the 1967 pronouncement was certainly an
incremental or marginal change, even if the Bonin Island concession is figured in. It was, moreover, a
small change not merely over the policy of the 1965-67
period between the most recent bilateral communiques,
it was, arguably, even a small change over the Kennedy-
Ikeda communique of 1961 and the executive order of

1962. An examination of the decision sequence preceding the Johnson statement and interviews with officials involved with the President reveal a stronger commitment than the literal wording of the communique might indicate, however. Between 1967 and 1968 the United States greatly expanded the role of the Japanese in Okinawan affairs through the establishment of the Advisory Committee for the High Commissioner and approved popular elections for the Ryukyus Chief Executive, the latter virtually sounding the death-knell for control of Okinawan politics by the Okinawa Liberal Democratic Party. Independent voters who were not as effective in getting their voices heard in a legislature tightly organized into parties, would heavily support the moderate leftist Yara Chobyo over the OLDP candidate.29

There are two points to be made here -- one general, one more specific. The general point is that it is not always enough to examine a decision at the end of a sequence and characterize the decision as incremental or "quite limited" because the decision itself does not effect a profound change. A given decision sequence can dramatically alter the climate of elite opinion surrounding a problem even if the immediate steps taken appear inconsequential. The specific point highlighted by the 1967 decision sequence on Okinawa is that bureaucratic political processes contributed to an immediate outcome of minimal change, but-- along with events in Japan and Okinawa -- also wrought a substantial shift in the balance of forces in favor of returning Okinawa, probably before the 1960 security treaty became subject to alteration in 1970.

The rational actor decision analyst might well characterize the 1966 and especially the 1967 Working Group studies of the reversion question as exemplifying the synoptic policy-making approach that Lindblom describes as seldom possible in real life. A great deal of research energy -- not only by the Working Group study, but also by a parallel RAND study of the question -- was trained on a limited and clearly defined problem and, theoretically at least, a wide variety of options and eventualities were being considered. It seems clear however that Sneider and his colleagues were heavily oriented toward reversion at the outset and were seeking through the studies mainly to demonstrate and get a consensus that returning the archipelago to Japan in the late 1960's was entirely consistent with United States' security requirements. This assessment is based on the detailed study of

199

Clapp and Fukui, as well as the statements of most of the participants themselves.[30] The process corresponded closely in this regard to Lindblom's description of a policy alternative regarded as "do-able" and desirable in advance being selected and the justification (or rationalization) coming after that selection is already made, tailoring values to practical policy.[31] This may be a question of semantics as much as anything else: if reversion is regarded as a practical policy alternative (i.e., easier than resisting reversion) and values are attached to it ex post (better relations with Japan, thus better Pacific security in the long run) then the fit with Lindblom's incremental model, with ends frequently adapted to means rather than the reverse is easy to see. If reversion is considered a value or end in itself (consistent, for example with other American values like the avoidance of overt imperialism) then the Sneider strategy, while not comprehensive in its consideration of a wide variety of options, was rational in seeking to prove diligently that reversion would not endanger other values like military security. One is not completely comfortable, then, with a depiction of the President's Okinawa pronouncement as wholly incremental, even though it was decentralized in the sense of being a product both of the foreign affairs bureaucracy and the will of the military per Senator Russell, that is a Presidential compromise. If the tip of the iceberg was the actual communique statement, the under-part contained strong rational elements: means-ends analysis, interdepartmental coordination, etc., which were to have effects beyond merely incremental ones.

Conclusion

The climate for significant change on American Ryukyus policy was not particularly good between 1962 and 1966. Americans were faced with an unstable and unsettling situation in Indochina and the Cold War exchanges of insult with the Communist Chinese were intensifying. After modest but promising adjustments of the Kennedy executive order of 1962 and the replacement of Gen. Caraway with more pliable High Commissioners after his retirement in 1962, the issue of appeasing Japan on the Okinawa question seemed to die. In spite of increasing dissatisfaction on the part of the Okinawan and Japanese political opposition and the reiteration of the occasional request for the archipelago's return by Sato in conference with Johnson early in

200

1965, the Okinawa problem was essentially in a kind of political-military limbo until 1966. In that year both bureaucratic politics in Washington and external events came together to create new momentum in the push to return the islands to Japan. The coincidence of dramatically heightened interest in Okinawa by civilian officials (led by Sneider and Halperin, new in their posts), more diplomatic and conciliatory high commissioners, and renewed pressure on the LDP to get action did give new life to the reversion issue, as evidenced in the interdepartmental studies in Washington. Some of the outcome of the 1967 communique can be explained in purely rational-actor terms, borrowing from Allison's vocabulary, a decision to give further assurances on the Ryukyus and throw in the Bonin Islands as both a token of Washington's sincerity and a palliative. But a healthy portion of the outcome can also be explained by bureaucratic political considerations: the reluctance of the Secretary of State to endorse recommendations for major changes in the Ryukyus, the intervention of Senate hawks in the person of Mr. Russell of Georgia, and the subsurface tension between the Joint Chiefs and the civilian officials who felt they were preparing the way for a rational compromise on the reversion question in good faith.

The Lindblom incremental model stands up fairly well in this decision-sequence in spite of the superficially strong rationality and apparent coordination of the consideration of the problems of the Ryukyus. The fragmented nature of the sources of authorative input on the disposition of Okinawa (Senate, White House, SIG/IRG, and military) plus the fact that the decision was shaped in the end by considerations strongly political (the President's respect and awe of Senator Russell) detract from rationalist explanations and give weight to the more pluralist, incremental ones.

NOTES

[1]See for example Destler et al., op.cit., p.30-31.

[2]I have entitled this chapter "The Johnson Reversion Promise of 1967" aware that the extent to which there was "a promise" is debatable.

[3]Testimony of Lt. Gen. Paul W. Carraway before the House Committee on Appropriations, Foreign Operations Sub-Committee, 88th Congress, 1st Session, 1963, pp. 264-265.

[4]Telephone interview with Lt. Gen. Albert Watson II (Ret.), March 24, 1976.

[5]The majority of the officials we interviewed for this decision sequence reflected a personal sensitivity to the needs of the Vietnam conflict (if varying degrees of enthusiasm about the wisdom of the original commitments) in 1967; similarly, public backing of the war, as reflected in the public opinion polls lasted through 1967 although by a sharply reduced majority. In answer to Gallup's question: "In view of the developments since we entered the fighting in Vietnam, do you think the United States made a mistake sending troops to fight in Vietnam?" the percentage in February 1967 answering "no" was 52% and "yes" 32%; in July the figures were 48% and 41%; in October 44% and 46%; and in December 46% and 45%. In 1968, the percentage calling the war a mistake shifted (as it had briefly in October) to a majority and continued to increase after that. Cited in Hazel Erskine, "Is War a Mistake?" in Public Opinion Quarterly, (Spring, 1970), p. 141.

[6]Watanabe cites declarations in favor of Okinawan "liberation" at the Afro-Asian People's Solidarity conferences in Cairo (1957) and Tanzania (1963), op.cit., p. 146.

[7]The faction headed by Foreign Minister Miki Takeo, for example, regarded the Prime Minister as "soft" on the United States and not as tough on the Okinawa question as he should have been or, indeed, as his own rhetoric indicated.

[8]The speculation that the Cultural Revolution in China directly affected the thinking of the Joint Chiefs on the Okinawa problem, articulated in the study by James H. McBride, _op, cit._, p. 101, is very plausible; however, there was no mention of this particular source of concern in interviews we conducted with policymakers.

[9]In an interview with the Japan Socialist Party's Sasaki Kozo on April 10, 1966, Mao Tse-tung, after noting that "The Soviet Union has occupied too much," is quoted as saying "...as for your Kuril Islands (sic), there is no problem as far as we are concerned. They should be returned to you, I think." Cited in Eto Shinkichi, "Attitude of Peking and Taiwan Governments on Okinawa Issue," (sic), Kyoto Conference paper (January, 1969), p. 5-6.

[10]Watanabe, _op. cit._, p. 146.

[11]Clapp, _op. cit._, pp. 18-19 and 26.

[12]Letter-interviews with the author, dated June 30 and July 29, 1976.

[13]Clapp, _op. cit._, pp. 20-21.

[14]_Ibid._, p. 26.

[15]_Ibid._.

[16]Interview, _cit_.

[17]The Canal Zone, administered by the Army, represents the most truly comparable international situation to Okinawa's. Among the more obvious comparison-worthy factors are: the unique strategic position of the areas; the special legal arrangements (backed by subtle but undeniable power) for the American admin-

17
istration of foreign sovereign territory; a restive
local population nevertheless heavily dependent for
its economic well-being on the American presence,etc.
We did not mention it in the strategic discussions of
the global paradigm chapter because of its largely
defensive, hemispheric importance, compared with Okinawa, Hong Kong, Djibouti, Cyprus, etc. all of which
had the potential for the projection of interregional
power.

18Impressions based on several interviews already cited
as well as conversations with former Russell aides.

19Interview with Morton Halperin, Washington, D.C.,
March 16, 1976.

20Clapp, op. cit., pp. 23-24. Also interviews cited
with Halperin, Sneider, and Emmerson.

21Clapp, op. cit., p. 26.

22Clapp and Fukui cite evidence that American officials
with whom Miki talked made it clear to the Foreign
Minister that Japan would have to be prepared to
shoulder greater security responsibilities in the Far
East as a "sine qua non" for official negotiations on
Okinawan reversion. They also note that the Japanese
minister must have been impressed by the increased
concern with overall Asian security threats on the
part of the Pentagon, especially because of McNamaras
anti-China ABM deployment. Priscilla Clapp and
Haruhiro Fukui, "Decision-Making in U.S.-Japanese Relations," 1974, p. IV-10.

23It should be remembered that an important related
feature of the 1967 communique, and one which also
underscored a desire to please on the part of the
United States, was the pledge to allow the Bonin Islands to revert to Japan. If this was a disappoint-
ing substitute for immediate guarantees of Okinawa
reversion from the standpoint of the Japanese, it was
also a concession from the military of the United
States, who had received no guarantees on nuclear
storage rights (although they had strongly requested
these).

[24] I.e., the consequences of administrative reversion for conventional American military capability.

[25] Clapp, op. cit., p. 22 and Halperin interview, cited.

[26] Clapp and Fukui, op. cit., p. IV-212.

[27] According to Clapp and Fukui, op. cit., pp. IV-25, 26 and the accounts of some of the officials we interviewed, the original discrepancy between the Japanese (ryosan-nen) and American ("within a few years") was deliberate, but the resulting uproar was not anticipated. It was assumed that the Japanese version would be specific enough to placate the Japanese opposition and that the English-language version would be sufficiently vague not to be regarded by pro-military forces, including Congressmen, as endangering America's Far East security efforts. Sato indicated in statements to the Japanese press that the President had privately assured him that in fact two to three years was what Washington had in mind. A New York Times story shortly after the communique was released did not help matters, characterizing the document as "laced with vague phrases soothing to the Japanese ear..." The New York paper's reputation for reliability and authoritativeness could not have but increased Tokyo's uneasiness; for all the Sato government knew this impression may have come from insiders at the White House itself.

[28] Most of the left-leaning political party experts and the scholars we interviewed made this assessment of the 1967 summit. See also Hong N. Kim, "The Sato Government and the Politics of Okinawan Reversion," in Asian Survey, (November, 1973), pp. 1021-1035.

[29] Yara beat the OLDP candidate in the November, 1968, election by a margin of 237,643 to 206,209 (52% to 48%).

[30] Sneider and James Siena declared themselves openly sympathetic to the Japanese position on the Okinawa question from the outset of the Working Group's mission; Halperin was a bit more circumspect but essentially of the same orientation. (Sneider and Halperin interviews cited; Siena interview-letter from

[30] Stanford, California dated May 10, 1976).

[31] Lindblom and Braybrooke, op. cit., p. 118. Also Lindblom, Strategies for Decision-Making, op. cit., pp.12-13.

CHAPTER SEVEN: THE NIXON REVERSION DECISION OF 1969

Discussion of the "deep background" of the final
reversion decision-sequence in 1969 need not be as detailed as that of earlier chapters - in a sense the
four decisions I have already analyzed plus the accounts of the 1968-69 period in the historical chapter
have accomplished this already. What may be seen as
more proximate or close-in background events occurring
in 1968 and encouraging fast action on the Okinawa
problem in 1969 deserve to be mentioned, however, and
related more explicitly to the situation facing the
Nixon administration as it took office in January of
that year.

An important change took place in 1968 which constituted a somewhat ironic refutation of the military's
argument that Okinawa was essential for the conduct of
the war in Indochina. In February the Air Force's
long-standing demand that B-52's be allowed to make
their bombing runs (much more efficiently) from Kadena
Air Base in Okinawa rather than being limited to Guam,
was finally agreed to. The Army, as the service responsible for administrating the Ryukyus, warned that
the cost-savings and operational efficiency gained by
this policy change might well be outweighed by the losses to the American position there caused by inflamma-
tion of opposition groups, which were already highly
uncomfortable with Okinawa's role in supporting the
United States' activities. If the most dire predic-
tions were not confirmed, the mass demonstrations and
Ryukyus election campaign rhetoric generated in the
fall of the year by the bombing missions came close
enough to a "worst case" situation to cause USCAR administrators many sleepless nights. A general strike
set for early January of 1969 was narrowly averted by
the intercession of Prime Minister Sato and the partial
loss of nerve by the strike leaders and the new Chief
Executive, Yara.[1] The B-52 controversy was only one of
the more attention-getting aspects of the Vietnam-
caused expansion of activity in Okinawa. Between 1967
and 1969 Vietnam related expenses reportedly increased
from $89 million to $126 million (nearly 40%) and more
than 50,000 troops were stationed on the island by the
end of 1969.[2]

Closely related to the Vietnam-connected causes of domestic unrest in Okinawa were the security treaty-connected effects. As early as November of 1966, USCAR had been actively discouraging the linking of the Okinawan reversion issue to that of the security treaty's possible cancellation, a linkage by which the pro-immediate-reversion people would have made return of the political control of the Ryukyus to Japan a condition of allowing the 1960 treaty to remain in effect (obviously requiring close coordination with Tokyo).[3]

A third development, more on the minds of those in Washington and Tokyo than of those in Naha, was the belated but rapid development of hard proposals and positions from Japanese officialdom on how reversion negotiations might be carried out and how American military capabilities on Okinawa might be safeguarded in the post-reversion era. In December of 1967 the Prime Minister had announced his "blank-slate" policy, meaning that he did not want to be committed to specific boundaries imposed by Japanese political infighting. This was followed in May of 1968 by his statement to the House of Councillors Foreign Affairs Committee that he would not be bound by a Japanese non-nuclear condition for reversion: his priority would be the early return of the archipelago, preferably, but not necessarily, with the area nuclear-free. In February and March the activities of the Base Problems Study Committee and the Advisory Committee to the High Commissioner, respectively, got under way, both of which served to enhance the Japanese government's familiarity with the problems of the American military in Okinawa.

It would be fair to say that between the Sato-Johnson meeting of November, 1967 and the accession to power of the Republicans, events conspired to weaken further the American position in the Ryukyus and at the same time the Japanese enhanced their own negotiating position by getting a much better grasp of American requirements there and developing arguments of their own. All of this, of course, affected the more immediate decision-setting of early 1969.

Background

Internal setting - By 1969 the domestic environment for all foreign policy-making in the United States had undergone some notable shifts from that of the early and mid-1960's. The process of disenchantment

208

with great-power global politics and American commitments abroad--discernible but tentative during the
1966-67 decision sequence just studied--had become
quite pronounced. Looking at the Snyder group's category of non-human factors, however, it seems safe to
say that not much had changed since the last sequence.
Okinawa continued to be vital because of its location,
especially for the Indochina war (and this type to conflict generally),[4] which showed no sign of abating.

Within the society category - i.e., American
society- under common values, major public opinion indicators had shown a steady decline in support for the
Vietnam effort since late - 1967/early 1968 and an increased tendency to view armed American involvements as
undesirable.[5] And while opinion polls reported Americans continuing to defer to and back specific governmental policies in the conduct of the war well into
1968, public support for the Vietnam intervention as a
whole - i.e., as an original step - declined.[6] This
does not mean, as Rourke, among others, has emphasized,
that isolationism was again ascendent, but rather that
the kind of internationalism to be viewed as desirable
was of a more circumspect and conservative variety.[7]
Societal structural and institutional factors are closely related to values: as with the values category one
has to be careful to distinguish between deep-seated
changes and more immediate trends (we have mostly been
concerned in these analyses with the latter). The
standard - and probably correct - interpretation of
American societal developments in the late 1960's saw
a breakdown in support of a wide range of traditional
institutions: governmental, religious, educational,
military, corporate, etc. At the most general level
such a trend would be supportive of government policies
to increase the quality of performance in a given area
by scaling down the range of undertakings, setting more
realistic goals with a higher probability of success,
and focusing energies on these goals. In the area of
foreign policy, the Nixon administration employed precisely such a general strategy, placing a high priority on the successful conclusion of the Indochina involvement and arriving at more stable and politically
advantageous relationships with each of the Communist
giants, Russia and China. This also involved a greater role for American allies as regional powers, a
natural consequence of which might be the political return of Okinawa to a proven and competent ally, Japan.

An important and very indirectly related factor
under this heading would be the demands placed on the
Nixon administration through an important element of
its Southern domestic constituency: the textile manufacturers. In a special kind of linkage politics,
they were able to tie concessions on export controls of
Japanese textiles to the Okinawa reversion negotiations.
I avoid the temptation to attribute the flow of influence in this particular case to some inherent responsiveness of the Republican Party to manufacturing interests; rather I credit the electoral politics of 1968
and the Nixon debt to the Carolinas.

As for internal cultural factors or human environment, again we are confronted with a category from
which a large variety of factors might be plucked, and
which is in any case not terribly specific. Presumably the Nixon international affairs people continued
to be influenced by the socio-cultural assumption of an
American interest in Pacific affairs, but with democratic and ideological tutelage rather than territorial
expansion (for the long term) the desired goal. If we
continue to view American foreign policy generally as
operating like a pendulum between the two extremes of
missionary activism and provincial isolationism, then
the former, with Nixon's revisions, embodied in the
Guam Doctrine, Okinawa reversion and other innovations,
a swing toward the latter.

External setting - In several earlier chapters we
have observed that the primary relevant non-human environment factor in the Okinawa policy equation had been
the island's strategic location. During the early
1960's the Ryukyus contributed in a limited way to nuclear deterrence through the presence of the obso-
lescent but functional MACE-B missiles, which could be
used against China.[8] The islands were really more important, however, for their convenient location at
something of a center-point between Southeast Asia and
the Philippines, Japan, Korea and China. By 1965 they
had become regarded as "indispensible" as a supply de-
pot, training and staging ground for the United States
effort in South Vietnam - in 1968 B-52 bombing missions
routinely originated there as we have pointed out.[9]
By 1969, however, the usefulness of Okinawa for Indochina was seen to be at its peak and likely to decline
rapidly as the war itself wound down. As the sort of
regionally oriented security strategy of the Nixon administration took hold, it appeared likely that the
geographic factors which had made the Ryukyus so ad-

210

vantageous a position for the Vietnam War would now serve Japan well as a regional power, and that although the United States and Japan would garrison the archipelago jointly, political administration might well be turned over to Tokyo. Advances in intercontinental ballistic missilery, moreover, had made Okinawa largely irrelevant as a platform for intermediate-range missiles targeted for China.

External cultural factors, as we have identified them for the other decisions, were largely the historical ties which the reversionists in both Japan and the Ryukyus constantly alluded to when making their case for reunification. While it is true that Okinawan reversionists such as Chief Executive Yara became much more critical of Tokyo and what they regarded as the Sato government's excessively conciliatory stance toward the United States during the reversion negotiations, this was all more in the nature of a family quarrel than anything else. What the Okinawans were saying was, in effect, "we look to you fellow-Japanese for support as kinsmen and your leaders treat the Americans, who have given us so many headaches these last twenty-five years, with kid gloves."

In the external societal factors category, we have been concerned with the sorts of phenomena which Rosenau has characterized as linkages, i.e., in this case social phenomena within Japan which are perceived by and directly impinge upon the American policy-makers' activities. In 1969 Japanese economic and social links to the United States were stronger than they had ever been, and there was an awareness on the part of key American actors in the Japanese policy-drama that the Liberal Democratic Party, which once had the iniative on the Okinawa issue, now had its back to the wall on the reversion question. There was, moreover, a new factor that seemed likely to be felt in any final solution to the Okinawa problem: the textile question. The men in power in Washington apparently felt they were in some measure responsible for the interests of the American (especially Southern) textile industry, which resented the encroachments of Japanese exporters of cheap fabrics. The actions of the Japanese manufacturers directly stimulated their counterparts in the United States, who in turn put pressure on the Nixon administration which would not likely have the effect of impeding reversion itself, but which would apparently force some harder bargaining on the Japanese.[10]

Within the final analytic compartment in external setting, that of other governments, only four governments could be thought to have had any effect on American decision-making - and of these three were marginal: the USSR, China, and Korea. Their influence paled by comparison with that of Japan. In fact, of the major decision participants I talked with, regarding the 1969 decision, only one was willing to directly connect considerations of the Soviets and Communist Chinese to the NSC - and in particular the President's - decision strategy.[11] That does not mean that detente was irrelevant to the action on the Ryukyus (i.e.,enabling reversion to go forward more easily), but rather that the demands of the alliance were paramount and dominated the thought-screens of those doing the deciding. Most of those I interviewed characterized detente and the policies of friendliness toward the Communist giants as coinciding conveniently with the Okinawa reversion issue rather than actively affecting it.[12]

Judging from the content of the communique in November of 1969, which contained a fairly explicit Japanese commitment to a greater role in regional defense, including regarding Korea as essential to the security of Japan (diplomatic code for a pledge to assist the United States in assisting Korea in case of attack) there was a marked increase in concern over Korea under the new administration. The Pueblo capture of 1967 and the shooting down by North Korea of a flying reconnaissance team in 1969 heightened tensions on that peninsula and led to an increase in maneuvers and defensive preparations undetaken jointly by the United States and South Korea. It is certain that the concern of the Park government and American strategists looking at Korea had some impact on the Okinawa decision and in getting a more explicit commitment by Japan to a recognition of Korea's importance to Japanese security than had ever been made, in part in return for the American concessions on the Ryukyus.

The central actor in the international environment perceived by President Nixon's foreign policy specialists participating in the 1969 decision was Japan - there was universal agreement on this by the men we interviewed. A majority of those with whom we talked also agreed that concern for the Sato wing of the LDP and its continued good health made it imperative that fast action be obtained on the Ryukyus question.[13]

Individual actors - Of the seven decision-makers who seem to have been most active in this sequence, we were able to interview five: National Security Council Staffmen Sneider and Halperin, Assistant Secretary of Defense for International Security Affairs Warren Nutter, Deputy Under Secretary of the Army James Siena, and Secretary of State William Rogers. The first two of these continued to have a crucial role by virtue of their transfer of assignment from the State and Defense Departments to Henry Kissinger's National Security Council.[14] For obvious reasons I was not able to interview former President Nixon; it was possible to get, I believe, a fairly thorough picture of his role from our other sources, though. The other participant I omitted was the Joint Chiefs of Staff (considered as a unit: it is very difficult to determine the roles of individuals in the JCS, especially for so recent an event as the 1969 decision). I feel that Mr. Nutter was able to provide a number of insights into the role of the JCS as a body and was supportive and sympathetic to their position.[15] He was also knowledgable about the role of Secretary Laird who, although certainly in a position to get heavily involved in the Okinawa reversion negotiations, evidently chose not to do so.[16]

<u>Richard Nixon</u>

In spite of the analysis by Graham Allison and others to the effect that the Nixon administration was woefully inadequate in its Japan policy, the President was sympathetic from the outset on the Okinawa issue. It is believed that he had pretty well finalized his decision for a solid reversion commitment in the November 1969 summit as early as May of 1969. The <u>conditions</u> of reversion, including the sensitive nuclear weapons question, represented the other side of the coin of the 1969 sequence and the matter was conclusively settled only a short time before the fall meeting with Sato, according to most accounts. Personal factors may have played a noteworthy role in Mr. Nixon's readiness to see the Japanese viewpoint on reversion. A number of participants whom we interviewed commented on the President's appreciation for the friendly and respectful receptions he always received in Tokyo during his years out of power; one commented that Mr. Nixon was impressed by the remarks made to him by former Prime Minister Kishi visiting the United States for the Eisenhower funeral in April of 1969.

213

William Rogers

In contrast to most other foreign policy issues, there is impressive evidence that Secretary of State Rogers rather than Special Assistant for National Security Affairs Henry Kissinger was the prime mover on matters concerning the Ryukyus. Certainly after the Spring, 1969 National Security Council Decision Memorandum, Rogers' importance eclipsed that of Kissinger and the latter's expert assistants, Richard Sneider and Morton Halperin. Rogers personally conducted negotiations on the terms of reversion with the Japanese Foreign Minister, Aichi Kiichi, between June and September. The Secretary of State was definitely globally rather than Japanese alliance oriented (as demonstrated by his rather tough and aloof negotiating tactics with the Japanese) but eventually developed a personal rapport with Aichi and a respect for the Japanese position that assured Tokyo that progress toward its goal would not be impaired.

Warren Nutter

Nutter was the most active Defense Department participant in the early 1969 planning on reversion strategy (except for the Army's James Siena). His role was a representative rather than a personal one; he saw his responsibility to be that of articulate advocate of the JCS and the civilian ends of the Pentagon jointly. He also handled most of the day to day DOD/ISA work on the issue for Secretary Laird and Deputy Secretary David Packard. Nutter's personal predilections ran toward maintaining the American global-strategic position in Okinawa to the greatest extent possible and toward hard bargaining with the Japanese. He indicated that he felt he was on the losing side from the beginning, however, as were the Joint Chiefs. He therefore took the position of deferring to majority opinion and simply acting as "minority spokesman" giving the military position on such matters as nuclear weapons storage rights and prior consultation on base use.

James Siena

The Army's Deputy Secretary for International Affairs played a part similar to that in 1967, although

214

by this time he had gained considerably more experience
in dealing with the Ryukyus problem and consequently
more "clout." Closely associated with Sneider and Halperin and disposed as they were to cooperate with Ja-
panese-alliance interests, Siena, with his colleagues,
contributed to a degree of continuity and expertise on
a long-term problem not always to be had at such a high
level. As the other major spokesman for USCAR besides
the Army Chief of Staff, Siena could have potentially
been a foot-dragger on Okinawa, but instead chose to be
a pace-setter and bring the military around to the political necessity of what was being done.

Richard Sneider

The choice of Richard Sneider, as well as Morton
Halperin, to be on Henry Kissinger's National Security
Council staff implied strongly that the administration
gave high priority to the settling of the Ryukyus matter as one of those pressing and important - if not
first-rank - foreign policy problems. Sneider's familiarity with the problem and organizational abilities
were unparalleled and he continued to play an activist
role, although under the auspices of Kissinger and the
NSC instead of the Working Group of the 1966-67 period.
He was of course strongly trilateralist-alliance poli-
tics-minded rather than globalist in orientation.

Morton Halperin

Halperin continued to monitor the Okinawa situation alongside IRG colleague Richard Sneider when he
moved to the National Security Council staff assignment.
Nixon's NSC was considerably upgraded from what the
Council had been under Johnson, so Halperin's new location kept him at the center of decision-making power
for an issue in which he had invested a lot of time.
The two men together supervised the NSDM and related
position papers in the spring, having worked with Kissinger on Okinawa at the Pierre Hotel in New York
shortly after Nixon was elected. Halperin left his assignment in September, two months before the Nixon-
Sato summit, but the NSC staff's role had been eclipsed by Secretary Rogers and the President himself by
this time. Although Halperin noted that Kissinger was
interested in Okinawa and had in fact been further persuaded of the issue's importance by Kyoto Conference
participants Thomas Schelling and Albert Wohlstetter

after that January, 1969 gathering had concluded, all indications are that Sneider and Halperin worked much more closely on the Ryukyus than did Kissinger.

The Joint Chiefs Of Staff

In 1969 the Joint Chiefs were the following: Chairman, Gen. Earl Wheeler; Army Chief Gen. Harold Johnson; Navy Chief Admiral Thomas Moorer; and Air Force Chief Gen. John Ryan. I learned virtually nothing about their roles as individuals and their collective position papers are still insurmountably classified. What is known of their role comes from impressions of other decision-makers and applies to the Chiefs as an organizational component rather than interested individuals, so discussion of them is deferred until the next section, organizational actors.

Alexis Johnson

One final participant in the 1969 decision who may (but not necessarily should, according to our information) be included in the inner circle is Deputy Secretary of State U. Alexis Johnson, who moved to that position from the ambassadorship in Tokyo in the spring of that year. As a senior source of advice and one of that rare breed of State Department careerist who enjoyed Richard Nixon's confidence, Johnson may well have been the catalyst moving the Ryukyus matter quickly through the National Security Council System. He did mention having briefed the President shortly before the latter made a White House commitment to reversion at an NSC meeting in April of the year.

Organizational actors - As with the 1967 decision case-study, the discussion of individual roles in the 1969 sequence allows me to be more brief in our treatment of organizational ones. We noted that in 1966-67 the cockpit of action on the Okinawa question was the Ryukyus Working Group of the Inter-departmental Regional Group for the Far East (IRG). This group continued to function in 1969 as a research body, but was less important than two years earlier because Sneider and Halperin had moved on to the NSC staff (where they could continue to direct work on the Ryukyus). The Group's most important function in the spring was to prepare a final study on Okinawa for the NSC (pursuant to National Security Council Study Memorandum Number 5

216

- NSSM-5 - of January 21, 1976) and to look at the related issues of American Japanese relations: the 1970 possible-renegotiation-date of the security treaty and trade problems (but apparently not the textile issue).[18]

The role of the State Department was enlarged after the NSDM #13 virtually guaranteed reversion, in principle, but left the terms open to negotiation and, ultimately, Presidential decision. Mr. Nixon approved the Decision Memorandum in May and although that document was officially highly classified, the administration's predisposition toward reversion was no secret. Beginning in June, Secretary Rogers met with Foreign Minister Aichi in Washington negotiating sessions (Rogers met with Aichi briefly in Tokyo in July) and a second set of sessions was held in September. The two cabinet men centered their discussions on such pivotal communique-related questions as the nuclear weapons policy for Okinawa, (though very little came of this until the November summit), the actual date of reversion, the use of the prior consultation system (by which Japan was technically in a position to veto the use of American military facilities for certain purposes), and, finally, the textile issue.

Another American governmental department, Commerce, can be considered a marginal organizational actor for this decision sequence. Secretary of Commerce Maurice Stans met with Foreign Minister Aichi during the latter's first trip to Washington in an apparently coordinated American attempt to reinforce the importance of satisfactory Japanese action to limit textile exports and an implicit relating of the promise of such action to the Okinawa negotiations. Because nothing was really settled regarding textiles until well after the November communique, however, the extent of the influence of the Commerce Department -- and indeed the whole issue of export controls -- on the Ryukyus settlement remains obscure.

The role of the Defense Department and the Joint Chiefs of Staff, other than those functions specifically related to the NSC, was that of information bank (USCAR, after all, was always central to the Okinawa question and a Defense component) and permanent advocate of positions which would preserve the flexibility and effective striking power of the Ryukyus bases (e.g., nuclear weapons storage rights, continuation of B-52 missions, nuclear submarine docking, etc.) By 1969 much of the fight had gone out of the Okinawa

217

question, probably in part because of the much greater time demands of the Vietnam War and in part because the military really were sold on the arguments (which they had resisted for years) that no tactical advantages to be gained from the preservation of American authority in Okinawa could outweigh the strategic costs to the Japan-American relationship. Thus, from most of the evidence I have been able to gather, the Joint Chiefs and the Secretary of Defense played a largely passive and deferential role during the last months of the negotiations.

The Department of the Army continued to speak with its own voice on the Ryukyus question, by virtue of its charter for administering the archipelago and managing problems in the Pentagon. Mr. Siena's free hand in approaching the problem (given to him by Army Secretary Stanley Resor) from the Washington end assured that the Department would not be an obstacle for the last stages of eight years of Reischauer-Sneider diplomacy. The Deputy Under Secretary was very much in favor of reversion, especially when it became apparent that it could be gotten on terms not injurious to the United States' strategic position. He was served by High Commissioners (Unger in 1967 and 1968, Lampert in 1969) who were hand-picked because of their intellects and diplomatic skills so that there were no significant pockets of resistance to giving up Okinawa left.

Situational properties - Describing the immediate situational characteristics of the 1969 decision sequence, we have to recall that that sequence is logically considered best as in two separate parts: first, the internal governmental decision in April to return Okinawa to the Japanese, and second, the process of negotiating a minimum set of concessions from Tokyo which would allow the United States to make good on that decision. Both aspects of the decision sequence were certainly contemplated well in advance; they were as anticipated as any of the Okinawa decision-cases I have examined have been, as Kissinger's hiring of Richard Sneider and Morton Halperin to assist him personally as senior staff members illustrates. Whether the final decision to defer to Japanese wishes not to have nuclear weapons on Okinawa, as revealed in the November communique, was fully anticipated is subject to some question. Clapp reports Alexis Johnson as having gotten President Nixon's tacit agreement in April of 1969 that reversion with nuclear weapons remaining in Japan was rather pointless in one respect-

218

TABLE VII - Snyder Framework Applied to the
Nixon Reversion Decision

INTERNAL SETTING

Non-Human Environment - American mainland distance
from action spots in Asia;
virtually no economic need
for Okinawa itself

Society -
Values - Declining public support for
foreign interventions (tendency to regard Vietnam involvement as mistake)

Social Structure - Generally diminishing support
for institutions: military,
governmental, religious, educational; textile manufacturers complaint

Human Environment -
Culture - Heritage of Pacific involvements balanced against provincialism and anti-imperial
ideals

EXTERNAL SETTING:

Non-Human Environment -Geographic importance contrasted with economic unim-
portance; greatly diminished
value as strategic missile
base

Other Societies - Close American economic and
social ties; irritant over
competition from Japanese exports, especially textiles

Other Cultures - Much emphasis on cultural
closeness and inevitability
of re-unification of Ryukyuans and Japanese (this despite some Japanese-Okinawan
discord)

Other Governments - Great power detente a factor
but an indirect one compared
with alliance needs; Korean
situation may have promoted
reversion caution

(CONT.)

219

TABLE VII - (Cont.)

INDIVIDUAL ACTORS: President Richard Nixon; Sec. of State William Rogers; Asst. Secretary Defense ISA Warren Nutter; JCS; Army Deputy Under Secretary James Siena; NSC staff men Richard Sneider and Morton Halperin; Under Secretary of State Alexis Johnson

ORGANIZATION NETWORK: White House and NSC Staff; State Department (mainly Secretary); Defense Department ISA; Joint Chiefs; Interdepartmental Group; Army

SITUATIONAL PROPERTIES: Problem fully anticipated; time-frame tight but not crisis-like; value magnitudes somewhat high

namely that it would undermine the whole ethos of "no
nuclear weapons on Japan-controlled territory." The
time pressures on the Ryukyus decision as perceived by
the administration were not negligible: the security
treaty headaches of 1960 were well remembered ("night-
mare" might be the more appropriate metaphor from Tokyo's standpoint), 1970 might well be a problem if Okinawa were not handled with proper dispatch.[19] While
Okinawa was not seen as a crisis per se, the fact that
it was the exclusive subject of one of Kissinger's five
original National Security Study Memoranda in January
indicates that it was anything but peripheral. This
sheds some light on the third Snyder-Robinson situation analysis factor, magnitude of values. As we have
seen throughout, the magnitude of the issues involved
in the decision on whether and how to return the Ryukyus to Japan was fairly high, if not in a class with
disarmament questions or NATO policy. The vital matter of having a unique and desirable base situation
like Okinawa provided for twenty years (before political pressures undermined this) was seen as paling
alongside the vivid strokes being painted by opposition
parties and other Sato critics who were beginning to
argue successfully that three summits and five years
should be more than enough to secure territory that was
already legally Japanese anyway. The decision-makers
and organizations just outlined can thus be seen as
operating in an environment with well-staked-out problems, (anticipated), certain very real time constraints,
and value-stakes which were far from routine, although
not of the dimensions of certain other foreign policy
problems.

Alternative Explanatory Models

Of all of the cases we have studied, the Nixon reversion decision-sequence offers the richest source of
argument and example for the rational actor paradigm:

The Nixon administration's first year
witnessed the culmination of ten years of
concessions to Japan over the Ryukyus and
twenty-four years of debate of interrelated
factors - some very much a part of the mainstream of policy, others fortuitous - combined to make the decision process an efficient and remarkably satisfactory one from
the point of view of each side.[20] Contributing to the superiority of the Model I, uni-

221

tary actor explanation's superiority over models which seek answers in organizational or bureaucratic politics needs is the degree of central control and management of the problem by the National Security Council.

The Republicans had another advantage in handling the Ryukyus besides their well-oiled, hierarchical decision-making apparatus: they also had the substantial body of background preparation bequeathed to them by the Johnson administration and the SIG-IRG structure. They even had the two leading bureaucratic experts on the substantive questions surrounding Okinawa: Sneider and Halperin. One of the five original NSSM's dealt with Japan (another with Vietnam options, another with China, etc.), but for the Nixon agenda it was clearly Vietnam and the Ryukyus which would command most of the attention of the early months, and NSSM-5 reflected that.

Richard Nixon's foreign affairs vision was more coherent, if not necessarily more consistent, than that of most presidents and the corner of his eye reserved for Japan was no exception. In his October 1967 Foreign Affairs article he had asserted that with its tremendous economic growth "Japan will surely want to play a greater role both diplomatically and militarily in maintaining the balance in Asia."[21] He is known to have expressed considerable interest in resolving the Ryukyus situation early in his presidency; the enlarging of Japan's regional "partner" role symbolized by the overdue return of Okinawa, would fit in nicely with his over-all Asian strategy, first articulated at Guam in the summer.[22]

One entire NSC meeting in April was given over to an airing out of opinions on Okinawan reversion and a discussion of the study pursuant to NSSM-5. Here Secretary Laird and JCS Chairman Wheeler apparently reiterated their department's position (also contained in the study) that nuclear weapons storage rights should be retained there, but did not insist on this. It was clear from the meeting that Nixon and the committed "reversionists" were going to prevail on the degree of concession to be made to Japan, and the NSDM issued on May 28, summarizing the thinking of the April meeting, kept open the option of guaranteeing to the Japanese that nuclear weapons would be removed (the President was known to be leaning in this direction). Secretary of State Rogers began formal negotiations with Foreign Minister Aichi in June. By this time two major concessions had crystallized as those expected from Japan in return for nuclear-free reversion: 1. some cooperation from the Japanese on the textile problem, 2. a "clarification" of the "prior-consultation" clause of the 1960 security treaty, which would assure that Japan did not envision that clause as a pretext to veto any controversial American security proposal it had a mind to. The fact of Okinawa's reversion and its bases' coming under the same status as any other Japanese base apparently necessitated this second demand. Related to the prior consultation clarification was Washington's effort to get the Japanese to agree to the importance of the defense of Korea, Taiwan and Southeast Asia.

Rogers and Aichi solved most of the communique wording-problems by September, but there was no agreement on whether the option of storing nuclear weapons would be retained by the United States. Finally it was decided that the President and Prime Minister should resolve the matter at the summit, which it was, in Japan's favor. The Nixon administration's total bargaining strategy can be described as tough - tougher than the Japanese anticipated in some ways - but ultimately satisfactory to them. Considering the degree of the President's commitment to reversion and the long standing nature of this Japanese territorial grievance, the United States came away with an impressive array of small concessions from Tokyo. Reversion itself can be viewed as a gain for American prestige and an opportunity to dramatically demonstrate the seriousness with which the implementation of the Nixon doctrine of regional defense was viewed.

To the organizational paradigm analyst, the notion that the Republican policy on Ryukyuan reversion was controlled centrally from the top and carefully focused to assure maximum bargaining gains is an illusion. His account might run as follows:

223

The Nixon administration inherited far
more than expertise and key personalities for
dealing with the Japanese policy problems.
It was also the "beneficiary" of many years of
established organizational procedures and
priorities. The solution of the November summit
was at least as much a product of these as of
administrative innovations.

To begin with the Army Department's role,
which had begun to liberalize under Under Secretary Ailes in 1961, was crucial: with James
Siena working in Washington and the third of
three consecutively open-minded and cooperative
High Commissioners running things in the field,
the Nixon policy was immeasurably facilitated.
The working of the IRG structure remained basically intact, even though the top Okinawa-in-
volved personnel had migrated to the NSC staff,
so the underlying fabric of America's alliance
policy was really not changed. The alliance
of politically sensitive civilians in the
Defense Department and traditional State Department and traditional State Department advocates of the maximum number of pro-Japan policy adjustments on the Ryukyus (which could be
tolerated by the generals) combined to enable
Mr. Nixon to fashion a policy which happened
to benefit his desired strategy of overtures
toward China and more regional defense self-
sufficiency in the Far East.

Organizational innovations under Mr. Nixon
counted for as much or more than his substantive negotiating proposals which were in any
case quite flexible). The revitalized National
Security Council allowed the Joint Chiefs of
Staff to present their views on such specifics as retention of nuclear weapons storage
rights and desired troop levels in front of
the President and his top cabinet officials
rather than merely speaking with him on an ad
hoc basis or issuing memoranda. This may well
explain their willingness to have nuclear storage rights as a negotiating option rather than
a demand and in turn sheds light on why the
Chiefs were able to write off the possibility
that these rights might be lost as "administrative inconvenience" rather than an irre-
placable strategic loss. The commitment of the
Nixon foreign policy-makers to press the Japanese for a stronger statement of their regional

224

defense duties and a broadened conception
of the "prior consultation system" also contributed to the JCS acquiescence.[23]

Attention to organizational biases and changes represents an important advance over the rational-actor
explanation, but is as usual at a loss to explain certain anomalies and inconsistencies which are best accounted for by recourse to the Model III perspective:

The total Okinawa policy-output of 1969
cannot really be understood unless it is conceived of in terms of a group of simultaneous
or over-lapping "games", the progress of each
of which affected the outcome of the others.
The first game might be thought of as the administration's vision of Okinawa reversion as
part of its broad strategy in the Far East:
the lessening of American involvement in
Indochina, the upgrading of regional defensive capabilities, the increasing responsibility given to a not always eager Japan. The
principal players in this game were Nixon,
Kissinger and his staff, and the foreign policy establishments of Japan and the other
Pacific allies: Korea, Taiwan, the Philippines,
and Thailand. The American press may also be
considered a participant here.
In the area of interdepartmental bargaining, a second game was being played in which
the heads of the military services, the JCS
and their best civilian ally, Assistant Secretary Warren Nutter argued for various limitations on the reversion agreement, including
the concessions from Japan already mentioned.
Clapp has pointed out that the military were
aware that their trump card in this game
could be the more hawkish members of the
Senate Armed Services Committee (harking back
to Senator Russell's intervention) but it was
by no means certain that this card would be
played.
A third game, and this one at the very
heart of Rosenau's linkage politics, was the
textile issue, about which we have only fragmentary knowledge. Here certain Senators,
principally Southerners like Strom Thurmond,
were able to affect the content of the Okinawa negotiations by cashing in certain domestic political chips which Nixon and Rogers

225

knew needed to be honored. Thus it was that Foreign Minister Aichi's trip to Washington in June included an important visit to the office of Commerce Secretary Maurice Stans, the logical administration trouble-shooter for the textile problem. The general impression conveyed in the accounts we were able to get hold of is that there was at least an attempt to keep the textile question separate from the Okinawa bargaining to keep things relatively neat and reduce the crasser aspects of the trade-off. Most of the Americans, and interestingly virtually all of the Japanese officials we interviewed refused to acknowledge that there was anything but the most indirect connection between the reversion agreement favorable to Japan on the nuclear question and the voluntary restrictive guidelines which the Japanese adopted with regard to textile exports.[24] In any event the slippery nature of communique commitments was revealed later when, according to Binendijk, President Nixon learned that Prime Minister Sato did not regard Japan's obligations on export restrictions to be as manifest or concrete as Nixon himself had understood them.[25] Binendijk even goes so far as to argue that the President's wrath explains his high-handed disregard for the Japanese in his 1971 unilateral monetary policy changes and the overtures toward Communist China.[26]

The continued access of the articulate and committed duo of Sneider and Halperin to the decision-making on Okinawa - at least until the late summer of 1969 (when Halperin left the administration and Sneider had been installed as Deputy Chief of Mission under Ambassador Armin Meyer in the Tokyo Embassy). Their superior knowledge of the problem, plus the powerful presence of former Ambassador Alexis Johnson, now Under Secretary of State for Political Affairs assured that what the armed services were having taken from them in the Ryukyus was taken with style and also with promises from Tokyo which clearly softened the impact of the archipelago's bases coming under the 1960 security treaty.

The Decision: Rational-Comprehensive or Incremental?

In keeping with the pattern we have tried to establish, an assessment of the relevance of Lindblom's contrast of synoptic and incremental decision-making strategies can be helpfully combined with the discussion of Allison's rational actor vs. Models II and III in the Okinawa cases. Intellectually there is no reason to doubt that the final agreement on the Ryukyus reached in the joint communique of November 22 comported splendidly with the stated intentions of the Nixon people to grant greater roles and privileges to willing regional powers and the administration's not yet explicit, but germinating plan for rapprochement with Peking. More specific to the actual substance of the Okinawa planning was the effort - and it was considerably more than simple lip-service - to explore a number of avenues toward a settlement with Japan. In spite of the extensive ground-work done by the IRG working group in 1967, a new and thorough study was ordered on Inauguration Day of 1969 (through NSSM-5), reportedly considering a spectrum of options ranging from simply postponing the reversion commitment indefinitely because of continued uncertainties in the Far East (heightened by the Indochinese and Korean situations) and a total military as well as administrative withdrawal.[27] Another factor which casts doubt on any explanation of the 1969 events which relies heavily on metaphors of multiple bureaucratic games or mechanistic organizational output and pluralist decision-centers is that of the President's deciding himself on the nuclear question very late in the bargaining sequence. Finally, based on the accounts given by the advocates of a tougher-line bargaining posture, such as former Assistant Secretary Nutter, the battle for such a posture had been lost almost from the beginning; in effect the interdepartmental squabbling and maneuvering had played out in all but the most superficial senses during the 1967 sequence.[28]

There are several counter-arguments which the incrementalist and bureaucratic politics analyst can make here. First he can point to the results of our interviews with the major participants in the 1969 decision, the majority of whom explicitly denied that the Nixon Doctrine, retrenchment policies, or detente ever fig-

227

ured importantly in discussions on Okinawa. Theory
and grand design, according to almost all of these
former officials, took a backseat to the pragmatics of
negotiating and getting the kind of intra-United States
government, not to mention Japanese, cooperation necessary to make healthy adjustments in Pacific strategic policy. The Japanese found to their surprise that
hard-pressed Southern textile interests were helping
make American foreign policy and affecting matters
which might have been considered "very personally Japanese," i.e., the ultimate disposition of an entire
archipelago containing nearly one million Japanese.
The JCS in turn found that what might once have been
regarded as sacred prerogatives, such as the storage of
nuclear bombs on Okinawa had become expendable when Japanese domestic politics forced them to be. Even less
directly related, although highly salient national security questions such as the scheduling of American
troop withdrawals from South Vietnam may well have de-
flected the kind of top-level military attention from
monitoring the specifics of the Okinawa strategy that
one might have expected had there been no Indochina
problem and no Vietnamization preparations.

Bureaucratic political factors are therefore very
easily understated when looking at a bold and brainy
"new" system of making international affairs decisions
like the Nixon-Kissinger one. The central arguments of
Allison's account of the policy-making process appear
to stand up fairly well in this case; but can the same
be said for disjointed incrementalism? In its most
typically encountered form as described by Lindblom,
incremental policy means various progressions of small
steps which, taken together can add up to major changes
or to relatively insignificant ones. Central coordination, if any, is of the most superficial sort and for
the most part simply formalizes the difference-splitting among diverse nodes of decision-making power, giving a strongly (and Lindblom would claim healthily)
conservative bias to the policy-making process. The
reversion decision of the Nixon administration could
conceivably fit within this description: after all, the
1967 communique outcome was viewed from almost every
angle as a last redoubt for those who wished to put off
this long-awaited promise to Japan, the United States
government was teetering on the edge of a hard commitment to Okinawa's return just millimeters short of actually making the commitment.

The plugging in of the Lindblom model would be

easily achieved here if it weren't for the fact that so
much effort was expended by the Nixon people to stage
- and perhaps "stage" is a bit misleading - a careful
reconsideration of the Ryukyus problem in light of the
painfully sluggish progress in Southeast Asia and the
stirred up situation in Korea. A final review of the
consequences of reversion was made, the administration
held on to the nuclear option to the last possible moment, and the textile question - theretofore never linked to the terms of Ryukyuan reversion to our best knowledge - was introduced in a calculated bit of realpol-
itik. The self-conscious attempt by the National Security Council to incorporate the caveats of the Joint
Chiefs into the spring study and the NSDM was viewed
by some as a sham,[29] but it is a fact that Nixon and
Rogers used JCS-style arguments and the concerns of the
Chiefs themselves to extract some surprisingly assertive, if unspecific, statements on Far Eastern security
from Mr. Sato. Again we are left with the feeling that
disjointed incrementalism as a model around which to
build an explanation for our decision deprives us of
too much. If the 1969 decision was something less than
the synoptic ideal, it was something more than disjointed incremental, if the latter term is to have any
meaning. Events were not coldly and facilely controlled by a foreign policy nerve-center, but there was in
fact a nerve-center, and it did not simply respond to
sensations and motor impulses from the periphery.

Conclusion

     The decision-making setting for the 1969 reversion
policy of the Nixon administration was in many ways
structured by commitments by the previous President,
but there was an important element of flexibility in
the terms of the communique - or more properly speaking the options for bargaining positions leading to
the desired terms. The fact that the Nixon administration finally settled on terms fairly close to what
the Johnson administration people had been heading toward should not be taken as an indication that the
negotiating position was an inevitable one. This position, moreover, in terms of the Allison models, was
by no means determined (although it was unquestionably
influenced and colored) by the ebb and flow of bureaucratic politics. There were strong "rational-actor
forces" operating in the centralizing tendencies of the
Kissinger National Security Council to offset the effects of Commerce-Congressional versus Pentagon versus
State Department haggling. Consequently aspects of

both the Model I and Model III explanation-types of
Allison are convincing in accounting for this episode.
This of course closely relates to the Lindblom dichotomy between rational-comprehensive policy-making and
his preferred disjointed-incremental model. While the
direction given to the policy-development process for
the Okinawa issue by Sneider and Halperin of Kissinger's staff was impressive, there were a number of aspects of that process which were not subject to option-
paper evaluation and were very much subject to the kind
of limited-alternatives solutions posited by the in-
crementalists. We have in mind here particularly the
subtle, slowly changing, and not-centrally controlled
impact of the textile matter on the negotiations as
well as the uncertain and fluid nature of the nuclear-
rights option once the negotiations for reversion passed into the hands of Secretary of State Rogers.

[1] A detailed account of the 1968-69 B-52 bomber controversy can be found in Herbert Kampt, The United States
and Okinawa: A Study in Dependency Relationship, (unpublished Ph.D. dissertation, Department of Political
Science, City University of New York, 1972), pp. 571-
577 and 600-607.

[2] Binnendijk, "Political-Military Aspects..." op.cit.,
p. 14.

[3] From USCAR position paper "The Tendency of Okinawans
to Relate the Question of Reversion to the Possibility
of Revision of the GOJ-US Security Treaty in 1979,"
dated November 30, 1966 (USCAR files, National Archives, Suitland, Maryland).

[4] The value of the Ryukyus in the strategic equation
with the Chinese (not to mention the USSR), that is,
as a base used for medium-range ballistic missiles had
long since become negligible.

[5] See statistics on the increasing American support for
the proposition that the original American troop commitment to Vietnam was a mistake in Public Opinion
Quarterly (Erskine article cit.), Francis Rourke cites
comparable Gallup polls in his article "The Domestic
Scene," in Robert Osgood et al., America and the
World, (Baltimore: The Johns Hopkins Press, 1970),
p. 152. He characterizes the American attitude of the
late 1960's in the wake of Vietnam as more cautious
about commitments abroad, but still not isolationist.
Ibid., p. 187.

[6] Erskine in Public Opinion Quarterly, op. cit., and
Rourke, ibid., p. 152

[7] Rourke, ibid., p. 187

[8] Binnendijk discusses the MACE-B missiles in "Political-Military Aspects..." op. cit., p. 52.

[9] CINCPAC Commander Admiral U.S. Grant Sharp was quoted in the December 10, 1965 Pacific Stars and Stripes, as calling Okinawa "indispensible" to the Vietnam War effort. Cited in Binnendijk, "Political-Military Aspects..." op. cit., p. 15.

[10] For a detailed discussion of the role of the textile issue in the 1969 negotiations on Okinawa see Destler et al, op. cit., pp. 35-45.

[11] That individual was former Assistant Secretary of Defense for International Security Affairs, G.Warren Nutter, interview, cit. Nutter recalls administration discussions on the Ryukyus as making explicit the connection between great power detente and the return of Okinawa. Others we interviewed described the connection as more implicit, or remembered no connection at all.

[12] For example William Rogers, former Secretary of State, in a telephone interview, March 22, 1976, characterized the connection between reversion negotiations and the administrations overall strategy as implicit and a demonstration of American rejection of territorial ambitions in Asia.

[13] Among those who emphasized this consideration most strongly were Sneider, Halperin, Alexis Johnson, and two other individuals we talked with: former Ambassador to Japan Armin Meyer (interview in Washington, March 15, 1976) and Rodney Armstrong, a former State Department Japan expert who assisted with the 1969 NSSM study (Interview in New York, November 20,1975). See also Armin Meyer, Assignment: Tokyo (New York: Bobbs-Merrill, 1974). pp. 38-39.

[14] Kissinger himself played a relatively minor role in the actual working out of a position on Okinawa during 1969, although of course he was interested in the progress of the matter and consulted closely with Sneider and Halperin on it. According to Halperin, Kissinger was impressed with the reports of Thomas Schelling and Albert Wohlstetter, participants in the January, 1969 Kyoto Conference on Okinawa that

14

the issue had become one of wide concern and top
priority in Japan, and that the conventional strategic arguments did not justify further delaying tactics.

15My interview with Halperin, William Bundy, and
Siena, cit., also contributed valuable insights on
the JCS position and bargaining techniques.

16Nutter described Laird's performance as low-key,
stating basic JCS positions but generally acquiesc-
ing to "the inevitable" and simply watching to see
that no specific military function performed by the
Ryukyus was needlessly jeopartized (interview, cit.).

17Allison in Rosovsky, op. cit.

18Clapp, op. cit.,pp. 34-36.

19Remember that, according to Clapp, Secretary of
State Rusk had succeeded in delaying the implementation of the Sneider Working Group recommendations until after the 1968 election. Clapp op. cit., p. 26.

20Francis Rourke emphasizes the uncanny ability of the
Nixon administration to capitalize on unique historical opportunities and marry them to its foreign
policy in "The President Ascendent" in Robert Osgood
et. al., Retreat From Empire?, (Baltimore: The Johns
Hopkins University Press, 1973), p. 108.

21Richard Nixon, "Asia After Vietnam", in Foreign Affairs, (October, 1967), pp. 111-125.

22Clapp op. cit., p. 34

23Ibid., p. 37

24By contrast, left-leaning Japanese foreign policy
authorities (i.e.,of the Socialist and Communist
parties) and writers were only too happy to point to
textiles as "the price of reversion." Interview with
Warashina Hiroto of the Japan Socialist Party, Tokyo,
August 7, 1975, and interview with Nihara Shoji of

[24]
the Japan Communist Party, Tokyo, August 23, 1975.

[25]Binnendijk, "Political-Military Aspects..." op.cit.,
p. 29.

[26]Ibid.

[27]Clapp, op. cit., p. 35 Former Secretary of State
Rogers indicated that the administration could have
reversed the trend toward reversion in American policy but chose not to. (interview, cit.)

[28]Nutter interview, cit.

[29]Ibid.

several years it should be added).[1] To cite just one
example from the present cases, this writer would not
have been disposed to examine the possibility that Okinawa somehow helped protect American domestic economic
interests by providing a base for military power which
could be used to protect Asian markets as some have
said it was used.[2] After considering this possibility,
it appears that this component of the non-human environment (economic/resources) was of marginal importance
(Korea and Vietnam were not of great economic consequence to the United States; Japan could be defended,
if not as well, from its own bases in the main islands)
but that does not eliminate the value of confronting
the possibility that market-protection factors were of
more marginal consequence. The same thing could be
said for the Snyder group's other categories - individual and organizational actors, for example - which, if
they are used in the way that Snyder and Paige have
prescribed, force the historian or political scientist
to determine fairly precisely who the men who made the
decision were and what agencies were involved and how.

These strengths of the Snyder approach provide the
clues to its weaknesses and risks. To begin with, the
process of filling the analytic boxes - "human environment," "external societal" factors, etc., - is a complex one and relies heavily on the analyst's personal
judgment in the long run.[3] For many of these boxes,
the number and range of factors which could be used to
fill them is large indeed. A case in point is the
1949 (NSC 13/3) decision, under the internal setting/
societies/ common values heading (ref. p.96) in which
we selected public sentiments on demobilization, rejection of isolationism, and the nascent Cold War-men-
tality as the salient ones, based on our reading of accounts of the period and such documents as we had access to. We could have listed any of a number of other
plausible public values considerations important to
Truman and his men: concern with holding down military
spending; possible public reaction against the takeover of Japanese territory (independent of the isola-
tionist-internationalist debate); resentment over the
Pacific war and the desire to "keep Japan in her place;"
humanitarian concerns for the people of the Ryukyus,
whose islands had been battered in the war and largely
re-made in peacetime into a conglomerate of bases,
etc.[4] Because the analyst working with these categories must put his own ordering on the salience of these
factors and which need actually be included in a narra-
tive of the decision, use of the Snyder framework is

236

TABLE VIII-A - Snyder 'Situational Properties'
Applied to Okinawa Decisions

	Anticipated v. Unanticipated	Routine v. Crisis	Magnitude of values involved
NSC 13/3 Section 5 1948-49 Truman	Anticipated	Closer to routine but not exactly	Qua Okinawa decision of moderate import;as part of NSC 13/3 rather high values involved
Residual Sovereignty 1950-51 Dulles	Anticipated	Neither	Moderate to high (territorial and security question and treaty)
Executive Order 11010 1961-62 Kennedy	Anticipated	Neither	Moderate(how to rule another state's former province without jeopardizing military facilities)
1967 Communique Promise 1966-67 Johnson	Anticipated	Neither	High(U.S.-Japanese future relations)but not of highest variety
	Anticipated	Neither	High(continued good U.S/ Japan relations,security treaty, etc.)but not of highest order

237

open to the charge of being an exercise in arbitrary judgments little different from the activity of the most conventional historians. The objection could be met in part by having more than one researcher looking at the same materials to see how consistently the same factors were assigned to the same categories as a reliability check, but that would be an expensive and time-consuming process.[5]

Another alternative would be to stress the psychological environment of the decision rather than the operational one and include as data for the Snyder classification system only those factors mentioned by the actual participants in the decision process, ranking these factors when appropriate (e.g., under "common values" in 1969, six of the eight major decision participants might have cited disaffection with costly American involvements like Vietnam, three of the eight might claim to have been influenced by their reading of an isolationist surge in public opinion, etc.). This example is completely hypothetical; while I certainly used the accounts of decisions by participants to guide our cataloguing of inputs into the decision sequence according to the Snyder categories, I did not attempt to quantify these. Too much depended, it was felt, on the original selection of the individual decision-makers to be interviewed, and in any event there was no reason to suspect that they could reconstruct the many and often subtle influences on their thinking in anything like a manner lending itself to quantitative analysis.[6]

The Snyder-Robinson concept of "occasion for decision," which is referred to by the earlier Snyder-Paige designation of situational properties, proved to be of mixed value for analyzing the Okinawa cases. As Table VIII-A implies, all of the decisions were anticipated, i.e., in Snyder's usage of the term, meaning that it was known well in advance that a decision would be necessary, although the content of the decision might not be known to the decision-makers until very shortly before the decision itself. The anticipated v. unanticipated distinction (the latter applicable to crisis situations or other, unexpected occasions for action) was a useful one: all of our decisions allowed for some planning and the rather detailed consideration of options. The one possible exception to this was the Johnson decision of 1967, in which the President's options, as he saw them, changed very suddenly shortly before the summit meeting with Prime Minister Sato. The other categories were less helpful

238

because they were more difficult to operationalize satisfactorily. The time-frame category, distinguishing <u>routine</u> and <u>crisis</u> varieties was problematic because, although none of the decisions, again, involved a crisis, neither was any of them routine in the sense of having well-established action procedures or any kind of repetitive sequence as with, say, annual budgetary decisions. The final category, <u>value magnitudes</u> is also difficult to handle, much less operationalize satisfactorily, although by carefully studying a decision and interviewing participants one can develop an intuitive feel for the value stakes involved. All of the decisions have been characterized as having fairly high value magnitudes (far higher than a routine decision such as a budgetary appropriation, yet certainly lower than a decision about whether to go to war with another country or whether to approve an important treaty),,like the Nuclear Test-Ban Treaty. Four of the five decisions involved the question "what was the United States going to do with Okinawa?" - the 1961-62 decision centered on how the United States would <u>run</u> Okinawa. Each of the decisions except the first <u>was</u> made public. To the extent that an analyst is willing to allow the decisions to be regarded as dealing with Okinawa as a very important military complex, though not by itself critical to the defensive viability of Asia, they can fairly be regarded as of middle magnitude, <u>i.e.</u>, important but not all-important to the alliance, to Far East security, to America's sense of its rightful global role, etc.[7]

A final point of interest in the Snyder approach concerns his focus on identifying and describing individuals and their roles in decisions (which he describes as together comprising <u>decisional units</u>). This exercise forces the scholar to delineate clearcut - if somewhat arbitrary - boundaries of participation in any decision sequence. Paige used it with some success in the <u>Korean Decision</u>. In this study I use, implicitly rather than methodically, Snyder's three individual actor variables (<u>personality characteristics</u>, <u>social backgrounds</u>, and <u>personal values</u>) to paint our portraits; from the nature of his presentation I suspect that Paige uses them in this way also. Although the technique of carefully selecting the men who really appear to have been the central decision-makers and presenting them concisely according to fairly specific guidelines is a good one for describing individual impact on a given decision, it is not very helpful in depicting role-types that are useful for comparisons of

TABLE VIII-B- Utility of Allison Models in Okinawa Case-Studies Summarized

	Rational Actor Model I	Org. Process Model II	Bur. Politics Model III
NSC 13/3 Sect. 5 1948-49 Truman	Of modest explanatory value and only after NSC started coordinating	Of considerable value, especially organizational positions of SCAP, Defense, and State	Of considerable value, especially role of Kennan and MacArthur
Residual Sovereignty 1950-51 Dulles	Of considerable explanatory value; single decision maker	Of limited value; organizational positions formed background but did not determine outcome	Of limited explanatory value; some bargaining games occurred but rational actor dominant
Executive Order 11010 1961-62 Kennedy	Of considerable explanatory value; central coordination, detailed study and options consideration	Of some explanatory value; especially in terms of organizational input into Kaysen Task Force	Of some explanatory value, especially interaction between Task Force and USCAR
1967 Communique Promise 1966-67 Johnson	Of some explanatory value, especially during coordinated 1967 studies; outcome subject to State, JCS, Russell bargaining, however	Of some value, i.e., organizational needs (JCS) outlasting perceived need for complete control of Ryukyus	Of considerable explanatory value; interaction of Sneider group (IRG), JCS, Russell, Rusk, and the President

240

TABLE VIII-B (Cont.)

	Rational Actor Model I	Organizational Process/Model II	Bureaucratic Politics/ Model III
Nixon-Sato Communique Reversion Commitment 1969 Nixon	Of some explanatory value because of the President's reservation of final decision-making power to himself and NSC structuring of Okinawa studies	Of limited explanatory value; near-consensus precluded posturing	Of considerable explanatory value, especially concerning textiles and nuclear storage issue

roles played by different participants within such decisions or across several decisions. To facilitate this kind of comparison - to move from configurative portraits of roles - it may be desirable to develop a typology of roles to be used in comparisons of decision cases.

The Allison Models

As should be clear from the five case studies, the importance of Allison's decision-making models is considerable for analyzing cases like these (although perhaps not in the way he might like to have his models termed "important"). Certainly for these purposes the thrust of his contribution goes more in the direction of enriched description and explanation from a first-class heuristic device than toward radically new source of explanations which renders traditional ones obsolete. Allison's Models II and III (especially Model III) supplement rather than supplant Model I, but they supplement in a particularly valuable way not justly conveyed in the faint praise of a term like "enrichment." To demonstrate this let us move to the five cases.

In only one of the five decisions studied did the bureaucratic politics model appear to be of doubtful value, i.e., the Dulles residual sovereignty formula of 1950-51. In that case the rational-actor Model I is seen at its strongest: a single individual was given a tremendous amount of responsibility to act and decide on behalf of his country, albeit within certain boundaries. In the NSC 13/3 (1949) and Nixon (1969) decision sequences, bureaucratic politics contributed heavily to explaining the outcome and in the Kennedy and Johnson decisions it added a lot (all of this is summarized in Table VIII-B). The organizational process paradigm (or Model II), we found useful for explaining all of the decisions except the Dulles one, especially the 1949 Truman/NSC sequence. Model II is perhaps not as fertile a source of new insights as Model III, mainly because its focus - organizational processes and positions - is more the stuff of traditional analysis then the focus of bureaucratic politics. This latter model depicts decision outcomes as a less than rational - though not necessarily unpredictable - process involving one or more political games played more or less simultaneously by powerful men who may or may not be acting on behalf of organizational interests.

242

From this study's perspective, the failure of Model III to add much to an explanation of the Dulles decision casts serious doubt on any statement implying that satisfactory explanations of all international affairs decisions need rely on the premises of bureaucratic politics.[8] The old truisms of "the more cases examined the better" and, up to a point, "the more examinations of a case the better" apply here: ideally, as promising and innovative a model as Allison's bureaucratic politics should be tried out in a number of different contexts. It may be that in certain kinds of decision-making situations Model III may be more effective than others. Our own case-studies indicate that the model was most useful in A. explanations of decisions in which the issues were defined by the most skillful bureaucratic gamesmen within agencies and not by a central figure such as the President (e.g., especially the 1949 decision and to some extent the 1967 decision) or B. where if the central figure and his immediate staff did tend to define the issues, there were enough complex inputs from other sources (e.g., the textile lobby in the 1969 decision) that the decision was in effect shaped in part by agencies representing those sources (e.g., the Commerce Department through Mr. Stans by way of Mr. Rogers in the Nixon decision-sequence).

When the President and his staff tended to monopolize the issues (the Kennedy decision in 1961-62) or when a decision was handed over to a negotiator subject to later approval (the Dulles decision), Model III seemed a less fruitful source of explanations, and a less accurate shaper of description. Propositions based on this assessment of bureaucratic politics are fully subject to skepticism because of the limited number of cases used, but if that skepticism is a trigger to further investigation the propositions will be justified. I suggest that:

1. Bureaucratic politics explanations are likely to be fruitful and convincing when the initiative on and definition of issues is not centrally controlled by the President during the decision sequence (i.e., the President and the White House staff),

2. Bureaucratic politics explanations are likely to be fruitful and convincing when the initiative on and definition of issues is largely

243

centrally controlled by the White House but
when the White House is responsive to bureaucratic and constituent interests as well as
what it feels to be the interest of the nation
as a whole,

3. Bureaucratic politics explanations are not
   likely to be fruitful or convincing when the
   White House defines and controls issues and no
   single bureaucratic or outside interest is
   clearly favored, and

4. Bureaucratic politics explanations are not
   likely to be fruitful or convincing when a
   single individual is given responsibility and
   authority for a decision and can thus be said
   to be acting on behalf of his or her government,

To these propositions I add a fifth based on my
brief consideration of the organizational process model:

5. Organizational process explanations are likely
   to be fruitful and convincing when organizations have had time to control and define
   issues and when the White House is inclined to
   conform to rather than superimposing control
   on those organizations.

Thus in the 1948-49 decision sequence, when the White
House accepted the joint recommendations of the Defense
Department and State Department through the National
Security Council, organizational process has maximum
interest and credibility for the analyst. When the
White House or a White House delegate like Dulles or
Kaysen is allowed to manage an issue and present it to
the President for decision (as in 1969, 1951 and 1961-
62 respectively) organizational process is less central.
When the White House overrides or steers around organizational recommendations, even if it does not have an
independent source of expertise on the issue, as was
the case with President Johnson in 1967, the organizational process explanation is also not likely to be
very relevant.

On the whole the Allison models - whether regarded
as based on competing paradigms or as different "cuts
of reality" - make a substantial contribution to our
foreign policy decision analysis. If Snyder and his

244

colleagues have given us a comprehensive and detailed system for classifying and describing decision inputs, Allison has provided us with two highly imaginative alternative sets of premises which enable us through his models to detect certain kinds of phenomena that we would pick up incidently or at least much less directly using traditional rational-actor methods.[9] Numerous examples could be cited from my own investigations: the parts played by organizational interests - especially the State and Defense Departments - hardening antagonistic interests between 1945 and 1948; the USCAR-Tokyo-Washington triangle of 1961-62; the inter-organizational consensus-building of Sneider and Halperin in 1966-67.

The tools of bureaucratic politics analysis, although in need of improvement, are well worth incorporating into any framework that purposts to analyze the foreign policy making of conglomerates of agencies. If I belaboured Allison's three-model analysis in my development of the Okinawa decisions, it was to show that his dismissal of the rational Model I could be as questionable, and indeed myopic, as the traditional reliance on rational actor metaphors had been for theoreticians and practicioners these many centuries. It was found that there are some types of decision-sequences in which the single-rational-actor classical model is at least as appropriate as his Models II and III. The cataloguing and charting of what kinds of decisions are most susceptible to organizational process and bureaucratic politics analysis and what kinds to the problems of the rational actor are eminently worthy research goals.

The Lindblom Models

The reader is reminded that when the Lindblom models have been referred to in this study and rational comprehensive decision making contrasted with incremental, this has merely been an extension of Lindblom's own contrast between his real theoretical innovation (incrementalism) and a kind of paradigm of the rationalist conventional wisdom of policy analysis. Lindblom may thus be closely identified with incrementalism in much the same way that Allison is with bureaucratic politics.

Unquestionably the Okinawa cases offer a certain amount of support for a model of foreign policy based on disjointed and incremental processes of choice making. The initial case study fit most closely with this perspective: decisions regarding the Ryukyus evolved tentatively and experimentally in several military and non-military centers of power. By 1948 the thinking of these diverse centers, including SCAP in Tokyo, the Secretary of State's office and the Policy Planning Staff of the State Department, and the Defense Department (particularly the Army) had converged around the idea of a dramatic economic and social, as well as military, build-up on Okinawa. Although the National Security Council became a vehicle for drawing together points of view on Okinawa policy, it was not really acting as the kind of central coordinating mechanism which Lindblom terms essential to the rational comprehensive brand of policy formation.

At the other extreme from this fairly clearly incrementalist case were the 1950-51 residual sovereignty decision and the 1961-62 Kaysen-Kennedy reforms. It is something of an overstatement to say "other extreme," but these sequences do contrast sharply with that of 1948-49 in the degree of focused authority determining the decision outcomes. In the case of the Dulles episode, apparently a great deal of weighing of alternatives went on with the interested parties in both Washington and Tokyo, but the last word was, at least formally, Dulles'. This is not to argue that residual sovereignty came about by anything like a synoptic, all-options-considered process, but rather that incrementalism does not do adequate descriptive justice to Dulles either. As for the decision sequence leading to the Kennedy executive order, while a certain amount of bureaucratic pluralism and limited-options decision making did characterize the early stages, there was also a remarkable amount of central coordination of agencies and a wideranging weighing of options by the Kaysen group. Because the low-level classified documents to which I had access (comprising, in all likelihood, 95 percent of the total paper records of the Kaysen Task Force) indicated that the Task Force was a true investigatory body, not a mere cosmetic device, I assume that the few top-level discussions and highly classified memoranda that came out of the sequence probably touched on even more controversial options (e.g., conceivably even the return of the Ryukyus). What the Dulles and Kennedy decision sequences suggest is not that foreign policy decision making on the Ryukyus resembled ideal rational models, but rather that the sequences did not particularly fit with the increm-

246

ental either and that therefore some other model seems in order. Such a model would have to take account of the conservative-incremental and the rationally coordinated aspects of decisions and offer a guide to when one aspect or the other is likely to be dominant.

The Johnson and Nixon decision sequences, I would contend, fell between the other three in their closeness of resemblence to incremental models. There was a certain amount of central coordination and rationalization of the options weighing process in both cases. This was accomplished through the Sneider-led Ryukyus Working Group in 1966-67 and the Sneider-Halperin NSC staff management of the issue in 1969. Because in both cases the range of options was bi-modal and boiled down to "promise to give Okinawa back" or "not promise to give Okinawa back" the analysis of multiple alternatives which Lindblom characterizes as so strongly favoring change-at-the-margins was not really necessary. Hence a great deal of energy could be focused on debating the pro's and con's of a two-proposition issue. Incrementalist critics might well respond that for the 1969 decision, in spite of former Secretary of State Rogers' statement to the contrary, that there was really no consideration of the option of not returning Okinawa to the Japanese. This might lead to the conclusion that the brand of decision-making which occurred in that year was one-option-only, with only the nuances and terms of the communique subject to negotiation. According to this analysis the implicit promise of a prompt return of the Ryukyus in the Sato-Johnson comcunique of 1967 forced a single-option, "no alternatives seriously considered" (thus incremental) situation on the Nixon people. As with the 1966-67 sequence, in which there was a rational, centrally directed re-thinking of Ryukyus policy within the bureaucracy but ultimately a decision which reflected demands from diverse bureaucratic components as well as Congressional input, the 1969 decision was a hybrid of synoptic and incremental elements. Neither model, again, is entirely satisfactory as a depiction of the organic workings of the decision sequence.

On balance, then, if Lindblom provides some important departure points for a foreign policy analytic framework, his incremental model and analysis do not fare that well in light of the Okinawa cases. It may well be that specialized foreign policy making areas such as Ryukyus policy lend themselves to centrally coordinated and carefully studies on-going considerations of alternatives and that the Lindblom formulations are more appropriate to exceedingly complicated foreign policy decisions or to domestic decisions with much broader input. Okinawa decision-making, although not centralized in the sense that, say, United States policy in the UN Trusteeship Council or of the Securities and Exchange Commission is, always involved comparatively few agencies and very little domestic input.

Inferences from the Okinawa Case-Studies

Here the objective is to offer some policy implications of this research that go beyond the banal and pro forma codas óf altogether too many otherwise meritorious studies in international relations. One particularly painful and intractable facet of the whole analysis centered on the external setting of decision-making of what might be called the Sprout-Snyder school and the individual actors in a decision (in effect a decision "cast"). If one takes seriously the notion--and it is really a common sense one -- that elements of foreign governments and societies actually enter into the process of decision-making in Washington and are not just perceived out in some phenomenological distance, then does it really make sense to limit consideration of decision actors to American governmental participants? Why could not Yoshida or Sato or Miki be bona fide members of decision "casts?" Surely they were as central to the action as, say, Acheson, Rusk, and McNamara in their respective sequences. This gets close to the heart of a problem which Snyder, Rosenau, Singer and a host of other students of international events have been grappling with: the dichotomy between national foreign policies and the process by which two or more national policies combine in patterns in the international system. Does it make sense to dichotomize always along national lines -- e.g., America v. Japan? Were not Sato and Nixon and Johnson more of a common mind on some aspects of Ryukyus policy (and alliance policy in general) than with the Japanese left on one side of the Pacific and some of the more orthodox minds in the American military on the other? These are not purely academic questions. They have been taken up seriously, although far from systematically or meticulously, in the literature on linkage politics. I submit that it may well be desirable in future analyses of decision participants, to experiment with a typology that includes the key performers from all sides. Allison's solution (already alluded to), that of dis-

248

carding the theatrical metaphors for those of "team competition" is no solution at all: often the members of one so-called team are playing with members of the other side at the expense of their own team-mates. This is especially true of alliance politics decision-making. One particularly telling case in point from this study would be a comparison of the position of Ambassador Reischauer and Japanese leaders and the American Joint Chiefs of Staff respectively for closeness of fit on the Ryukyus question.

A second difficult but important area surrounds the arguments about rationality in international political choices. The Okinawa studies strongly suggest that rationality and coordinated central control are not dead or beyond the reach of modern bureaucratic establishments. In the case of the Kaysen commission, for example, the path of least resistance may well have been to let the issue continue to drift rather than bringing together diverse and contentious elements of the defense and diplomatic establishments. Kennedy and his staff could have settled for a purely symbolic "fact-finding" panel and some high-blown presidential rhetoric (there are a few in the United States and Japan who suggest that this is in fact what happened). But the Kaysen investigation was far from superficial. It kicked up an enormous amount of bureaucratic dust and, if its results seemed incremental and token, its reverberations were certainly felt and felt widely. Okinawa policy was never again the same after 1962; most Japanese I talked with regarded the Task Force as the most important Ryukyus-related happening since the Peace Treaty, and--if partially symbolic--an important first step in the return of their territory.

Blue-ribbon panels are nothing unusual in American government. As often as not they appear to poke around, uncovering dust and chipped surfaces, but ignoring the really debilitating dirt and dangerous fissuring in the policy forming structures of government. But not always. Sometimes house cleaning and repairs are actually called for, as in the case of the Kaysen investigation. The real issue is whether policies can be turned around by any other means as effectively (or otherwise dramatized). The critics of Allison have been right to contend that a method for cutting through much of the bureaucratic gamesmanship and intrigue does exist: i.e., simply capturing the attention and interest of the President or a key member of his staff. Once Kennedy became convinced that United States rule in the Ryukyus was becoming a burden to Japanese-Ameri-

can relations, it did not matter that an interdepartmental body challenging long-held assumptions was offensive to some important men in the armed services.

Regardless of the extent to which rational policy
making can be said to have occurred within the critical Okinawa decisions, there was an extraordinary degree of agreement, in the case of the last three decision sequences, that successful, desirable, exemplary
decision-making had taken place, in spite of some deficiencies and disappointments. For William Bundy,
Okinawa was a "dream case"---and he was not alone.
Clapp, in her account of the resolution of the Okinawa
problem between 1966 and 1969 frequently alludes to
fortunate circumstances, talented individuals and dili-
gent consensus building. Perhaps the most salient
question, then, is: to what extent was the relatively
efficient functioning of the decision making process
for Okinawa the result of favorable circumstances
unique to that case or a small class of such cases and
how much of that effectiveness can be explained and
then applied to other cases?

A number of factors certainly aided the guiding of
Ryukyus policy and do appear to be limited to a small
number of potential situations, or to have been the
product of happy historical coincidence: 1. the fact of
Japan's total defeat in the Second World War and its
great dependence on the United States; 2. the management of the issue in the mid-1960's by a remarkably
broadminded group of individuals, including Reischauer,
Sneider, Halperin, and Alexis Johnson; a perception of
Okinawa problem as one important enough to argue out
but not central enough to have blood-letting or show-
downs between governmental interests; and 4. the near
total lack of public interest or participation in the
issue within a foreign affairs arena dominated by Vietnam, the Middle East, weapons systems battles, and the
Communist "threat." In the case of number four I wish
to make it clear that I do not equate the lack of American public interest with a "desirable" or "effective"
decision-making environment for foreign policy, but two
realities   be kept in mind. First, public discussions of international security matters such as the
Panama Canal Zone, troops in Europe, and bases in Asia
have tended to degenerate into exaggerated confrontations between exponents of so-called "strong defense
postures" and "free world security" and those of "America keeping out of where it doesn't belong" or avoiding
"colonialist adventures." Second, aside from the ques-

tion of whether the arrival of foreign policy issues
in the public forum is healthy or detrimental to the
resolution of those issues such public debates do sometimes interfere with the work of dedicated professionals of good will who are attempting to work out realistic compromises, as was the case with Okinawa policy
-- at least after 1961.

The case studies demonstrate, however, that there
were positive aspects of the handling of Okinawa which
might be applicable to many kinds of policy making.
These do not guarantee enlightened outcomes, if for no
other reason than that only a modest part of international affairs problems are manipulable by governments,
and only a portion of that part manipulable by any one
government.[10] But some of these affirmative aspects
may increase the prospects for success. As a general
rule, for example, it is probably best not to allow
a single agency or department to achieve the degree of
stake in and control over a definable foreign policy
area that the Army had over Okinawa, regardless of such
an agency's apparent success in managing its bailiwick.
Ad hoc and/or interdepartmental review groups do not
constitute a guarantee to the flow of new ideas and
methods, but they increase the odds that innovation can
take place, and that grievances, inside or outside of
the policy formulating mechanism, can be heard and
dealt with. There has been too much emphasis in the
literature and in the recommendations of Hoover Commis-
sions and Wriston Committees (themselves ad hoc enter-
prises) on permanent, structural changes, watchdog
committees, weekly review boards and the like, which
tend to become routinized, acclimated or co-opted by
the policy makers they are established to oversee. If
a permanent mechanism is desirable, it would be the
kind of mechanism which can assemble a Kaysen Task
Force with real teeth and purpose at the first sign of
trouble that appears to call for more than minor adjustment attempts. And whatever the merits of a
finely tuned coordinating instrument like the Kissinger
National Security Council, there should be more than
one source of potential policy review. The sort of
pluralistic base for policy innovation called for in
different ways by Lindblom, Alexander George[11] and
others is particularly appropriate to the process of
internal criticism of given foreign affairs positions.

Where some degree of central coordination and at
least the attempt of rationality and comprehensiveness

in the review of new alternatives is desirable is in
the process of actually undertaking that review. What
must be nurtured and carefully coordinated is the access and input of as many intra-governmental and extra-
governmental interest groups as possible. The substantive issues, ranges of choices and options should not
be centrally determined. A conscious effort should be
made to allow for suggestions and directions from policy globalists and generalists -- the Dulleses and Kay-
sens and Johnsons -- but not to the exclusion of the
specialists, alliance advocates and bilateralists: the
Reischauers, Sneiders, and Ungers. The most felicitous
aspect of the three critical decision sequences leading
to the reversion decision by the end of the 1960's was
that key policy actors were able to see to it that men
of quite different casts of mind but similar weight and
influence were brought together and convinced that they
had to produce solutions.

The close and systematic examination of a succession
of related decision episodes can yield a certain amount
of wisdom from hindsight and experience with or without
the analytic structuring of models for policy-making.
But the use of such models, besides providing a way of
simplifying reality that lets us see the common denomi-
ators of complex chains of events and laying foundations
for theoretical explanations of why those events occur
in certain patterns, is that they also make the process
of policy recommendation easier. It is here that they
go beyond the function of providing the historian and
social scientist with a kind of compass for traversing
the reconstructed past and offer pay-offs to the patient
and introspective policy practitioner as well. Insights
generated from models which are seen to have a highly
imperfect fit with the events they attempt to "structure"
retro-actively are not sufficient to furnish either the
academician or the practitioner with a great deal of confidence and satisfaction. This is certainly true of the
Okinawa cases discussed in the preceding pages. What remains to be accomplished, then, is the setting forth of
a more finely drawn framework for analysis and model,
which-- while not discarding totally or relying too heavily on its predecessors-- offers the prospect of a more
reliable basis for both understanding and correcting decision episodes still unfolding. It is to this that we
turn in the final section.

A Critical/Incremental Decisions Model

The recognition that decision processes, including those churning out Ryukyus policy, did often strongly conform to Lindblom's "muddling through" incrementalism, but tended to depart dramatically from it on certain occasions was an inducement to construct a new model to account for such departures. The object here is to use the investigation of the Okinawa cases to attempt to bridge the sharp gaps between rational/incremental and rational-actor/bureaucratic politics gaps which have puzzled Lindblom and Allison in different ways. The model I am introducing should be viewed as informal and empirical rather than formal deductive in character. The model is based on the case studies only (although I believe it may have very wide applicability) and is rather more similar to the kind of modeling done by Allison than the more abstract and general models of, say, Riker, Downs, or Mancur Olson. That is not to imply that it is tentative, loose, or purely descriptive; however, it probably will require refinement and further empirical-case investigation which is well beyond the scope of the present study.

Essentially the model is a rejection of Lindblom's dichotomy between rational and incremental policy-creation, preferring to see these processes as opposite ends of a continuum. Many decisions, including some of these cases, contain strong elements of both of these styles. I do not, however, want to equivocate and level cheapshot criticism at Lindblom, which in effect says: "you oversimplify: it's really a matter of a little of this and a little of that mixed together." That kind of superficial complaint misconstrues the whole purpose of modeling in the social sciences: the production of parsimonious, streamlined, and inevitably somewhat oversimplified representations of social processes--the search for common denominators. Rather, my model sees some decision-making as clearly incremental in character, some as highly rational, some as a mix of both, and in any given foreign policy arena (e.g., Latin American policy, Ryukyus policy, arms control policy, economic aid policy) a switching back and forth across these different modes depending on the substantive issues, time-frame, manpower, and various related factors. What I call critical decisions within the model often are preceded by comparatively rational and comprehen-

253

sive reviews of existing policies and options, characterized in both journalistic jargon and "bureaucratese" as "fact finding missions," "full-scale investigation," "House-cleaning" and so forth.

For a concise picture of what the critical/incremental decision model is all about I offer some descriptive postulates, sequentially arranged:

1. Foreign policies may initially evolve by improvisation, serendipity, short-term consideration views to historical and legal precedent, or wide ranging, highly self conscious processes often involving high-level studies (e.g., NSSM's) and sometimes public debate,

2. Regardless of how they begin, policies tend to proceed pragmatically, incrementally, and without rigid adherence to a grand design, especially in pluralist foreign policy-making establishments (as described by Allison, Kissinger, Lindblom, and others) but not necessarily limited to them,

3. Occasionally a truly comprehensive review and overhaul of a policy occurs due to a variety of factors in the internal or external policy-making settings (cf.Snyder)or both, and this critical decision sequence entails processes falling outside the more routine, incremental decision pattern,

4. Critical decision-sequences involve marked changes in the decision cast (i.e., participants) in a particular policy arena (e.g., Ryukyus policy); after the critical decision, which normally brings clearly identifiable changes in policy, the decision cast may or may not return to the way it was before,

5. Changes in decision-cast which accompany and often signal critical decisions usually involve greater numbers of participants than for incremental decisions, but at the same time this participation is usually more centrally controlled, i.e., from a higher policy-making level such as the White House, the National Security Council, or a high-level interdepartmental committee, and

6. <u>Critical decisions</u> usually, although not
necessarily, <u>call for</u> Presidential participation or approval, at least in the final
stages.

In essence the model says: "Watch the cast of
characters participating in an issue-arena; when it be-
gins to change, something's afoot (even if no formal
announcement to that effect is made); watch it more
closely. If the change is permanent, or, if after what
appears to be a <u>critical decision</u>, there is a <u>subse-
quent</u> change in <u>the cast most centrally involved in</u> the
issue, look for substantive policy changes of major dimensions. Conversely, "if the decision-cast appears to
return to exactly its composition before the <u>critical
decision</u>, be wary of any claims or prospects <u>for major
changes</u> occurring," might be added as a corollary. It
may be thought, at first glance, that the model states
the obvious: "Routine, incremental decisions are
churned out at the middle and lower bureaucratic echelons; when higher-ups or outsiders step in it is usually because of some turbulence or negative feedback in
the policy process, and one can expect to see some
changes made." But the model also says that <u>decision-
cast</u> changes <u>can</u> involve coordinated, qualitative improvement in <u>the</u> degree of rationality and the comprehensiveness of policy-option review undertaken. And
this is not truism, for it fundamentally opposes the
direction taken by Lindblom and, to some extent, Allison, a major current-perhaps even the main-stream-of
bureaucratic policy-analysis today.

The Okinawa Decisions: Another Look

Having advanced a foreign policy analytic framework which draws heavily but selectively on the work of
Snyder <u>et al.</u>, Allison and Lindblom, we return to the
five case-studies to see how some refinements might be
applied. These accounts focus only on those refinements, so the reader is referred to the individual decision-case chapters to recall any background features
needed (and   Tables VIII-D through <u>VIII-H</u> summarize the
individual decision casts).

255

TABLE VIII-C- Decision Cast Role-Category Criteria

Role-Type	Presence of Distinguishing Characteristics		
	Formal authority and responsibility criterion	Perceived creative input criterion	Extent of interest and involvement criterion
DECISION-EFFECTOR	High	Variable	High
DECISION-INFLUENCER	Variable: Low to high	High	Variable
DECISION-APPROVER	High	Low	Low

256

The 1948-49 Build-Up Commitment

Recall that the original lists of decision actors for each case were composed from three sources of data: documents, interviews with known participants, and secondary source accounts. For the Truman decision of 1949 I relied heavily on the first and third of these to compose and refine my list of individual actors for the Snyder framework. These same sources form the basis for composing the decision-cast (see Table VIII-C); here I discuss the conversion of that descriptive listing into the more analytic role-type categories of the decision-cast.

In all of the foreign policy decisions studied, the important participants were frequently shapers of the outcomes not to the degree of seniority or the political status of their formal position, but rather to the degree that they chose to become involved (e.g., Richard Sneider), happened to become involved (Ball), had the time to become involved (Kaysen)-- or some combination of these and related circumstances. The construct of the decision-cast attempts to take this often overlooked fact into account--i.e., that formal authority and responsibility criteria are only one set of determinants of how and to what degree an individual participates in a decision. It is more useful to focus on an official's role in a particular sequence (often heavily influenced by criteria such as simple creative input or extent of interest) in arriving at the constellation of decision-maker influence than to rely on formal roles and expectations. This in itself is common sense. The utility of establishing the three simplified role-types depicted in Table VIII-C is that it provides a wide range of possibilities for comparing an individual's "clout" in a variety of contexts and over time and permits the depiction of numerous influence patterns-- not perfectly-- but manageably.(What determines effector, influencer, and approver roles is illustrated in Table VIII-C).
President Truman is rather easily classified as decision effector (ref. p. 102); although his interest in and "time for" the Ryukyus was not great, it was his signature and concern about in Japan policy as a whole which activated NSC 13/3 (including section 5 on the Ryukyus) and made it United States policy. The list of influencers, i.e., those who may and usually did have more creative (substantive) input and involve-

ment than the President but did not have the authority
to execute as wide-ranging a document as NSC 13/3, is a
long one, including: Secretary of State Marshall, Secretary of Defense Forrestal, George Kennan of Policy
Planning in the State Department, Army Under-Secretary
Draper, SCAP MacArthur, and The Joint Chiefs of Staff.
The extent of their influence varied considerably with
Kennan, MacArthur, and the JSC deeply involved in the
substance of the commitment in Okinawa, and Forrestal,
Draper, and Marshall less so. They all did share two
attributes, however: 1. making identifiable inputs into
the content of the NSC document, and 2. lacking the
authority to make the kind of commitment to an economic
as well as military pledge to Okinawa that the President could. In the approver category I have placed
Army Secretary Royall and NSC Executive Secretary
Souers, with authority approximately equal to or greater than several of the decision-influencers, but who
chose to play a more formal and perfunctory role (at
least on the basis of the available evidence. It is
conceivable that the sorts of changes which were initiated in Okinawa as a result of NSC 13/3 could have
been effected at the Secretary of Defense or Secretary
of State level, had the decision-makers not wished to
incorporate them into part of the broader Japan policy
statement contained in the NSC paper. But the fact
that the President did endorse that document made it
the most important Ryukyus decision in the five years
following the islands' conquest.

The 1949 commitment was not only an important decision, but also a critical decision in the sense defined by this model. For the first time since 1945
there was a truly coordinated interdepartmental statement of Okinawa policy, and, significantly, the State
Department and the White House became directly involved for the first time, too (helped by the coordinating mechanism of the NSC). As a result of the tacit
agreement reached by MacArthur and Kennan regarding
Okinawa's future, a decision process was initiated
which forced some degree of structured inter-departmental communication on the matter, although bureaucratic politics and uncoordinated games probably played
an even larger role.

The NSC decision was dominated by policy globalists rather then those who placed top priority on Japanese sensitivities: Kennan, Marshall, the JCS, the
President himself. Even MacArthur, who might be seen
as so Japan-oriented by 1948 as to be more of an al-

258

TABLE VIII-D- Decision Cast for the 1948-49 Build-Up Commitment

Decision and Time Frame	Decision Cast	Organizational Participants
To make a commitment to a permanent or open-ended American military presence in the Ryukyus	President Harry Truman (effector)	White House
Spring 1948 - May 6, 1949	Secretary of State George Marshall (influencer)	State Department
	Policy Planning Staff Head George Kennan (influencer)	
	Secretary of Defense James Forrestal (influencer)	Defense Department
	Army Under Secretary William Draper (influencer)	Army
	The Joint Chiefs of Staff (influencer)	JCS
	SCAP Douglas MacArthur (influencer)	SCAP
	Army Secretary Kenneth Royall (approver)	Army
	NSC Executive Secretary Sidney Souers (approver)	National Security Council

259

liance politics figure, was ultimately concerned about
Okinawa as a center of gravity for American military
power in East Asia. Although there were alliance
boosters within the State Department who encouraged the
return of the Ryukyus between 1945 and 1948, none was
numbered among those who acted as influencers in the
decision sequence which really counted, that leading
to NSC 13/3. Strictly speaking there were no bilateralists either, although men like Draper and Kennan did
push for the economic and social development of the
Ryukyus (which found its way into the final document in
order to make the United States strategic position
there more dependable).

The 1950-51 Residual Sovereignty Formula

With the second decision-case we have the only instance of a decision-effector below the Presidential
level in the five cases. That was of course the
special negotiator, John Foster Dulles, who by all accounts conceived and delivered residual sovereignty
himself, and had the authority to endorse it again on
behalf of the President at the San Francisco conference. According to the best information I could get
paramount influencers in this decision were General
Douglas MacArthur in the field and the Joint Chiefs of
Staff in Washington, especially Generals Bradley and
Collins. All advised Dulles to minimize the concessions made to the Japanese on the Ryukyus. Some whom
I interviewed indicated that Dulles wanted to make more
guarantees to the Japanese concerning their residual
rights in the islands. I characterize President Truman and Secretary of State Acheson as approvers in this
decision sequence. They had little personal expertise
in Japanese (much less Ryukyuan) affairs and formally
delegated virtually unimpaired negotiating power to
Dulles.

Although Dulles was fairly clearly a globalist, he
was more sensitive to alliance concerns than any others
member of the decision-cast, including General Mac-
Arthur. If the residual sovereignty formula can be
seen as a victory for global strategists from one angle,
it can also be seen as a concession of considerable
value to the Japanese, as the military readily pointed
out between 1961 and 1969. As for the applicability of
the critical/incremental decisions model, there was
never much doubt that the negotiation of the peace

260

TABLE VIII-E— Decision Cast for the 1950-51 Residual Sovereignty Formula

Decision and Time Frame	Decision Cast	Organizational Participants
To use the residual sovereignty formula to relieve Japanese fears about the legal status of the Ryukyus without undermining complete American freedom of military action there	Negotiator John Foster Dulles (effector)	State Department
	SCAP Douglas MacArthur (influencer)	Defense Department SCAP
	Joint Chiefs of Staff, especially Generals Bradley and Collins (influencer)	JCS
Summer 1950 - Summer 1951	President Harry Truman (approver)	White House
	Secretary of State Dean Acheson (approver)	State Department

treaty with Japan would be a crucial time for American policy in the Ryukyus. Any American negotiator would have to become involved in the affairs of the archipelago as would the White House and the Congress for that matter, although less directly. Although it is not clearly known just how much freedom Dulles felt he had in his disposing of the Ryukyus matter or how "comprehensive" his review of alternatives really was, it is certain that the possibility that the islands would be returned or their status substantially modified was far greater during those negotiations than during the five years preceding or the five years following them.

The 1961-62 Kennedy-Kaysen Innovations

The decision effector in the 1961-62 cast was the President, who had the review of Okinawa policy initiated and who signed the executive order effecting the decision six months later. There appear to have been no fewer than seven separate, though not equal, influencers in the inner decision-cast: Carl Kaysen of the White House Staff, Ambassador Reischauer, Atty. Gen. Kennedy, Army Under-Secretary Ailes, General Lemnitzer and the JCS, High Commissioner Caraway, and George Ball, Deputy Under-Secretary of State. With the exception of Mr. Ball and Mr. Kennedy, I interviewed each of these individuals (Gen. Lemnitzer representing the Joint Chiefs) and each characterized the other five as central to some phase of the decision sequence, substantively as well as formally. The names of McGeorge Bundy, Secretary of State Rusk, and Secretary of Defense McNamara came up, but they were described more as overseers or, in the case of Bundy, coordinators who let others get much closer to the issue. These latter I call approvers, although the line between, say, Secretary Rusk as an approver and JCS Chairman Lemnitzer as an influencer is a thin one indeed. At the high end of the influence scale, of course, were Kaysen, who led the Task Force and made personal recommendations to the President, and Reishauer and Caraway, who in very different ways helped get the Kaysen mission started in the first place. Mr. Ball's period of influencer and involvement was extremely short, but as Table VIII-F indicates, influencers need not have heavy, lengthy, or extensive involvement: a short conversation will suffice as influence. The vast majority of those interviewed concerning the 1961-62 sequence agreed that Ball was pivotal in this respect: getting the Presi-

262

TABLE VIII-F— Decision Cast for the 1961-62 Okinawa Administrative Reforms

Decision and Time Frame	Decision Cast	Organizational Participants
To amend Executive Order 10713 to allow for a civilian Civil Administrator on Okinawa and increased Japanese participation in the economic development of the Ryukyus and related changes	President John F. Kennedy (effector)	White House
August 1961 – March 1962	Presidential Assistant Carl Kaysen and his Task Force Associates (influencer)	
	Presidential Assistant McGeorge Bundy (influencer)	
	Deputy Under Secretary of State George Ball (influencer)	State Department
	Under Secretary of the Army Stephen Ailes (influencer)	Army Department
	High Commissioner Lt. Gen. Paul Caraway (influencer)	USCAR
	Secretary of Defense Robert McNamara (approver)	Defense Department
	Secretary of the Army Elvis Stahr (approver)	Army Department
	The Joint Chiefs of Staff (approver)	Joint Chiefs of Staff
	Secretary of State Dean Rusk (approver)	State Department

263

dent's attention fastened on Okinawa.

In spite of the President's and Kaysen's globalist orientation, the 1962 decision was in an important sense a victory for the Japan-partisans like Reischauer. Mr. Kennedy and his Deputy Special Assistant regarded the concessions to the Okinawans and Japanese embodied in Executive Order 11010. as a long run gain for global strategy even if it appeared to be a short run loss. High Commissioner Caraway and the Joint Chiefs of Staff disagreed but were overruled. The Kaysen Task Force and the executive order temporarily but effectively removed control of Okinawa policy, which had been dominated by the High Commissioner and the JCS through the Army Deputy Chief of Staff for Military Operations in the Pentagon and, before 1958, the Military Governor in Tokyo, from the military and subjected it to White House and State Department scrutiny. The review of past policy conducted by the Task Force came as close to rational-comprehensive decision-making as one is likely to get in modern foreign policy, with a two-week study mission on top of several weeks of inter-departmental information gathering and sharing in the fall of 1961.

The 1967 Johnson Reversion Promise

As the final spokesman for the United States in the 1967 summit and communique, President Johnson was the single decision-effector for the 1966-67 Ryukyus policy-review sequence. No fewer than eight decision participants seems to warrant the designation influencer: Secretary Rusk, Ambassadors Reischauer and Johnson, Asst. Secretary William Bundy, Japan Country Director and Ryukyus Working Group head Sneider, Deputy Assistant Secretary of Defense Halperin, Army Commissioner Unger, and Senator Russell. The Joint Chiefs of Staff and Army Deputy Under-Secretary Siena I have chosen to classify as approvers, the former because they supported the final watered down commitment made by the President and their specific influence role is not well established, the latter because he entered the decision sequence rather late, in June of 1967, and seems to have been more of a "facilitator" on behalf of the Army in the Working Group, than a source of substantive recommendations. Secretary McNamara almost certainly falls within the approver category by his own account and that of others. General Unger's designa-

TABLE VIII-G— Decision Cast for the 1967 Johnson Reversion Promise

Decision and Time Frame	Decision Cast	Organizational Participants
To express desire to return Ryukyu Islands to Japan when feasible and offer return of the Bonin Islands as a good-will gesture	President Lyndon Johnson (effector)	White House
Early 1966 – November 1967	Secretary of State Dean Rusk (influencer)	State Department
	Assistant Secretary of State William Bundy (influencer)	
	Japan Country Director and Ryukyus Working Group Head Richard Sneider (influencer)	
	Ambassador to Japan Edwin Reischauer (influencer)	
	Ambassador to Japan U. Alexis Johnson (influencer)	
	Senator Richard Russell (influencer)	Senate
	Deputy Assistant Secretary of Defense Morton Halperin (influencer)	Defense Department
	The Joint Chiefs of Staff (approver)	Joint Chiefs of Staff
	Deputy Under Secretary of the Army James Siena (approver)	Army Department
		(CONT.)

265

TABLE VIII-G (Cont.) - Decision Cast for the 1967 Johnson Reversion Promise

Decision Cast	Organizational Participants
Secretary of Defense Robert McNamara (approver)	Defense Department
High Commissioner Lt. Gen. Ferdinand Unger (influencer)*	USCAR

*influencer with many elements of approver

tion may be subject to question: he was chosen as an influencer because his reporting on the unsettled conditions on Okinawa and the reality of the impending political crisis seems to have affected other influencers, including Ambassador Johnson and probably the Joint Chiefs, the latter in the direction of moderation and open-mindedness regarding the policy reassessments in progress in the IRG.

As indicated in Chapter 6, the 1967 decision can be called a temporary and unexpected setback for the alliance-partisans: the Sneiders, Bundy's, Halperins, and Reischauers in favor of those with a more world-wide military strategy bent like Senator Russell, the JCS, and perhaps Secretary Rusk. But it was also noted that the 1966-67 sequence left the climate of thinking in Washington about the Ryukyus profoundly changed, doubtless making easier the Nixon administration's job in 1969. This decision-sequence was a most important empirical source for the critical/incremental decisions model and thus, logically, conforms to it very well. The activation of an inter-departmental review group to reconsider the Okinawa question, allowing substantial State Department input for the first time, was a dramatic department from past procedure, as was persuading the Joint Chiefs of Staff to actually participate in the review in 1967. The President would almost certainly have been far more in touch with and receptive to this activity had it not been for the Vietnam War. As it was, he did not have the opportunity to directly confront the work of the IRG because of the decision of Secretary Rusk not to pass it on to him. Even if he had, however, it is doubtful that the Bundy-supervised recommendations could have survived the hard skepticism of Senator Russell. Evidence for this lies in the fact that Bundy himself helped work on the communique draft, talked with the President and had supported the stronger commitment to the return of Okinawa version that was finally rejected.

The 1969 Nixon Reversion Decision

Mr. Nixon reserved the right of final decision on reversion and the most salient terms of the reversion agreement to himself, thus qualifying as decision-effector. Secretary of State Rogers, from whom one might have expected an approver's role given the influence of the Kissinger staff and the fact that

Sneider and Halperin were on that staff, comes very close to being a second effector because of his integral role in the process of negotiating the communique with Foreign Minister Aichi. Instead, however, I place him in the influencer category because of the President's authority in signing the communique and his reservation of the right to decide the nuclear question and pass on other questions himself. Other influencers were Asst. Secretary of Defense for International Security Affairs Nutter, Sneider and Halperin of the NSC Staff, Deputy Secretary of State Alexis Johnson, and Army Deputy Under-Secretary Siena. The Joint Chiefs of Staff were the major approver (and a reluctant one) and although I did not include Secretary Laird or Special Assistant Kissinger in the decision-cast in Chapter II they might be seen as decision approvers as well (the categories are descriptive and suggestive rather than rigid).

By the spring of 1969 the long process during which global strategy and the strengthening of the Japan alliance, (rather than the holding of prerogative in Okinawa) came to be seen as tightly interrelated, reached fruition. There was no longer a preconceived conflict between giving back the Ryukyus and keeping the American Western Pacific position strong; rather, the conflict was between maintaining that position and damaging it by antagonizing the Okinawans with delays and frustrating the LDP, guardians of the close alliance. Although the Nixon administration's moves to make good on the tacit pledge of the Johnson administration to return the archipelago "within a few years," might have been predicted, they were hardly routine or incremental in character. A major review of earlier politico-military assessments was undertaken by the National Security Council staff and the links between both the nuclear storage question and the textile issue and reversion were explored in depth for the first time. The management of Ryukyus policy, which had been returned to the hands of the Joint Chiefs and USCAR (for the most part) during the December 1967-January 1969 period, was again coopted by interdepartmental committees and the White House (and after June, the Secretary of State's office). Former members of the Nixon administration revealed that holding on to Okinawa until the Indochina conflict was under better control was an option considered, but rejected because of its unacceptable cost to the Japanese-American alliance. The decision-sequence culminating in Mr. Nixon's announcement that Okinawa would be returned nuclear-free (but

268

TABLE VIII-H- Decision Cast for the 1969 Nixon Reversion Commitment

Decision and Time Frame	Decision Cast	Organizational Participants
To promise the return of the Ryukyus to the Japanese by 1972 January 1969 - November 1969	President Richard Nixon (effector)	White House
	Secretary of State William Rogers (influencer)	State Department
	National Security Council Staff Member Richard Sneider (influencer)	National Security Council
	National Security Council Staff Member Morton Halperin (influencer)	
	Assistant Secretary of Defense Warren Nutter (influencer)	Defense Department
	Deputy Under Secretary of State U. Alexis Johnson (influencer)	State Department
	Army Deputy Under Secretary James Siena (influencer)	Army Department
	The Joint Chiefs of Staff (approver)	Joint Chiefs of Staff

269

without prejudicing the right to consult with the Japanese about using these weapons at any Japanese base) was the fifth time the supervision of Ryukyus policy was taken out of military hands and re-fashioned since the original occupation in 1945, i.e., the fifth critical decision.

[1]Snyder, Bruck, and Sapin began work on decision-making in 1954 with a paper published by Princeton University; their major publication on decision theory, op. cit., was published in 1962. Rosenau's book on linkages, op. cit., came out in 1969; Allison's major work on bureaucratic politics, Essence of Decision, cit., appeared in 1971.

[2]E.g., Selden, op. cit., and Halliday & McCormack, op. cit.

[3]This was a major criticism of Herbert McCloskey, op. cit., in Snyder-Bruck-Sapin., cit.,pp. 186-205.

[4]We did, however, select the most relevant and demonstrably salient public values.

[5]McCloskey, op. cit.

[6]Richard Snyder has distinguished between "in order to" motives and "because of" motives. The former are conscious which the decision-maker recalls and can be verbalized, the latter are normally semi-conscious or unconscious motives. Citation by James Rosenau in "The Premises and Promises of Decision-Making Analysis," in James C. Charlesworth, ed., Contemporary Political Analysis (New York: Free Press, 1967), p. 208.

[7]This is the assessment made by Destler, et al. op.cit.

[8]A major criticism of Allison's work has been that he has sometimes confused cuts or aspects of reality with competing explanations of reality when developing his paradigms. The paradigms/models actually provide aspects of perspectives on social reality rather than different explanations per se. See Ernest J. Yanarella "Reconstructed Logic and Logic-In-Use in Decision-Making Analysis: Graham Allison," in Polity, Fall,1975 p.169.

[9] In developing his models Allison presents us with a new and sometimes bewildering vocabulary with a mix of analogies, metaphors, jargon and neologisms: "players in positions," "Chiefs and Indians," action channels," "dominant inference patterns" and so forth.

[10] In reconstructing the decision environments, it was clear that individual participants at the top level could have some impact on events (e.g., a Dulles or a Kaysen-cum-Kennedy), but equally clear that they were circumscribed by organizational factors over which they had limited influence and environmental "givens" over which they had none.

[11] See George's "The Case for Multiple Advocacy in Foreign Policy Decision-Making." American Political Science Review (September 1972) pp. 751-785

A P P E N D I C E S

NOTES ON METHODOLOGY

It was noted earlier in this study that three major sources of information were relied upon for the reconstruction of the critical decisions and the development of the competitive historical perspectives: 1. official records, 2. elite interviews, and 3. secondary source materials. The third of these, secondary accounts and analyses, included the books mentioned in the Introduction and cited frequently thereafter as well as numerous periodical and newspaper articles also cited. The focus of this section, however, is on the first two data sources, how they interrelate, and how together they were put into the service of checking hypotheses, propositions, and questions.

The crucial data source, initially, for information about what seemed to be the landmark decisions as well as the lesser decisions and transitional periods is the official records, including: memoranda, internal correspondence, proclamations and various executive order types, reports, position papers, etc. Because the Department of the Army was mandated the administration of the Ryukyus for 23 of the 24 years covered by the study, Army records at the National Archives contained copies of the needed official records of all other agencies involved, i.e., the Department of State, the White House, the Office of the Secretary of Defense, the Department of the Navy, the Central Intelligence Agency, etc. It was from these massive collections of papers that "for the record" accounts, as well as a great deal of classified material useful in reconstructing what happened, were gathered. Even in the case of classified documents, however, the research has to assume that the "for the internal record" effect operates to modify -- and in some cases to inhibit or obscure -- a complete reflection of what was going on in the discussions of the decision-makers. This is to say that if highly secret materials can be expected to allow the scholar who obtains access to them to penetrate a layer of information not formerly available, it cannot be assumed that it gives him entry into the innermost layers, which are likely not to be recorded on paper anyhow.

The most useful check on the information contained in official records, for my purposes, was the existence and the surprisingly easy accessibility of the decision makers themselves as well as people close to the decisions, i.e., those who may have helped implement them or at least communicate them within the bureaucracy and to the attentive public. From the interviews I was able to confirm and compare impressions from a variety of perspectives in order to arrive at a kind of composite account to be compared against the more contemporary documentary ones. It should be emphasized that this procedure is by no means one hundred percent reliable, as any competent researcher knows, for various reasons related to memory, self-esteem, etc., discussed below. It should also be pointed out that confirmation and clarification of specific points can be gotten to an impressive extent within the official record themselves by comparing the accounts of different individuals and organizations or of the same ones over time. From both head-on clashes and quibbling over nuances within government documents I was able to learn a lot about everything from MacArthur's differences with the Joint Chiefs of Staff in 1948 to Lyndon Johnson's staff's Ryukyus-related public relations ploys in the late 1960's. Nevertheless, there are certain kinds of enlightenment which cannot really be obtained in any systematic way from archives, and it is here that the interviews were most useful. I turn now to a somewhat more detailed consideration of the research strategy related to the two major data sources.

I. Archival data -- were for the most part obtained between June, 1975 and June, 1976. Because of my having been involved in Okinawa research during 1971-72 with a security clearance to view highly (and in some cases overly) classified materials, the task of sifting through twenty-four years of multi-agency paperwork on the Ryukyus three years later was made much easier. In the intervening time a number of documents from the late 1940's-1950 had been declassified, including high level studies like NSC-68 and the NSC-13 series. Excerpts from some of these appear for the first time outside the archives in this dissertation and, I think it fair to say, shed some interesting new light on American foreign policy thinking during the period -- and not just Ryukyus policy.

By far the most productive sources of information were the National Archives in Washington, D.C. and its branch record center in Suitland, Maryland, nearby.

The former contains documents of the Armed Services known as "headquarters files," i.e., the records of policy-making in Washington, while the latter holds a vast accumulation of material from the USCAR files, shipped back to the United States from Okinawa during 1972, the year of reversion.

As indicated, the Army Department files are the central locus of data, but the National Archives contained additional valuable records in the Joint Chiefs of Staff files. Most of the Army materials had been declassified through 1947, and I was able to obtain a researcher's clearance to see materials through 1949. Headquarters materials for the period 1949-69 were not available; many of the more recent files are still housed in the Pentagon, State Department, etc. The USCAR or "theater" files at Suitland, however, were for the most part at a low classification level and therefore accessible for the entire period that I was interested in. The combination of the two collections provided an excellent documentary base for the period 1945-49 and a modest but very helpful one for the 1950-69 period. Interviews were vital for supplementing my understanding of events after 1949; for the pre-1949 period the abundance of available documentary materials was fortunate, because most of the participants in the Truman decision sequence are either dead or of advanced age.

Two other sources of official data, one semi-official and the other private, should be mentioned here: the Lyndon Baines Johnson Library in Austin, Texas, and the Dulles Oral History collection at the Princeton University Library. We were able to obtain useful material by mail from the former and to visit the latter in person. The Princeton collection was especially valuable in providing information and interview transcripts of conversations between Dulles Collection researchers and former colleagues of the late Secretary of State. I say "especially valuable" because the Dulles 1950-51 decision-sequence was the most difficult of the five to research: few classified materials have yet been opened up for scholars and only a couple of the key individuals working with Dulles on the negotiations for the treaty interviewing.

It almost goes without saying that in raw form, documents related to any given topic are often of very little use. Army files, which as indicated included many copies of documents originating in other depart-

277

ment or agencies, were voluminous. Indexes provided dim initial clues; truly satisfying answers, however, required a great deal of detective work, sometimes more than I was willing or able to give. A final word on the declassification process: I was able to get favorable action on requests for approval of over 80 documents or document excerpts used in this study. The proportion of rejections of these requests was very small and tended to involve the bureaucratic complications of getting a coordinated inter-agency document approved rather than the sensitive nature of the material actually being sought.

II. Interview data -- The interviews, again, were part of a symbiotic research process, complementing and reinforcing information obtained from archives and in turn being complemented by archival materials. In general, for information on the last three decision-sequences I relied more on the interview data, while for the earlier periods it was necessary to depend more on the written, official records. What effect this change in the source of raw data may have on the final product -- the five case studies -- is difficult to measure, but in any event it is essential to acknowledge that the mix of archival and interview data did change. One buffer against distortion resulting from parallel analyses drawn from qualitatively different primary source-types is the use of secondary sources, which of course are available for the entire 1945-1969 period. Another protection lies in the fact that I did have access to some official records for the later years and previously had had access to more highly classified recent material which, although it could not be cited in this study, did help me to avoid misleading statements or giving undue emphasis to this or that point. Conversely, there were available a few individuals, like Mr. Freimuth of USCAR (see Acknowledgments), whose careers dated back to the early occupation years and who could help confirm impressions gained from the archival research (although neither he nor any other individual consulted bears any responsibility for the judgments made).

Describing the functions of the interviews as uniform, as has been done thus far, may be somewhat misleading in that those conducted in Japan had a rather different, though related purpose from those undertaken in the United States. At this point it becomes desirable to discuss the two phases of the research separately.

278

A. Interviews in Japan/Okinawa -- From the very beginning of this project, it was deemed essential to get certain kinds of impressions and recollections from Japanese and Okinawans* who were most directly involved as "recipients and/or implementers" of American policy in the Ryukyus, the latter including those in Tokyo and Naha who negotiated with Americans or who were otherwise in official contact with United States officials responsible for decisions and decision-implementation in the archipelago. The interview schedule on the following page gives the core questions asked during the field research in Tokyo and Naha during July and August of 1975, and developed during the six-month period before that (the only modifications made in these core questions after arriving in Japan were semantic ones for purposes of translation clarification). As the questions themselves suggest, the focus of the interviews was on four objectives: 1. knowledge of certain historical details and interpretations placed by the Japanese and Okinawans most intimately involved on specific American and Japanese actions (e.g., "Amami reversion," "Japanese interest in the Ryukyus" and so on) and particularly useful for the development of the historical chapter, 2. establishing whether the five really critical decisions identified for the 23-year period of American policy-making struck the Japanese as the most important ones, or whether there were other equally important decisions (from their perspective) which had been neglected, 3. perceptions of "the Americans who counted" and their roles, useful for getting an additional slant on decision participants, and 4. getting a sense of what many observers have characterized as differences within the Japanese and Okinawan leadership over various issues related to American policy.

A word now about the techniques for selecting which Japanese were to be interviewed. Attention is called to the four subsequent pages: the next two pages contain a complete list of the Japanese and Okinawans actually interviewed, the two pages after that divide the 28 major interviewees by professional back-

---

* Although the Okinawans are and have been considered Japanese for many decades, we continue to make the distinction in our study for purposes of clarity, because of the unusual situation separating them between 1945 and 1972.

279

INTERVIEW LIST AND DATES: JAPANESE AND OKINAWANS

Twenty-Eight Major Former Officials, Present Officials and
Policy Experts --
    (listings are with the Japanese surname first, according
    to current scholarly practice)

Yoshida Shien, former high-level official in Nampo Doho
Engokai, July 28, 1975

Suetsugu Ichiro, former head of quasi-official LDP Okinawa
Okikon (Committee), July 30, 1975

Usui Soichi, head of LDP Diet committee on Okinawa, July
30, 1975

Ohama Nobumoto, former head of Nampo Doho Engokai, July
30, 1975

Ota Seisaku, former Chief Executive of the Ryukyu Islands,
August 1, 1975

Takeshita Shuzo, former chief Okinawa correspondent for
the Mainichi Shimbun, August 4, 1975

Sakanaka Tomohisa, former chief Okinawa correspondent
for the Asahi Shimbun, August 5, 1975

Tokonami Tokuji, former head of LDP Diet Committee on
Okinawa and author of the Tokonami Plan, August 6, 1975

Warashina Hiroto, foreign affairs specialist of the Japan
Socialist Party, August 7, 1975

Kusumi Tadao, LDP military affairs expert, August 7, 1975

Funada Naka, LDP representative and former Speaker of the
House in the Diet, August 8, 1975

Watanabe Akio, Japanese scholar of Okinawa as an issue in
US/Japan relations, August 9, 1975

Kimura Toshio, former head of the Prime Minister's Office (Sorifu) and later Foreign Minister, August 11, 1975

Makise Tsuneji, marxist historian, August 8, 1975

Watanabe Ichiro, Komeito party foreign affairs specialist, August 11, 1975

Higa Mikio, Okinawan political scientist and leading
scholar of American occupation, August 13, 1975

Ota Masahide, Okinawan sociologist, August 13, 1945

Matsuoka Seiho, former Chief Executive of the Ryukyu Islands, August 14, 1975

Asato Tsumichiyo, Diet member and Okinawa specialist (and native) of the Democratic Socialist (Minshato) Party, August 15, 1975

Yara Chobyo, former Chief Executive of the Ryukyu Islands (and presently Prefectural Governor), August 16, 1975

Miyasato Seigen, Okinawan political scientist, August 16, 1975

Uema Seiyu, editor of the Okinawa Times newspaper, August 18, 1975

Kudeken Kenji, prominent OLDP member, August 18, 1975

Yamano Kokichi, former director of Okinawa Liason Office in Sorifu, August 21, 1975

Saito Akira, former Okinawa correspondent (and now staff member of) Yomiuri Shimbun, August 22, 1975

Nihara Shooji, foreign policy specialist of the Japan Communist Party (Kyosanto),August 23, 1975

Sato Yukio, Foreign Office specialist on Okinawa and North American Affairs, September 3, 1975 (Washington, D.C.)

Chiba Kazuo, North American Affairs official in Foreign Office (presently consul in Atlanta), November 12, 1975 (Atlanta)

Other Interviews --

Kitazawa Ichiro, former private secretary to the late Japanese Prine Minister Yoshida Shigeru, August 7, 1975

Masuoka Ichiro, Secretary of the Diet, August 6, 1976

Takara Shintaro, former USCAR aide (presently advisor to the American Consul in Naha), August 13, 1975

Roll Call: Yoshida Shien, Suetsugu Ichiro, Ohama Nobumoto, Usui Soichi, Ota
Seisaku, Takeshita Shuzo, Sakanaka, Tomohisa, Tokonami Tokuji,
Warashina Hiroto, Kusumi Tadao, Funada Naka, Watanabe Akio, Kimura
Toshio, Makise Tsuneji, Watanabe Ichiro, Higa Mikio, Ota Masahide,
Matsuoka Seiho, Asato Tsumichiyo, Yara Chobyo, Miyasato Seigen,
Uema Seiyu, Kudeken Kenji, Yamano Kokichi, Saito Akira, Nihara
Shoji, Sato Yukio, Chiba Kazuo

N=28

Journal	Party Experts	Legislators	Professional Lobbyists	Officials	Academics
Sakanaka, Asahi	Asato, DSP	Usui, LDP	Yoshida, Nampo	Ota, GRI	Watanabe, Tokyo
Takeshita, Yomiuri	Nihara, JCP	Tokonami, LDP	Ohama, Nampo	Matsuoka, GRI	Higa, Ryudai
Saito, Mainichi	Watanabe, Komeito	Asato *	Suetsugu, Okikon	Yara, GRI	Ota, Ryudai
Uema, Taimusu	Warashina, JSP	Funada, LDP		Sato, Gaimusho	Miyasato, Ryudai
				Chiba, Gaimusho	
				Kimura, Sorifu	Author
				Yamano,	Makise, Marxist
				Kudeken, GRI	
					Military Expert
					Kusumi, Tadao

* Both legislative and partisan-spokesman roles related to Okinawa

N=28

CLEARLY PRO-U.S.	LEANING PRO-U.S.	NEUTRAL	LEANING ANTI-U.S.	CLEAR ANTI-U.S.
Funada	Usui	Sakanaka	Uema	Warashina
	Tokonami	Takeshita	Asato	Nihara
	Chiba	Saito	Watanabe I.	Makise
	Sato	Ohama	Suetsugu	Yara
	Kudeken	Yoshida	Ota Masahide	
	Kimura	Kusumi		
		Matsuoka		
		Yamano		
		Ota Seisaku		
		Higa		
		Miyasato		
		Watanabe A.		
1	6	12	5	4

Tendency Pro-U.S.	Tendency Anti-U.S.
7	9

ground and also by ideological orientation. Criteria for characterizing the interviewees ideologically included: 1. party affiliation (if any), 2. writings and professional reputation as evaluated by myself and others, 3. specific answers to questions I asked. I think the table indicating ideological divisions is a useful one for conveying the diversity of those with whom I spoke and the sense of balance I was trying to achieve--this in spite of the fact that the designations were based ultimately on my own judgment and not a formal, rigorous operationalization process. I never intended to attempt a random sampling of policy-makers involved in Okinawa matters; I cannot even claim to have a scientifically stratified sample. What is claimed is that the major figures who were available were contacted, that the three major Japanese daily newspapers' leading Okinawa correspondents were spoken with at length, and that I was able to interview foreign policy experts from all of the major Japanese political parties, the leading Japanese and Okinawan scholars on the occupation of the Ryukyus, the Diet members most directly involved in Japan's Okinawa policy from about 1960 onward, and the most important Okinawan policy implementers, i.e., all three of the living former Chief Executives of the Ryukyus. In addition to this central group of 28, other Japanese, less directly involved in Okinawa policy concerns but knowledgeable about certain aspects of these problems and sources of information about them were interviewed, for example, the former personal secretary to the late Prime Minister Yoshida Shigeru, Mr. Kitazawa.

Before the interviews of the Japanese were begun, I discussed the interview format and the wording of the questions with my able interpreter, Ms. Yvonne Yung of Tokyo University. She worked on translating the questions into Japanese with her husband, Mr. Tsunekawa Keiichi, also of Tokyo University.* We were satisfied that we had minimized translation errors and ambiguities, but two additional checks served to confirm this further. As the interview process got underway a second interpreter-assistant, Ms. Shiraichi Aiko, was given Mr. Yung's Japanese-language version of the questions to translate back into English. The translation is given here on the next two pages for the

---

*My own knowledge of conversational Japanese is limited so that interpreters were essential.

INTERVIEW SCHEDULE: CORE QUESTIONS FOR JAPANESE / OKINAWANS

Following are questions asked of all 28 principal Japanese and Okinawan interviewees, with only the slightest variation in wording. Follow-up questions, although consistent in substance and general direction, were not consistent as to wording and so are not reproduced here.

1. /Introductory7 Could you please tell me a little of your own background, especially as it relates to the Okinawa policy of Japan and the United States?

2. What do you regard as the five or six most important American decisions affecting the Ryukyus between 1945 and the 1969 reversion promise? /after allowing interviewee to name as many decisions as he could or would, we turned to specific questions about important decisions7

3. Why do you think American policy-makers initially decided to retain Okinawa instead of returning it to Japan after the Second World War?

4. What is your understanding of the reaction of Okinawan leaders to the Dulles doctrine of residual sovereignty in the peace treaty record? /wait for answer7 What about Japanese leaders?

5. What was the reaction of Okinawans to the return of the Amami islands to Japan in 1953? /answer7 What about Japanese leaders?

6. What is your appraisal of the Kaysen investigation of the Ryukyus under President Kennedy in 1961?

7. Are you aware of any important American reviews of Okinawa policy in the 1960's. i.e., high level reviews concerning Okinawa's political status and the position of the Ryukyus in the total Asian strategic picture?

8. When did the return of Okinawa first become an important popular political issue in Okinawa itself? How about Japan? /if there is a difference7 How do you account for the gap?

9. Which Japanese do you consider most important in bringing about the reversion of the Ryukyus? Which Americans?

Original Re-Translation into English of Japanese Language
Interview Questions (of Ms. Y. Yung) by Ms. A. Shiraichi

Note: Numbers 1 and 2 are introductory items.
All spellings are as in the original.

1. I am sorry my Japanese is not good enough to have all
my interview in Japanese. But Miss Yon, my interpreter, will sufficiently help me to talk with you.

2. May I record this interview in Cassette tape-recorder?
If you mind please tell me frankly.

3. Would you please tell me a little about your background
concerning Okinawa Policy of Japan and the United States?

4. What was the most important American policy-making on
Okinawa between 1945 and 1969 when Ryuky's Return to
Japan was decided?

5. What do you think was the first reason for American
policy-makers to decide the occupation of Okinawa rather than returning it to Japan after the World War II?
How do you think of the fact that American side has
ever considered Return of Okinawa as a part of Peace-
Treaty?

6. What was the response of Okinawa people to the Return
of Amami Islands? How about the people of mainland
Japan?

7. What was the response of political leaders in Okinawa
to the doctrine of "Potential Sovereignty" by Dales?
How about the political leaders in mainland Japan?

8. How do you appreciate Kaysen Reprot on the situation of
Okinawa that was handed to President Kennedy in 1961?

9. Have you ever noticed that in 1960's United States had
reconsidered Okinawa Policy: a high-level reconsideration concerning political status and position of Okinawa in the strategical aspect of whole Asia?

10. When did Restoration of Okinawa first become the important, popular political issue in Okinawa? How
about mainland Japan?

11. How do you explain the gap of time to begin Restoration
Movement in mainland Japan and in Okinawa?

286

reader's inspection. A final safeguard against lin-
guistic inaccuracies derived from the fact that several
of the 28 major Japanese and Okinawan interviewees had
an extensive knowledge of English and in a few cases
the interviews were actually conducted in English but
with frequent reference to the Japanese translation of
the special terminology, phrases like "reversion"
(Okinawa henkan) and "residual sovereignty" (Sen
zaishu-ken). In the interviews conducted in Japanese
I would do the following: 1. exchange pleasantries and
introduce my interpreter, 2. request that the interview
be allowed to be recorded (there were no refusals) with
the understanding that the tapes would be kept confidential and that the machine would be turned off on request, 3. ask questions from the interview schedule in
a prescribed sequence (deviated from only when the interviewee had time-constraints) and have my interpreter
ask them in Japanese, and 4. briefly discuss the
answers as she translated them to me for use in follow-
up questions. In addition to the core-questions which
we attempted to ask each interviewee in the same way,
there were both follow-up questions and individually-
tailored questions appropriate to specific individuals
(e.g., asking former Okinawan Chief Executives about
the relationship with American officials).

B. Interviews in the United States -- These were
conducted between June, 1975 and May, 1976 (a complete
interview list and schedule of core interview questions
may be found on the following four pages). Although
considerable attention has already been given to the
American policy-actor interviews, some features of the
process deserve further explanation. There is no doubt
that the most original and in many cases useful date
came out of this particular phase of the research: I
was extraordinarily fortunate in having the great majority of the participants in the five critical decisions I analyzed make themselves available for
lengthy conversations* and allow these to be recorded
on tape. A great deal about the impressions and
thought processes of decision-makers was learned in the
course of these discussions some of which can be attributed and some of which cannot. In each instance
in the body of the dissertation in which reference has
been made to unspecific sources, e.g., "several high

*
As with the Japanese interviews, the average conver-

287

INTERVIEW LIST AND DATES: AMERICANS

Policy-Actors from Critical Decision-Sequences --

Edwin O. Reischauer, former Ambassador to Japan, June 13, 1975

William P. Bundy, former Asst. Secretary of State for Far Eastern Affairs, January 21, 1976

Carl Kaysen, former Deputy Assistant to the President for National Security Affairs, January 19, 1976

U. Alexis Johnson, former Ambassador to Japan and Under Secretary of State for Political Affairs (now Ambassador-at-Large), January 22, 1976

Lt. Gen. Paul W. Caraway, Ret., former High Commissioner of the Ryukyus, January 24, 1976

Lt. Gen. Ferdinand T. Unger, Ret., former High Commissioner of the Ryukyus, February 4, 1976

Stephen Ailes, former Secretary of the Army (and Under Secretary), February 6, 1976

Gen. Lyman L. Lemnitzer, Ret., former Chairman of the Joint Chiefs of Staff, March 15, 1976

Morton Halperin, former Deputy Assistant Secretary of Defense for International Security Affairs, March 16, 1976

Warren Nutter, former Assistant Secretary of Defense for International Security Affairs, April 5, 1976

William Rogers, former Secretary of State, (telephone)

> Also, interviews by correspondence with: former Secretary of State Dean Rusk; former Japan Country Director Richard Sneider; former Deputy Under Secretary of the Army James Siena

Other Interviews --

George H. Kerr, historial of Okinawa, July 5, 1975

Richard Petrie, American Embassy, Tokyo, July 31, 1975

Raymond Aka, American Embassy, Tokyo, July 31, 1975

John Sylvester, American Consulate, Naha, August 13, 1975

John Emmerson, former Deputy Chief of Mission, American Embassy in Tokyo (under Reischauer), Tokyo, August 4, 1975

Rodney Armstrong, former NSC staff member and State Department Japan specialist, November 20, 1975

General James E. Moore, Ret., former High Commissioner of the Ryukyus, January 7, 1976

Gerald Warner, former Civil Administrator of the Ryukyus, February 4, 1976

Stanley Carpenter, former Civil Administrator of the Ryukyus, February 5, 1976

Robert Fearey, former Civil Administrator of the Ryukyus, February 5, 1976

McGeorge Bundy, former Special Assistant to the President for National Security Affairs, March 22, 1976 (telephone)

Lt. Gen. Albert Watson II, Ret., former High Commissioner of the Ryukyus, March 24, 1976 (telephone)

Lt. Gen. James Lampert, Ret., former High Commissioner of the Ryukyus, April 1, 1976 (telephone)

Armin Meyer, former Ambassador to Japan, March 15, 1976

Paul H. Nitze, former Deputy Secretary of Defense for International Security Affairs, June 1, 1976

INTERVIEW SCHEDULE: CORE QUESTIONS FOR AMERICAN POLICY-ACTORS

The following questions were asked of all former policy-actors in the critical decision sequences and in very much the form stated here. The only deviations were slight variations in the wording to make dates appropriate for the individual being interviewed and in most cases questions regarding decision sequences in which the individual was not involved were omitted.

1. Could you briefly characterize your contact with the Okinawa problem and your recollection of your role in the _____ decision?

2. If one looks at the history of American policy making for the Ryukyus it is possible to categorize the chief participants in the following way: a. those most concerned with the relationship between the United States and the Okinawans, b. those concerned with the impact of Okinawa policy on U.S./Japanese relations, and c. those emphasizing the position of the Ryukyus in American global stretegy. Would you be willing to place yourself in any of the 3 categories? Which order would reflect your own ordering of priorities?

3. Did you regard your own role in _____ as one of actually making policy or could it better be characterized as influencing or approving the outcome of the decision?

4. I am going to list some individuals who are supposed to have participated in this _____ decision. To the extent that you feel comfortable in doing so, could you give your own impressions of each of their roles in that decision? /procede down checklist of decision sequence participants; ask if interviewee would have omitted any of these entirely or would add some names/

5. A major school of thought in American political and administrative science argues that policy decisions are often made in response to short-term expedient considerations and rarely subjected to high-level comprehensive reviews to determine their worth and continued workability. Does this, in your view, reflect accurately your experience with the making of Okinawa policy?

Following are questions that were widely asked (whenever applicable and when time permitted):

INTERVIEW SCHEDULE: CORE QUESTIONS FOR AMERICAN POLICY-ACTORS

1. How explicitly and how early did the smooth automatic renewal of the 1960 U.S./Japan security treaty weigh as an important factor in the timing and terms of Okinawa reversion?

2. Did the idea of detente and the lowered American military profile vis-a-vis the USSR and/or China explicitly figure in the discussions of the _____ decision? In 1969 did the Nixon or Guam Doctrine per se get associated with policy regarding Okinawa?

officials," great care has been taken to assure that the point being supported with unattributed references did in fact reflect accurately those references. In support of this most of the interview tapes can be made available to serious scholars who might be interested.

The general objectives of the American interviews, already touched upon, can be summarized as follows: 1. assistance with the determination and reconstruction of the critical decisions of the case-studies, 2. closely related, the characterization of participants in these decisions useful in reconstructing and evaluating the decisions, 3. uncovering historical details and checking the impressions of policy-makers against those derived from the documents and other archival materials as well as secondary source accounts and 4. shedding light on the theoretical interests of the case studies, as reflected in the questions about rationality in decision-making, the origins of the decision, etc. The interviews with United States policy elites and experts, it should be made clear, were of two principal types: 1. the questioning of those who from secondary-source accounts, archival references, or my first-hand knowledge appeared to have been central in the decision-sequences of 1961-62, 1966-67, and 1969, and 2. those who were close to such central decision-cast members or who were otherwise expert on some phase of Ryukyus policy. A sample data sheet based on one of the numerous elite interviews of the first type is presented on the following pages; interviews of the second type were less structured and did not lend themselves to this kind of standardized summarization.

I conclude this section with a short consideration of possible limitations of the interview methodology (the strengths presumably are self-evident). As regards the interview process itself, there is the problem of accurate recollection and retrospective distortion by interviewees well-documented in the social science literature (including works by Hyman, Dexter, Richard Snyder, and others). There were many evidences of this in the Okinawa interviews, especially

---

*sation with American policy-makers (i.e., present and former) ran about an hour. In unusual cases we were limited to 30 minutes or so and occasionally the interview went two hours or more. Covering the standardized core-questions normally took about 45 minutes.

292

AMERICAN POLICY-ACTOR DATA SHEET: WILLIAM ROGERS

Position: Secretary of State, 1/69-9/73

Decision Involvement: FINAL REVERSION DECISION, 1969

INTERVIEW INFORMATION: Telephone Interview: 22 Mar. 76

1. SELF DESCRIPTION -- Mixture of alliance and strategic
concern voiced, although Japanese alliance appeared
to have clear priority based on remarks; personal involvement with Okinawa issue voiced; was involved as
Naval officer in Battle of Okinawa; role with regard
to final decision one of strong influence (although
this implicit, not expressed)

2. ROLE IN DECISION -- Advisory to President from early
in administration, more active and participatory beginning summer 1969 with negotiations w. Foreign
Minister Aiichi; major figure in U.S. negotiating
position from June to Nov. 1969, when final terms
of reversion were ironed out between Nixon and
Sato at Summit

3. DETENTE -- termed implicit by-product of Okinawa
negotiations, which were primarily alliance policy
oriented (advantages to U.S. position vis-a-vis
USSR & CHINA relatively incidental) (see #4)

4. IMPERIALISM -- as issue not asked implicitly, but R.
did mention on his own that "no territorial ambitions
in Asia" aspect of administration well served by Okinawa reversion and, he feels, given added credibility

5. NIXON DOCTRINE -- "Compatible" with Okinawa decision
but not causally linked to it; essentially the Okinawa return seen as preceding Nixon Asian policy and
causally independent of it, although conveniently
compatible; does not recall any overt references in
high-level discussions

6. 1970 SECURITY TREATY -- Implicit in thinking on Okinawa but does not recall its coming out specifically
in discussions of problem; appears to have been case
that reversion at this time was an issue of independent
importance and not connected or conditional (or at
least on other security issues)

7. LDP DOMESTIC POSITION -- Again termed an implicit consideration, not explicit; R. did not seem to attach

293

much importance to this, although no specific comment
to this effect

8. EVALUATION OF OTHERS ROLES:

because of time factor no direct questions on this
except re: Nixon

a. Richard Nixon -- quite interested,
personal focus on Pacific affairs

b. Aichi Kiichi very highly regarded an individual and negotiator

9. OTHER INTERVIEW INFORMATION -- EMPH. that Nixon-Ad-
min. policy on Okinawa not determined; could have
been slowed down or aborted by doing nothing; instead they chose to act

OTHER EVALUATIONS OF ROGERS' ROLE: Most officials in
decision cast stressed Secretary's considerable involvement in actual pre-communique negotiations with the
Japanese and limited role in the initial determination
(Spring 1969) to return the Ryukyus under the most favorable terms possible.

in the case of those trying to reconstruct early decisions and events -- even the Kaysen-Kennedy decision sequence, now 15 years in the past, was a difficult one for some interviewees (and understandably as several were involved in dountless other decisions and issues, some more important than Okinawa, in the intervening years). The checks employed against bias and distortion were the obvious ones: trying to get a variety of perspectives, asking the same question twice in slightly altered form in a given interview if either the question or the answer appeared to have potential difficulties, and so forth. Documents and other primary source materials plus the comparison of notes with other researchers (e.g.,Priscilla Clapp, Higa Mikio, Watanabe Akio, George Kerr -- none of whom bears the slightest responsibility for my own impressions or misimpressions) were also helpful antidotes to interview data contamination.

Criticism might also be directed at possible biases in the selection of interviewees. Rather than getting a sample, I was attempting to work with the universe of policy participants in the five critical decisions, but precision in determining (operationalizing) such a universe was a formidable challenge. I think I met this challenge with reasonable success through some of the techniques already described, but even so there were some key figures who could not be interviewed. In these cases extrapolations and partial reconstructions of positions had to be made from the accounts of those who were accessible and from such other sources as I could find.

LIST OF INTERVIEWEES BY ORGANIZATIONAL AFFILIATION

State Department

E. Reischauer, Amb.
A. Johnson, Amb.
A. Meyer, Amb.
J. Emmerson, DCM
R. Petrie, DCM
R. Sneider, CD
D. Rusk, SecState
W. Rogers, SecState
R. Armstrong, 69 aide
W. Bundy, FE
M. Greene, FE

11

Uniformed Mil./USCAR

J. Moore, HC
P. Caraway, HC
A. Watson, HC
F. Ungar, HC
J. Lampert, HC
L. Lemnitzer, JCS
G. Warner, CA
C. Carpenter, CA
R. Fearey, CA
E. Freimuth, LO

10

Army Department

S. Ailes, USec
J. Siena, DUSec

2

Other DOD

P. Nitze, ISA
W. Nutter, ISA
W. Halperin, NSC

3

White House

C. Kaysen
McG. Bundy

2

Congress

R. Russell-man

1

N = 29

D O C U M E N T S

Note: Following are documents and a map referred
to in the text. All documents have been
re-typed for purposes of improved repro-
duction, but no stylistic, format, or wording changes have been made. The only departure from the original occurs at the
top of the first page of each document,
that being the identifying title and sequence number of the document.

Document 1 - SCAPIN-677

AG 091 (22 Jan 46)GS   A-O 500
(SCAPIN - 677)   29 January 1946

MEMORANDUM FOR: IMPERIAL JAPANESE GOVERNMENT.

THROUGH: Central Liaison Office, Tokyo

SUBJECT: Governmental and Administrative
                     Separation of Certain Outlying Areas
                     from Japan.

1. The Imperial Japanese Government is directed to
cease exercising, or attempting to exercise, governmental or administrative authority over any area outside of Japan, or over any government officials and
employees or any other persons within such areas.

2. Except as authorized by this Headquarters, the Imperial Japanese Governmant will not communicate with
government officials and employees or with any other
persons outside of Japan for any purpose other than the
routine operation of authorized shipping, communications
and weather services.

3. For the purpose of this directive, Japan is defined
to include the four main islands of Japan (Hokkaido,
Honshu, Kyushu, and Shikoku) and the approximately
1,000 small adjacent islands, including the Tsushima
Islands and the Ryukyu (Nansai) Islands north of 30°
North Latitude (excluding Kuchinoshima Island); and
excluding (a) Utsuryo (Ullung) Island, Liancourt Rocks
(Take Island) and Quelpart (Saishu or Cheju) Island,
(b) the Ryukyu (Nansei) Islands south of 30°North Lati-
tude (including Kuchinoshima Island), the Izu, Nanpo,
Bonin (Ogasawara) and Volcano (Kazan or Iwo) Island
Groups, and all other outlying Pacific Islands /Includ-
ing the Daito (Ohigashi or Cagari) Island Group, and
Parece Vela (Okino-tori), Marcus (Minami-tori) and
Ganges (Nakano-tori) Islands7 and (c) the Kurile
(Chishima) Islands, the Habomai (Hapomaze) Island
Group (including Suisho, Yuri, Akiyuri, Shibotsu and
Taraku Islands) and Shikotan Island.

4. Further areas specifically excluded from the governmental and administrative jurisdiction of the Im-

298

perial Japanese Government are the following:
(a) all Pacific Islands seized or occupied under man-
date or otherwise by Japan since the beginning of the
World War in 1914, (b) Manchuria, Formosa and the Pescadores, (c) Korea, and (d) Karafuto.

5. The definition of Japan contained in this directive shall also apply to all future directives, memoranda and orders from this Headquarters unless otherwise specified therein.

6. Nothing in this directive shall be construed as an
indication of Allied policy relating to the ultimate
determination of the minor islands referred to in
Article 8 of the Potsdam Declaration.

7. The Imperial Japanese Government will prepare and
submit to this Headquarters a report of all governmental agencies in Japan the functions of which pertain
to areas outside of Japan as defined in this directive.
Such report will include a statement of the functions,
organization and personnel of each of the agencies concerned.

8. All records of the agencies referred to in paragraph 7 above will be preserved and kept available for
inspection by this Headquarters.

FOR THE SUPREME COMMANDER:

                                /s/ H.W.Allen
        ENCLOSURE (B)   Colonel, AGD
                                Asst.Adjutant General

Document 2- NSC 13/3

Colonel Hugh C. Johnson

NSC 13/3   COPY NO 19

A REPORT

TO THE

NATIONAL SECURITY COUNCIL

by

The Executive Secretary

on

Recommendations With Respect To U.S. Policy Toward Japan

May 6, 1949

WASHINGTON

NATIONAL SECURITY COUNCIL

WASHINGTON

COPY NO. <u>19</u>

May 6, 1949

MEMORANDUM FOR THE NATIONAL SECURITY COUNCIL

SUBJECT: Recommendations with Respect to U. S.
             Policy Toward Japan

REFERENCES: A. NSC 13/2 and NSC 13/3
             B. NSC Action No. 214

          The President has this date approved paragraph
20 of NSC 13/2, on Japanese Reparations, as adopted by the
National Security Council in NSC Action No. 214, and directs
that it be implemented by all appropriate executive departments and agencies of the U. S. Government under the coordination of the Secretary of State.

          NSC 13/2, revised to incorporate the separately
approved paragraphs 5, 9, and 20, is circulated herewith as
NSC 13/3 for the information of the National Security Council.

                         SIDNEY W. SOUERS
                         Executive Secretary

                    301

NOTE BY THE EXECUTIVE SECRETARY

to the

NATIONAL SECURITY COUNCIL

on

RECOMMENDATIONS WITH RESPECT TO U. S. POLICY TOWARD JAPAN

References: A.   NSC 13/2
              B.   NSC Actions Nos. 124, 138, 143, and 214

      The National Security Council at its 23rd meeting adopted a report on the subject (Reference A) and agreed that paragraphs 5, 9, and 20, which were omitted, should be submitted separately (NSC Action No. 124). Paragraphs 5, 9, and 20 were subsequently adopted by the Council for incorporation into NSC 13/2 (NSC Actions Nos. 138, 143, and 214 respectively) and paragraph 5 was later amended (NSC Action No. 177).

      The enclosed revision of NSC 13/2, which incorporates the above actions and represents current U. S. policy toward Japan as approved by the President upon the advice of the Council, is circulated herewith for the information of the Council.

                                    SIDNEY W. SOUERS
                                    Executive Secretary

Distribution:
     The President
     The Secretary of State
     The Secretary of the Treasury
     The Secretary of Defense
     The Secretary of the Army
     The Secretary of the Navy
     The Secretary of the Air Force
     The Chairman, National Security
         Resources Board

May 6, 1949

on

RECOMMENDATIONS WITH RESPECT TO UNITED STATES POLICY TOWARD JAPAN

THE PEACE TREATY

1. Timing and Procedure. In view of the differences
which have developed among the interested countries regarding
the procedure and substance of a Japanese peace treaty and in
view of the serious international situation created by the
Soviet Union's policy of aggressive Communist expansion, this
Government should not press for a treaty of peace at this time.
It should remain prepared to proceed with the negotiations,
under some generally acceptable voting procedure, if the Allied Powers can agree among themselves on such a procedure.
We should, before actually entering into a peace conference,
seek through the diplomatic channel the concurrence of a majority of the participating countries in the principal points of
content we desire to have in such a treaty. Meanwhile, we
should concentrate our attention on the preparation of the
Japanese for the eventual removal of the regime of control.

2. The Nature of the Treaty. It should be our aim to
have the treaty, when finally negotiated, as brief, as general,
and as nonpunitive as possible. To this end we should try to
clear away during this intervening period as many as possible
of the matters which might otherwise be expected to enter into
the treaty of peace. Our aim should be to reduce as far as
possible the number of questions to be treated in the peace
treaty. This applies particularly to such matters as property
rights, restitution, etc. Our policy for the coming period
should be shaped specifically with this in mind.

SECURITY MATTERS

3. The Pre-Treaty Arrangements. Every effort, consistent with the proper performance of the occupational mission
as envisaged in this policy paper and with military security
and morale, should be made to reduce to a minimum the psychological impact of the presence of occupational forces on the
Japanese population. The numbers of tactical, and especially
non-tactical, forces should be minimized. In determining the
location of occupation forces, their employment, and support
from the Japanese economy in the pre-treaty period, full
weight should be given to the foregoing.

4. **The Post-Treaty Arrangements.** United States tactical forces should be retained in Japan until the entrance into effect of a peace treaty. A final U. S. position concerning the post-treaty arrangements for Japanese military security should not be formulated until the peace negotiations are upon us. It should then be formulated in the light of the prevailing international situation and of the degree of internal stability achieved in Japan.

5. **The Ryukyu, Nanpo and Marcus Islands.** The United States intends to retain on a long-term basis the facilities at Okinawa and such other facilities as are deemed by the Joint Chiefs of Staff to be necessary in the Ryukyu Islands south of 29° N., Marcus Island and the Nanpo Shoto south of Sofu Gan. The military bases at or near Okinawa should be developed accordingly. The United States agencies responsible for administering the above-mentioned islands should promptly formulate and carry out a program on a long-term basis for the economic and social well-being and, to the extent practicable, for the eventual reduction to a minimum of the deficit in the economy of the natives. At the proper time, international sanction should be obtained by the means then most feasible for United States long-term strategic control of the Ryukyu Islands south of latitude 29° N., Marcus Island and the Nanpo Shoto south of Sofu Gan.

The United States has determined that it is now in the United States national interest to alleviate the burden now borne by those of the Ryukyu Islands south of latitude 29° N. incident to their contribution to occupation costs, to the extent necessary to establish political and economic security. While it would not be in the interest of the United States to make a public announcement on this matter, and while it is not believed appropriate to obtain international sanction of this intent at this time, the United States national policy toward the Ryukyu Islands south of latitude 29° N. requires that United States Armed Forces and other Government agencies stationed therein pay their way to the extent necessary and practical to carry out the above-mentioned program for the economic and social well-being and towards eventual reduction to a minimum of the deficit in the economy of the natives in this area beginning sixty days after this date, and that these Islands must then no longer be financially dependent upon or obligated to any other occupied area.

6. **Naval Bases.** The United States Navy should shape its policy in the development of the Yokosuka base in such a way as to favor the retention on a commercial basis in the post-treaty period of as many as possible of the facilities it now enjoys there. Meanwhile, it should proceed to develop the possibilities of Okinawa as a naval base, on the assumption that we will remain in control there on a long-term basis.

This policy does not preclude the retention of a naval base as such at Yokosuka if, at the time of finalizing the U. S. position concerning the post-treaty arrangements for Japanese military security, the prevailing international situation makes such action desirable and if it is consistent with U. S. political objectives.

7. The Japanese Police Establishment. The Japanese Policy establishment, including the coastal patrol, should be strengthened by the re-enforcing and re-equipping of the present forces, and by expanding the present centrally directed police organization.

THE REGIME OF CONTROL

8. Supreme Commander for the Allied Powers. This Government should not at this time propose or consent to any major change in the regime of control. SCAP should accordingly be formally maintained in all its existing rights and powers. However, responsibility should be placed to a steadily increasing degree in the hands of the Japanese Government. To this end the view of the United States Government should be communicated to SCAP that the scope of its operations should be reduced as rapidly as possible, with a corresponding reduction in personnel, to a point where its mission will consist largely of general supervisor observation of the activities of the Japanese Government and of contact with the latter at high levels on questions of broad governmental policy.

9. Far Eastern Commission. The United States Government should ensure for its own part, and urge upon other FEC member Governments, that proposals considered by the FEC confined strictly to policy matters directly related to the fulfillment by Japan of its obligations under the Terms of Surrender, and be couched in broad terms leaving questions of implementation and administration to SCAP. The position of the United States should further be based upon the fact that these surrender terms, as envisaged by the Potsdam Declaration, have been substantially implemented. On matters still within the purview of the FEC, such as civil aviation policy in Japan, the United States Government should seek to establish as promptly as possible firm United States positions and then adopt an aggressive and positive attitude, by direct discussions with FEC member Governments and by forceful backing in the FEC of policies desired by the United States. In matters of urgency, where it has become evident that, after efforts to achieve maximum international support, agreement cannot be promptly reached, we should not hesitate to use the interim directive. SCAP should also be encouraged to make greater use of his authority as sole executive for the Allied Powers, asking where necessary for the United States Government's views. On the other hand, the United States Government should

not hesitate to render assistance to SCAP by elucidating its interpretation of previous directives and general policies, notably those appearing in the "Basic Post-Surrender Policy for Japan".

10. Allied Council. The Allied Council should be continued, with its functions unchanged.

OCCUPATIONAL POLICY

11. Relations with the Japanese Government. (See paragraph 8 above.)

12. Internal Political and Economic Changes. Henceforth emphasis should be given to Japanese assimilation of the reform programs. To this end, while SCAP should not stand in the way of reform measures initiated by the Japanese if he finds them consistent with the overall objectives of the occupation, he should be advised not to press upon the Japanese Government any further reform legislation. As for reform measures already taken or in process of preparation by the Japanese authorities, SCAP should be advised to relax pressure steadily but unobtrusively on the Japanese Government in connection with these reforms and should intervene only if the Japanese authorities revoke or compromise the fundamentals of the reforms as they proceed in their own way with the process of implementation and adjustment. If exigencies of the situation permit, SCAP should consult with the U. S. Government before intervention in the event the Japanese should resort to action of such serious import. Definite background guidance embodying the above principles and indicating the United States Government's view as to the nature and extent of the adjustment to be permitted should be provided SCAP in the case of certain reforms.

13. The Purge. Since the purpose of the purge has been largely accomplished, the U. S. now should advise SCAP to inform the Japanese Government informally that no further extension of the purge is contemplated and that the purge should be modified along the following lines: (1) Categories of persons who have been purged or who are subject to the purge by virtue of their having held relatively harmless positions should be made re-eligible for governmental, business and public media positions; (2) certain others who have been barred or who are subject to being barred from public life on the basis of positions occupied should be allowed to have their cases re-examined solely on the basis of personal actions; and (3) a minimum age limit should be fixed, under which no screening for public office would be required.

14. Occupation Costs. The occupational costs borne by the Japanese Government should continue to be reduced to the maximum extent consonant with the policy objectives of the pre-treaty period as envisaged in this paper.

15. Economic Recovery. Second only to U. S. security interests, economic recovery should be made the primary objective of United States policy in Japan for the coming period. It should be sought through a combination of United States aid program envisaging shipments and/or credits on a declining scale over a number of years and by vigorous and conscientious effort by interested agencies and departments of the United States Government to cut away existing obstacles to the revival of Japanese foreign trade, with provision for Japanese merchant shipping, and to facilitate restoration and development of Japan's exports. In developing Japan's internal and external trade and industry, private enterprise should be encouraged. Recommendations concerning the implementation of the above points, formulated in the light of Japan's economic relationship with other Far Eastern countries, should be worked out between the State and Army Departments after consultation with the other interested departments and agencies of the Government. We should make it clear to the Japanese Government that the success of the recovery program will in large part depend on Japanese efforts to raise production and to maintain high export levels through hard work, a minimum of work-stoppages, internal austerity measures and the stern combatting of inflationary trends including efforts to acheive a balanced internal budget as rapidly as possible.

16. Property Matters. SCAP should be advised to expedite the restoration or final disposal of property of United Nations members and their nationals in such a way that the process will be substantially completed by July 1, 1949. It should be the objective of United States policy to have all property matters straightened out as soon as possible and certainly well in advance of a treaty of peace in order that they may not hamper treaty negotiations.

17. Information and Education.

   a. Censorship. Censorship of literary materials entering Japan should be conducted with the minimum of delay and pre-censorship of the Japanese press should cease. This should not operate, however, to prevent SCAP from exercising a broad post-censorship supervision and from engaging in counter-intelligence spot-checking of the mails.

   b. Radio. The United States Government should immediately undertake a regular program of medium - and long-wave broadcasts to Japan from a suitably located transmitter station possibly on Okinawa. These programs should be carefully prepared with a view to developing an understanding and appreciation of American ideas and at the same time to maintaining as wide a Japanese radio audience as possible.

c. Interchange of Persons. The interchange between Japan and the United States of scholars, teachers, lecturers, scientists and technicians should be strongly encouraged. SCAP should continue the policy of permitting approved Japanese to go abroad for cultural as well as economic purposes.

18. War Crime Trials. The trial of Class A suspects is completed and decision of the court is awaited. We should continue and push to an early conclusion the screening of all "B" and "C" suspects with a view to releasing those whose cases we do not intend to prosecute. Trials of the others should be instituted and concluded at the earliest possible date.

19. Control of Japanese Economic War Potential. Production in, importation into, and use within Japan of goods and economic services for bona fide peaceful purposes should be permitted without limitation, except:

a. Japan's economic war potential should be controlled by restrictions on allowable designated strategic raw materials in Japan.

b. Japan's industrial disarmament should be limited to the prohibition of the manufacture of weapons of war and civil aircraft and the minimum of temporary restrictions on industrial production which can be advocated in the light of commitments already made by the United States regarding the reduction of the industrial war potential.

20. Japanese Reparations. It should be the policy of the United States Government that current transfers of reparations under unilateral U. S. directive should be terminated and every effort made to secure acceptance by the other reparations claimant countries of the principle that the reparations question as a whole should be reduced to the status of a dead letter. After advising friendly FEC nations of our intended course and of the considerations underlying our position, the United States should take the following specific actions:

a. Rescind the Advance Transfers Directive of April 4, 1947 (JCS Directive No. 75), except for allocations already processed under that directive.

308

<u>b</u>.   Withdraw its proposal of November 6, 1947,
on reparations shares.

<u>c</u>.   Announce to the FEC and publicly that it has
no intention of using its unilateral powers to make
possible additional industrial reparations removals.

<u>d</u>.   Announce to the FEC and publicly its views:

(1)   That all industrial facilities, including so-called "primary war facilities", presently
designated as available for reparations which can
contribute to Japanese recovery should be utilized
as necessary, except for scrapping, in Japan's
peaceful economy for recovery purposes.

(2)   That with regard to "primary war facilities", all of which were some time ago stripped of
their special purpose equipment and thus of their
"war facilities" characteristics, SCAP, under the
authority granted in paragraph 10 of the FEC decision on Reduction of Japanese Industrial War Potential, should as rapidly as practicable require the
dismantlement, dispersion or other action for the
utilization in Japan's peaceful economy of such of
these facilities as are required to meet the needs
of the occupation, which needs prominently include
economic recovery.   Under paragraph 10 SCAP may
develop a suitable system for using such facilities,
individually or collectively, upon notification and
explanation to the Allied Council for Japan.   Pursuant to the above-mentioned FEC decision requiring
their "impounding" remaining "primary war facilities" should continue to be protected, in the sense
of preventing loss or scrapping of individual items.
Impounding does not, however, include requirement
that the facilities be kept in their present loca-
tions or that the Japanese or the occupation authorities devote resources to preserve their value
or maintain them in working order.

(3)   That there should be no limitation on
Japan's production for peaceful purposes or on
levels of Japanese productive capacity in indus-
tries devoted to peaceful purposes.

<u>e</u>.   Submit to the FEC proposals, regardless of
likely unfavorable reception, for the rescission or amendment of existing and pending FEC reparations and "levels-
of-industry" policy papers so as to bring them in as close
conformity as possible with U. S. policy that there should
be no further industrial reparations removals from Japan
and no limitation on levels of Japanese peaceful productive capacity; and prevent action by the FEC contrary to
U. S. policy.

AMENDING EXECUTIVE ORDER NO. 10713,1 RELATING TO THE
ADMINISTRATION OF THE RYUKYU ISLANDS

By virtue of the authority vested in me by the Constitution, and as President of the United States and Commander-in-Chief of the armed forces of the United States, it is ordered as follows:

Section 1. Certain amendments of E.O. 10713. Executive Order No. 10713 of June 5, 1957, headed "Providing for administration of the Ryukyu Islands," is hereby amended by substituting the following for Sections 4, 6, 8, 9 and 11 thereof:

"Sec. 4. (a) There is established, under the jurisdiction of the Secretary of Defense, a civil administration of the Ryukyu Islands, the head of which shall be known as the High Commissioner of the Ryukyu Islands (hereinafter referred to as the 'High Commissioner'). The High Commissioner (1) shall be designated by the Secretary of Defense, after consultation with the Secretary of State and with the approval of the President, from among the active duty members of the armed forces of the United States, (2) shall have the powers and perform the duties assigned to him by the terms of this order, (3) may delegate any function vested in him to such officials of the civil administration as he may designate, and (4) shall carry out any powers or duties delegated or assigned to him by the Secretary of Defense pursuant to this order.

"(b) There shall be under the High Commissioner a civilian official who shall have the title of Civil Administrator. The Civil Administrator shall be designated by the Secretary of Defense, after consultation with the Secretary of State and with the approval of the President and shall have such powers and perform such duties as may be assigned to him by the High Commissioner."

"Sec. 6 (a) The legislative power of the Government of the Ryukyu Islands, except as otherwise provided in this order, shall be vested in a legislative body consisting of a single house. Members of the legislative body shall be directly elected by the people of the islands in 1962, and triennially thereafter, for terms of three years.

310

"(b)   The territory of the Ryukyu Islands shall continue to be divided into districts, each of which shall elect one member of the legislative body. The present 29 districts are continued, but the number or boundaries of districts may be altered by law enacted by the Government of the Ryukyu Islands with the approval of the High Commissioner. Any re-districting shall be done with due regard to obtaining districts which are relatively compact and contiguous and which have reasonably equal populations."

"Sec. 8. (a)   The executive power of the Government of the Ryukyu Islands shall be vested in a Chief Executive, who shall be a Ryukyuan. The Chief Executive shall have general supervision and control of all executive agencies and instrumentalities of the Government of the Ryukyu Islands and shall faithfully execute the laws and ordinances applicable to the Ryukyu Islands.

"(b)(1)   The Chief Executive shall be appointed by the High Commissioner on the basis of a nomination which is made by the legislative body herein provided for and is acceptable to the High Commissioner. A Chief Executive so appointed shall serve for the remainder of the term of the legislative body which nominated him and for such reasonable period thereafter as may be necessary for the appointment of a successor pursuant to this paragraph, or, failing such an appointment, pursuant to paragraph (2) of this subsection.

"(2)   In the event the legislative body does not make an acceptable nomination within a reasonable time as determined by the High Commissioner, or if by reason of other unusual circumstances it is deemed by the High Commissioner to be necessary, he may appoint a Chief Executive without a nomination. The tenure of any Chief Executive appointed pursuant to this paragraph (2) shall be as determined by the High Commissioner.

"(c)   The head of each municipal government shall be elected by the people of the respective municipality in accordance with procedures established by the legislative body of the Government of the Ryukyu Islands."

-2-

Executive Order 11010 (continued)

"Sec. 9. (a) Every bill passed by the legislative
body shall, before it becomes law, be presented to the
Chief Executive. If the Chief Executive approves a bill
he shall sign it, but if not he shall return it, with
his objections, to the legislative body within fifteen
days after it shall have been presented to him. If a
bill is not returned within the specified fifteen day
period, it shall become law in like manner as if it had
been approved by the Chief Executive, unless the legislative body by adjournment prevents its return, in which
case it shall be law if approved by the Chief Executive
within forty-five days after it shall have been presented to him; otherwise it shall not be law. When a bill
is returned to the legislative body with objections by
the Chief Executive, the legislative body may proceed
to reconsider it. If, after such reconsideration two
thirds of the legislative body pass it, it shall become
law in like manner as if it had been approved by the
Chief Executive.

"(b) If any bill approved by the legislative body
contains several items of appropriation of money, the
Chief Executive may object to one or more of such items
or any part or parts, portion or portions thereof, while
approving the other items, or parts or portions of the
bill. In such case, the Chief Executive shall append
to the bill, at the time of signing it, a statement of
the items, or parts or portions thereof, objected to,
and the items, or parts or portions thereof, so objected
to shall not take effect. Should the legislative body
seek to over-ride such objections of the Chief Executive,
the procedures set forth above will apply. In computing
any period of days for the foregoing purposes, Sundays
and legal holidays shall be excluded."

Executive Order 11010 (continued)

"Sec. 11. (a) The High Commissioner may, if such action is deemed necessary for the fulfillment of his mission under this order, promulgate laws, ordinances or regulations. The High Commissioner, if such action is deemed by him to be important in its effect, direct or indirect, on the security of the Ryukyu Islands, cr on relations with foreign countries and international organizations with respect to the Ryukyu Islands, or on the foreign relations of the United States, or on the security, property or interests of the United States or nationals thereof, may, in respect of Ryukyuan bills, laws, or officials, as the case may be, (1) veto any bill or any part or portion thereof, (2) annul any law or any part or portion thereof within 45 days after its enactment, and (3) remove any public official from office. The High Commissioner has the power to reprieve, commutation and pardon. The High Commissioner may assume in whole or in part, the exercise of full authority in the islands, if such assumption of authority appears mandatory for security reasons. Exercise of authority conferred on the High Commissioner by this subsection shall be promptly reported, together with the reasons therefor, to the Secretary of Defense who shall inform the Secretary of State.

"(b) In carrying out the powers conferred upon him by the provisions of subsection (a) of this section, the High Commissioner shall give all proper weight to the rights of the Ryukyuans and shall, in particular, have proper regard for the provisions of the second sentence of Section 2 of this order."

Sec. 2. Further amendments. Section 10 of the said Executive Order No. 10713 is hereby further amended as follows:

(1) By deleting from Section 10(a)(2)(b) the following: "even though not subject to trial by courts-martial under the Uniform Code of Military Justice (10 U.S.C. 801 et seq.)".

(2) By substituting the following for Section 10(b)(3):

-4-

Executive Order 11010 (continued)

"(3) Criminal jurisdiction over (a) the civilian component, (b) employees of the United States Government who are United States nationals, and (c) dependents, excluding Ryukyuans, (i) of the foregoing and (ii) of members of the United States forces."

Sec. 3. Transitional provisions. (a) This order shall not operate to terminate immediately the tenure of the Chief Executive of the Government of the Ryukyu Islands now in office. That tenure shall terminate when his first successor, appointed under the provisions of Executive Order No. 10713 as amended by this order, enters upon office as Chief Executive or on such other date as may be fixed by the High Commissioner.

(b) The members of the legislative body in office on the date of this order shall continue in office until the termination of their present terms as members.

(c) The amendment of Section 4 of Executive Order No. 10713 made by this order shall become effective on July 1, 1962. All other parts hereof shall become effective on April 1, 1962.

JOHN F. KENNEDY

THE WHITE HOUSE
March 19, 1962.

Extracted from FEDERAL REGISTER,
Volume 27, Number 55,
Washington, Wednesday, March 21, 1962

-5-

Document 4- Nixon-Sato Communique

Full Text of Joint Communique between President

Richard M. Nixon and Prime Minister Eisaku Sato

November 21, 1969

1. President Nixon and Prime Minister Sato met in Washington on November 19, 20 and 21, 1969 to exchange views on the present international situation and on other matters of mutual interest to the United States and Japan.

2. The President and the Prime Minister recognized that both the United States and Japan have greatly benefited from their close association in a variety of fields, and they declared that guided by their common principles of democracy and liberty, the two countries would maintain and strengthen their fruitful cooperation in the continuing search for world peace and prosperity and in particular for the relaxation of international tensions. The President expressed his and his government's deep interest in Asia and stated his belief that the United States and Japan should cooperate in contributing to the peace and prosperity of the region. The Prime Minister stated that Japan would make further active contributions to the peace and prosperity of Asia.

3. Efforts For Peace

The President and the Prime Minister exchanged frank views on the current international situation, with particular attention to developments in the Far East. The President, while emphasizing that the countries in the area were expected to make their own efforts for the stability of the area, gave assurance that the United States would continue to contribute to the maintenance of international peace and security in the Far East by honoring its defense treaty obligations in the area. The Prime Minister, appreciating the determination of the United States, stressed that it was important for the peace and security of the Far East that the United States should be in a position to carry out fully its obligations referred to by the President. He further expressed his recognition that, in the light of the present situation, the presence of United States forces in the Far East constituted a mainstay for the stability of the area.

4. The President and the Prime Minister specifically noted the continuing tension over the Korean peninsula. The Prime Minister deeply appreciated the peacekeeping efforts of the United Nations in the area and stated that the security of the Republic of Korea was essential to Japan's own security.

315

The President and the Prime Minister shared the hope that Communist China would adopt a more cooperative and constructive attitude in its external relations. The President referred to the treaty obligations of his country to the Republic of China which the United States would uphold. The Prime Minister said that the maintenance of peace and security in the Taiwan area was also a most important factor for the security of Japan. The President described the earnest efforts made by the United States for a peaceful and just settlement of the Viet-Nam problem. The President and the Prime Minister expressed the strong hope that the war in Viet-Nam would be concluded before the return of the administrative rights over Okinawa to Japan. In this connection, they agreed that, should peace in Viet-Nam not have been realized by the time reversion of Okinawa is scheduled to take place, the two governments would fully consult with each other in the light of the situation at that time so that reversion would be accomplished without affecting the United States efforts to assure the South Vietnamese people the opportunity to determine their own political future without outside interference. The Prime Minister stated that Japan was exploring what role she could play in bringing about stability in the Indo-China area.

5. In light of the current situation and the prospects in the Far East, the President and the Prime Minister agreed that they highly valued the role played by the Treaty of Mutual Cooperation and Security in maintaining the peace and security of the Far East including Japan, and they affirmed the intention of the two governments firmly to maintain the Treaty on the basis of mutual trust and common evaluation of the international situation. They further agreed that the two governments should maintain close contact with each other on matters affecting the peace and security of the Far East including Japan, and on the implementation of the Treaty of Mutual Cooperation and Security.

6. Vital Role

The Prime Minister emphasized his view that the time had come to respond to the strong desire of the people of Japan, of both the mainland and Okinawa, to have the administrative rights over Okinawa returned to Japan on the basis of the friendly relations between the United States and Japan and thereby to restore Okinawa to its normal status. The President expressed appreciation of the Prime Minister's view. The President and the Prime Minister also recognized the vital role played by United States forces in Okinawa in the present situation in the Far East. As a result of their discussion, it was agreed that the mutual security interests of the United States and Japan could be accommodated within arrangements for the return of the administrative rights over

Okinawa to Japan. They therefore agreed that the two governments would immediately enter into consultations regarding specific arrangements for accomplishing the early reversion of Okinawa without detriment to the security of the Far East including Japan. They further agreed to expedite the consultations with a view to accomplishing the reversion during 1972 subject to the conclusion of these specific arrangements with the necessary legislative support. In this connection, the Prime Minister made clear the intention of his government, following reversion, to assume gradually the responsibility for the immediate defense of Okinawa as part of Japan's defense efforts for her own territories. The President and the Prime Minister agreed also that the United States would retain under the terms of the Treaty of Mutual Cooperation and Security such military facilities and areas in Okinawa as required in the mutual security of both countries.

7. The President and the Prime Minister agreed that, upon return of the administrative rights, the Treaty of Mutual Cooperation and Security and its related arrangements would apply to Okinawa without modification thereof. In this connection, the Prime Minister affirmed the recognition of his government that the security of Japan could not be adequately maintained without international peace and security in the Far East and, therefore, the security of countries in the Far East was a matter of serious concern for Japan. The Prime Minister was of the view that, in the light of such recognition on the part of the Japanese Goverment, the return of the administrative rights over Okinawa in the manner agreed above should not hinder the effective discharge of the international obligations assumed by the United States for the defense of countries in the Far East including Japan. The President replied that he shared the Prime Minister's view.

8. The Prime Minister described in detail the particular sentiment of the Japanese people against nuclear weapons and the policy of the Japanese Government reflecting such sentiment. The President expressed his deep understanding and assured the Prime Minister that, without prejudice to the position of the United States Government with respect to the prior consultation system under the Treaty of Mutual Cooperation and Security, the reversion of Okinawa would be carried out in a manner consistent with the policy of the Japanese Government as described by the Prime Minister.

9. Economic Problems

The President and the Prime Minister took note of the fact that there would be a number of financial and economic

317

problems, including those concerning United States business interests in Okinawa, to be solved between the two countries in connection with the transfer of the administrative rights over Okinawa to Japan and agreed that detailed discussions relative to their solution would be initiated promptly.

10. The President and the Prime Minister, recognizing the complexity of the problems involved in the reversion of Okinawa, agreed that the two governments should consult closely and cooperate on the measures necessary to assure a smooth transfer of administrative rights to the Japanese Government in accordance with reversion arrangements to be agreed to by both governments. They agreed that the United States-Japan Consultative Committee in Tokyo should undertake over-all responsibility for this preparatory work. The President and the Prime Minister decided to establish in Okinawa a Preparatory Commission in place of the existing Advisory Committee to the High Commissioner of the Ryukyu Islands for the purpose of consulting and coordinating locally on measures relating to preparation for the transfer of administrative rights, including necessary assistance to the Government of the Ryukyu Islands. The Preparatory Commission will be composed of a representative of the Japanese Government with ambassadorial rank and the High Commissioner of the Ryukyu Islands, with the Chief Executive of the Government of the Ryukyu Islands acting as adviser to the two governments through the United States-Japan Consultative Committees.

11. The President and the Prime Minister expressed their conviction that a mutually satisfactory solution of the question of the return of the administrative rights over Okinawa to Japan, which is the last of the major issues between the two countries arising from the Second World War, would further strengthen United States-Japan relations. which are based on friendship and mutual trust ana would make a major contribution to the peace and security of the Far East.

12. Trade Relations

In their discussions of economic matters, the President and the Prime Minister noted the marked growth in economic relations between the two countries. They also acknowledged that the leading positions which their countries occupy in the world economy impose important responsibilities on each for the maintenance and strengthening of the international trade and monetary system, especially in the light of the current large imbalances in trade and payments. In this regard, the President stressed his determination to bring inflation in the United States under control. He also reaf-

firmed the commitment of the United States to the principle of promoting freer trade. The Prime Minister indicated
the intention of the Japanese Government to accelerate rapidly the reduction of Japan's trade and capital restrictions.
Specifically, he stated the intention of the Japanese Government to remove Japan's residual import quota restrictions
over a broad range of products by the end of 1971, and to
make maximum efforts to accelerate the liberalization of
the remaining items. He added that the Japanese Government
intends to make periodic reviews of its liberalization program with a view to implementing trade liberalization at a
more accelerated pace than hitherto. The President and the
Prime Minister agreed that their respective actions would
further solidify the foundation of overall United States-
Japan relations.

13. The President and the Prime Minister agreed that attention to the economic needs of the developing countries
was essential to the development of international peace and
stability. The Prime minister stated the intention of the
Japanese Government to expand and improve its aid programs
in Asia commensurate with the economic growth of Japan.
The President welcomed this statement and confirmed that
the United States would continue to contribute to the economic development of Asia. The President and the Prime
Minister recognized that there would be major requirements
for the post-war rehabilitation of Viet-Nam and elsewhere
in Southeast Asia. The Prime Minister stated the intention
of the Japanese Government to make a substantial contribution to this end.

14. The Prime Minister congratulated the President on the
successful moon landing of Apollo XII, and expressed the
hope for a safe journey back to earth for the astronauts.
The President and the Prime Minister agreed that the exploration of space offers great opportunities for expanding
cooperation in peaceful scientific projects among all nations.
In this connection, the Prime Minister noted with pleasure
that the United States and Japan last summer had concluded
an agreement on space cooperation. The President and the
Prime Minister agreed that implementation of this unique
program is of importance to both countries.

15. The President and the Prime Minister discussed prospects for the promotion of arms control and the slowing down
of the arms race. The President outlined his government's
efforts to initiate the strategic arms limitations talks
with the Soviet Union that have recently started in Helsinki.
The Prime Minister expressed his government's strong hopes for
the success of these talks. The Prime Minister pointed out

Document 5- Map from Central Intelligence Agency
Report "The Ryukyu Islands and Their
Significance," dated August 6, 1948.
(Section of original shown here).

THE WESTERN PACIFIC AND CHINA

SCALE 1:24,000,000

Stereographic Projection   Centered at 37°N, 135°E.

SCALE OF MILES: The linear scales printed on and at the bottom of the map indicate the scale (in statute miles) in all directions from the CENTER OF PROJECTION.

DISTANCE BETWEEN TWO POINTS: Find the respective distances of the two points from the center of projection, using either the scale on the map or the scale cut from the bottom of the map. Find the approximate average distance from the center of projection and use the appropriate scale in the lower right corner in measuring the distance between the two points.

EXAMPLE: Kunming is approximately 2000 and Nanking is approximately 900 miles from the center of projection. The average distance is 1450 miles. The 1500 mile scale is then used to measure the distance between Kunming and Nanking.

EQUIDISTANT CIRCLES ABOUT ANY POINT ON THE MAP:

1. Place the linear scale (cut from the bottom of map) on the map so that "0" is at the center of projection and the base line of the scale passes through any point, X.

2. From X, measure off in both directions on the scale the distance desired for the radius of a circle (500 miles, for example). These two points are the ends of a diameter of the desired circle. The center of this circle is midway between these two points on the base line of the scale.

The international boundaries shown on this map do not necessarily correspond in all cases to the boundaries recognized by the U. S. Government.

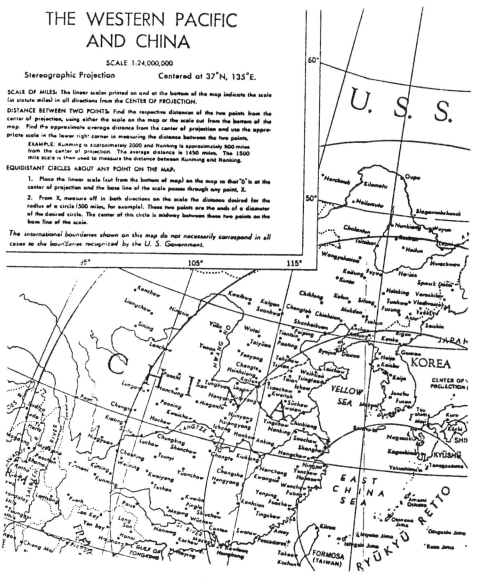

321

BIBLIOGRAPHY

The following is a selective bibliography. The two divisions are those which seemed most useful, namely: 1. Substantive (works related to historical events, the specifics of the Japan-America-Okinawa relationships, etc.) and 2. Theoretical (works on foreign policy and decision theory). These divisions of course do not preclude some overlapping of subject matter. Journal and newspaper listings are included in the "Substantive" section; Japanese sources are integrated alphabetically with English ones.

I. SUBSTANTIVE

Appleman, Roy et. al. Okinawa: The Last Battle. Washington: United States Army Historical Division, 1948.

Binnendijk, Johannes. "The Dynamics of Okinawan Reversion," in Public Diplomacy and Political Change, pp. 1-187. Edited by Gregory Henderson. New York: Praeger Publishers, 1973.

_____ "Political-Military Aspects of Reversion." Mimeo, March, 1974.

Braibanti, Ralph. "The Ryukyu Islands: Pawn of the Pacific," American Political Science Review, December, 1954. pp. 972-998.

Cameron, Allan W. "The Pacific Islands." Orbis , (Fall, 1975) pp. 1012-1036.

Clark, Keith C. and Laurence J. Legere. The President and the Management of National Security (Institute for Defense Analysis Report). New York: Praeger Publishers, 1969.

Destler, I.M., Priscilla Clapp, Hideo Sato, and Haruhiro Fukui. Managing an Alliance: The Politics of U.S.-Japanese Relations. Washington: Brookings Institution, 1976.

Dunn, Frederick S. Peace-Making and the Settlement with Japan. Princeton, New Jersey: Princeton University Press, 1963.

Emmerson, John K. Arms, Yen, and Power. New York: Dunellen Publishing Company, Inc., 1971.

Emmerson, John K. and Leonard A. Humphreys. Will Japan Rearm? Washington: The American Enterprise Institute, 1973.

Feis, Herbert. Contest Over Japan. New York: W.W. Norton & Company, 1967.

Ford, Clellan B. "The American Occupation Experience on Okinawa," Annals of the American Academy of Political and Social Sciences. (January, 1950). pp. 175-182.

Gibney, Frank. "Okinawa: Forgotten Island." Time, (November 28, 1949) p. 20.

Guntharp, Walter A. United States Foreign Policy and the Reversion of Okinawa to Japan. (Unpublished Doctoral Dissertation). George Washington University, Washington, D.C., 1973.

Halliday, Jon and Gavan McCormack. Japanese Imperialism Today. New York: Monthly Review Press, 1973.

Higa, Mikio. Politics and Parties in Postwar Okinawa. Vancouver: British Columbia University Publications Centre, 1963.

Iriye, Akira. Across the Pacific. New York: Harcourt, Brace & World, 1967.

Kampf, Herbert. The United States and Okinawa: A Study in Dependency Relationship, (Unpublished Doctoral Dissertation). New York: City University of New York, Graduate Department of Political Science, 1972.

Karasik, Daniel. "Okinawa: A Problem in Administration and Reconstruction," Far Eastern Quarterly (now Journal of Asian Studies). (May, 1948). pp. 254-267.

Kawaguchi, Hiroo. The Japanese Views on the Reversion of Okinawa, (Unpublished Master's Thesis) Charlottesville, Virginia: University of Virginia, 1969.

324

Kawai, Kazuo. Japan's American Interlude. Chicago: University of Chicago Press, 1960.

Kennan, George F. Memoirs: 1925-1950. Boston: Little, Brown & Company, 1967.

Kim, Hong N. "The Sato Government and the Politics of Okinawan Reversion," Asian Survey. (November, 1973), pp. 1021-1035.

Langer, Paul F. and Richard Moorsteen. The U.S./ Japanese Military Alliance: Japanese Perceptions and the Prospective Impact of Evolving U.S. Military Doctrines and Technologies. Santa Monica, California: The RAND Corporation (January, 1975), Paper No. P-5393.

Langdon, F.C. Japan's Foreign Policy. Vancouver: University of British Columbia Press, 1973.

Louis, William Roger. Imperialism at Bay. New York: Oxford University Press, 1978.

McPherson, Harry. A Political Education. Boston: Little Brown & Company, 1972.

Makise, Tsuneji. Okinawa no Rekishi ("The History of Okinawa").Tokyo: Sekibunsha, 1971.

Manchester, William. American Caesar: Douglas MacArthur, 1880-1964. Boston: Little, Brown & Company, 1978

Mendel, Douglas H., Jr. "Okinawan Reversion in Retrospect," Pacific Affairs. (Fall, 1975), pp. 398-412.

Meyer, Armin. Assignment: Tokyo. New York: Bobbs, Merrill, 1974.

Miyasato, Seigen. "Hopes and Realities in Okinawa," Japan Quarterly (April-June 1965), pp. 161-167.

Montgomery, John D. Forced to be Free-- The Artificial Revolution in Japan and Germany. Chicago: University of Chicago Press, 1957.

Nampo Doho Engokai (Relief Association for the Southern Areas). Okinawa Mondai Kihon Shiuyo-Shu (Basic Documents of the Okinawa Problem). Tokyo: Nampo Doho Engokai, 1968.

New York Times, 1945-1972.

Nishimura, Kumao. San Furanshisuko Heiwa Joyaku, in Nihon Gaiko Shi. Edited by Kajima Kenkyujo. Tokyo: Kajima Kenkyujo Shuppankai, 1971.

Ono, Setsuko. "Fragile Blossom, Fragile Super Power," Japan Quarterly (February-March 1976), pp. 12-27.

Osgood, Robert E. The Weary and the Wary: U.S. and Japanese Security Policies in Transition. Baltimore: The Johns Hopkins University Press, 1972.

Ota, Seisaku. Nichibei Anpo Joyaku no Kigentorai to Okinawa no Shisei-ken henkan. Tokyo: Gaiko Jiho, 1966

Rosovsky, Henry, ed., Discord in the Pacific. Washington: Columbia Books, Inc. 1972. See especially articles by Graham Allison, pp. 7-46 and Dwight Perkins, pp. 47-77.

Shiels, Frederick L. The American Experience in Okinawa: Case Studies for Foreign Policy and Decision-Making Theory (Unpublished Doctoral Dissertation) Ithaca, New York: Cornell University, 1977.

United States Army, Judge Advocate General's School, A Treatise on the Government of the Ryukyu Islands, 1959.

United States Civil Administration of the Ryukyu Islands, Annual Reports, 1961-1969.

United States House of Representatives, Committee on Appropriations. Hearings, Foreign Operations Appropriations. (Annual) 1961-1965.

United States Senate, Committee on Foreign Relations. The Japanese Peace Treaty and Other Treaties Relating to Security in the Pacific: Hearings, Eighty Second Congress, Second Session, 1952

United States Department of State, Conference for the Conclusion and Signature of the Treaty of Peace with Japan, Record of Proceedings, Washington: United States Government Printing Office, 1951.

326

Vinacke, Harold M. "United States Far Eastern Policy," Pacific Affairs (December, 1946), pp. 346-353.

Watanabe, Akio. The Okinawa Problem. Melbourne: Melbourne University Press, 1970.

Webb, James H., Jr. Micronesia and U.S. Pacific Strategy. New York, Praeger Publishers, 1974.

Weinstein, Martin E. Japan's Postwar Defense Policy, 1947-1968. New York: Columbia University Press, 1971.

II. THEORETICAL

Allison, Graham. Essence of Decision. Boston: Little, Brown & Company, 1971.

Bacchus, William I. Foreign Policy and the Bureaucratic Process. Princeton, New Jersey: Princeton University Press.

Bachrach, Peter and Morton S. Baratz. Power and Poverty. New York: Oxford University Press, 1970.

Bauer, Raymond A. and Kenneth J. Gergen, eds. The Study of Policy Formation. New York: The Free Press, 1968. See especially articles by Enid Curtis Bok Schoettle (pp. 149-179) and Kenneth Gergen (pp. 205-237).

Cohen, Bernard C. The Political Process and Foreign Policy. Princeton, New Jersey: Princeton University Press, 1957.

Coulam, Robert. Illusions of Choice: Robert McNamara, the F-111 and the Problem of Weapons Acquisition Reform, Princeton, New Jersey: Princeton University Press, 1977.

Crozier, Michel. The Bureaucratic Phenomenon. Chicago: The University of Chicago Press, 1964.

Davis, David Howard. How the Bureaucracy Makes Foreign Policy. Lexington, Massachusetts: D.C. Heath & Company, 1972.

327

DeRivera, Joseph H. The Psychological Dimension of Foreign Policy. Columbus, Ohio: Charles E. Merrill Publishing Company, 1968.

Destler, I.M. Presidents, Bureaucrats, and Foreign Policy. Princeton, New Jersey: Princeton University Press, 1972.

Dimock, Marshall E. and Gladys O. Dimock. Public Administration. New York: Holt, Rinehart and Winston, 1958.

Downs, Anthony. Inside Bureaucracy. Boston: Little, Brown & Company, 1967.

Eckstein, Harry. "Case Study and Theory in Political Science," in The Handbook of Political Science, Fred Greenstein and Nelson Polsby, eds. Reading, Massachusetts: Addison Wesley Publishing Company, 1975, pp. 79-137.

Fox, Douglas M., ed. The Politics of U.S. Foreign Policy Making. Pacific Palisades, California: Goodyear Publishing Company, 1971. See especially article by Chadwick Alger, "The External Bureaucracy in U.S. Foreign Affairs."

Frankel, Joseph. The Making of Foreign Policy. London: Oxford University Press, 1963.

George, Alexander. "The Case for Multiple Advocacy in Foreign Policy Decision-Making," American Political Science Review, (September,1972), pp. 751-785.

Halperin, Morton, with Priscilla Clapp and Arnold Kanter. Bureaucratic Politics and Foreign Policy. Washington: The Brookings Institution, 1974.

Hermann, Charles, ed. International Crises: Insights From Behavioral Research. New York: The Free Press, 1972.

Hanrieder, Wolfram F., ed. Comparative Foreign Policy, Theoretical Essays. New York: David McKay Company, 1971.

Hilsman, Roger. The Politics of Policy Making in Defense and Foreign Affairs. New York, Harper & Row, Publishers, 1971.

_____. To Move a Nation. New York: Doubleday & Company, 1967 .

Hirschman, A.O. and Charles Lindblom. Economic Development, Research and Development, Policy Making: Some Converging Views," Behavioral Science (April, 1962) pp. 211-222.

Holsti, Ole, Terrence Hopmann, and John D. Sullivan. Unity and Disintegration in International Alliances. New York: John Wiley and Sons, 1973.

Hyman, Herbert et. al. Interviewing in Social Research. Chicago: The University of Chicago Press, 1954.

Ilchman, Warren F. and Norman T. Uphoff. The Political Economy of Change. Berkeley, California: University of California Press, 1971.

Jensen, Lloyd. "Foreign Policy Calculations," in International Systems, ed. Michael Haas. New York: Chandler Publishing Company, 1974. pp. 78-97.

Kissinger, Henry A. "Domestic Structure and Foreign Policy," Daedalus (Spring, 1966) pp. 503-529.

Kolko, Joyce and Gabriel Kolko. The Limits of Power: The World and United States Foreign Policy, 1945-1954. New York: Harper & Row, Publishers, 1972.

Krasner, Steven. "Are Bureaucracies Important?" Foreign Policy (Summer, 1972) pp. 159-179.

Lindblom, Charles E. The Intelligence of Democracy. New York: The Free Press, 1965.

_____. The Policy-Making Process. Englewood Cliffs, New Jersey: Prentice-Hall, 1968.

_____. Strategies for Decision-Making. Urbana, Illinois: University of Illinois Bulletin, 1971.

_____ and David Braybrooke. A Strategy of Decision. New York: The Free Press of Glencoe, 1963.

_____ and David Cohen. Useful Knowledge. New Haven, Connecticut: Yale University Press, 1979.

Liska, George. Nations in Alliance. Baltimore: The Johns Hopkins University Press, 1967.

Lockhart, Charles J. "The Varying Fortunes of Incremental Commitment," International Studies Quarterly, (March 1975) pp. 46-66.

Lovell, John P. Foreign Policy in Perspective. New York: Holt, Rinehart and Winston, 1970.

Millar, T.B. "Naval Armaments in the Far East," in Sea Power in the 1970's, ed. George Quester, New York: Dunellen Publishing Company, 1976, pp. 159-177.

Neustadt, Richard E. Alliance Politics. New York: Columbia University Press, 1970.

Osgood, Robert E. Alliances and American Foreign Policy. Baltimore: The Johns Hopkins University Press, 1968.

Paige, Glenn D. The Korean Decision. New York: The Free Press, 1968.

Patchen, Martin. "Decision Theory in the Study of International Action," Journal of Conflict Resolution (June, 1965), pp. 164-176.

Robinson, James A. and R.R. Majak. "The Theory of Decision Making," in Contemporary Political Analysis, ed. James C. Charlesworth, New York: The Free Press, 1967. pp. 175-188.

Snyder, Richard C., H.W. Bruck, and Burton Sapin, Foreign Policy Decision-Making. New York: The Free Press of Glencoe, 1962.

Snyder, Richard C. and James A. Robinson. National and International Decision-Making: A Report to the Committee on Research for Peace. New York: The Institute for International Order, 1961.

Sorensen, Theodore C. Decision-Making in the White House. New York: Columbia University Press, 1963.

Steinbruner, John D. The Cybernetic Theory of Decision. Princeton, New Jersey: Princeton University Press, 1974.

Verba, Sidney. "Assumptions of Rationality and Non-Rationality in the International System," in The International System: Theoretical Essays, ed. Klaus Knorr and Sidney Verba, Princeton, New Jersey: Princeton University Press, 1961, pp. 77-92.

Vital, David. The Making of British Foreign Policy. London: George Allen and Unwin, Ltd., 1968.

Weil, Herman M. "Can Bureaucracies Be Rational Actors?" International Studies Quarterly (December, 1975) pp. 432-468.

Wohlstetter, Roberta. Pearl Harbor: Warning and Decision. Stanford, California: Stanford University Press, 1962.

Wolfers, Arnold. "The Actors in International Politics," in Theoretical Aspects of International Relations, ed. W.T.R. Fox. Notre Dame Indiana: Notre Dame University Press, 1959, Chpater 6.

Yarmolinsky, Adam. "Bureaucratic Structures and Political Outcomes," in Journal of International Affairs, New York: Columbia University Press, 1969, pp. 225-235.

State-Army-Navy-Air Force
   Coordinating Committee
   (SANACC), 103, 111
State-War-Navy Coordinating
   Committee Paper 249/1, 94
State-War-Navy Coordinating
   Committee Paper 38/20, 85
Stilwell, Joseph, 55
Strategic trusteeship, 71,
   94, 95, 105
Supreme Commander of Allied
   Forces in the Pacific
   (SCAP), 26, 53, 68, 100,
   101, 106, 115, 240, 246,
   259, 261
SCAP Directive 677, 72, 87

Taira, Osamu, 177
Taiwan, 59, 60, See also
   China, Republic of
Thailand, 74, 225
Third World, 178, 181,
   182, 189, 190
Thucydides, 11
Thurmond, Strom, 225
Toulmin, Stephen, 147
Toxic gas storage, 81
Trusteeship, 70, 98,
   116, 123, 138, 147
Truman, Harry, 20, 69,
   90, 100, 102, 103,
   106, 111, 120, 126,
   131, 132, 183, 237,
   240, 248, 259, 260,
   261
Typhoon Gloria, 120

Unger, Ferdinand, 177,
   181, 186, 218, 252,
   266
Union of Soviet Social-
   ist Republics (USSR),
   as ally, 258; navy of,
   31, 141; relations with
   China, 209; as strategic
   threat, 59, 60, 67, 68,
   73, 95, 104, 113, 124,
   184, 212

United Nations, 20, 70, 111,
   128, 136, 138, 143
United Nations Trusteeship
   Council, 248
United States, Air Force, 145;
   Army, 21, 35, 54, 61-78,81,
   82, 93-110, 117, 120, 135-195,
   217-229, 244-265; Central Intelligence Agency (CIA), 68,
   102; Civil Administration in
   the Ryukyus, 74, 164, 168, 171,
   194; Congress, 9, 27, 35, 73,
   78, 83, 110, 120, 150, 160,
   183, 247, 262; Department of
   Defense, 21, 29, 35, 99, 104-
   114, 134-138, 185-197, 214, 217,
   224, 244-246, 259, 269; Department of Labor, 160, 161; Department of State, 20-29, 35,
   57, 63, 64, 75, 79, 87, 89,
   94, 98-115, 133-149, 155, 160-
   169, 180-195, 217-224, 245, 246,
   256-269; Navy, 31, 58, 60, 61,
   62, 69, 95, 97, 110
Uphoff, Norman, 44

Vandenberg, Hoyt, 105
Verstehen, 46
Vietnam war, 26, 74, 75, 80,
   81, 178-181, 186, 189, 191
   193, 202, 208, 209, 211,
   217, 238, 250, 267
Vital, David, 22, 49
Vorhees, Tracy, 69

Watanabe, Akio, 1, 44
Watson, Albert, 78, 178,186,
   202
Weckerling, John, 65
Weiss, Leonard, 84
Wheeler, Earl, 216
Wilkie, Wendell, 120
Wohlstetter, Albert, 215
Wohlstetter, Roberta, 29, 50,
   232

Yoshida, Shigeru, 71, 127,
   136-139, 147, 248

ABOUT THE AUTHOR

Frederick L. Shiels is Assistant Professor of
Political Science at Mercy College in Dobbs Ferry,
New York. He also teaches public administration at
Baruch College / City University of New York. He
did field work in Washington,D.C. and Japan in 1975
and received his doctorate from Cornell University
in 1977.

Dr. Shiels is the editor of The New American
Foreign Policy: A Primer for the 1980's (1979). He
is currently working on a book about alliance politics, centered on recent trends in the Japanese-
American relationship.